A LIE OF REINVENTION

Black Classic Press
Baltimore

A LIE OF REINVENTION

CORRECTING MANNING MARABLE'S MALCOLM X

edited by Jared A. Ball and Todd Steven Burroughs

A Lie of Reinvention:
Correcting Manning Marable's Malcolm X

Published 2012 Black Classic Press

Cover photograph credit: Library of Congress, Prints & Photographs Division, U.S. News & World Report Magazine Collection, reproduction number LC-DIG ppmsc-01274.

Cover and book design by Nathaniel Taintor
Editing by D. Kamili Anderson

Library of Congress Control Number: 2012940681

ISBN: 978-1-57478-049-9

Printed by BCP Digital Printing, an affiliate of Black Classic Press, Inc.

To review or purchase Black Classic Press books,
visit: www.blackclassicbooks.com

You may also obtain a list of titles by writing to:
Black Classic Press
c/o List
P.O. Box 13414
Baltimore, MD 21203

CONTENTS

For Dr. John Henrik Clarke,
who stood with Malcolm
when it was not popular.

lie (lī), ***n.*** something intended or serving to convey a false impression; imposture; a flat contradiction.

A NOTE FROM THE PUBLISHER

Along with many others, I believe that Manning Marable's *Malcolm X: A Life of Reinvention* is a severely flawed and problematic biogaphy. Instead of it being a "a definitive work" as some have called it, it is a contradictory political reshaping and distortion—a lie really—of the life and times of Malcolm X. Its problems are multiple—excessive use of innuendo, glaring omissions, questionable sourcing, undocumented speculation, misdirected conclusions, and an unexplained and inexcusable lack of key primary sources, for example (and maybe especially) Malcolm's wife and family. The product of these many problems, we believe, is essentially a *LIE*. Such a "lie" demands a strong critical response, from scholars, activists, and others in the Black community, especially publishers like Black Classic Press, who have benefited so richly from Malcolm's example and legacy.

Searching for an editor to assemble a critical response led me to Jared A. Ball, who enthusiastically agreed to take on this task with the assistance of his comrade and co-editor, Todd Steven Burroughs. Halfway into the project, we decided that *A Lie of Reinvention* would be a perfect counter-title to Marable's *A Life of Reinvention*. We also agreed that our title would speak directly to the problems cited above.

To be clear, with our title selection, and with the book itself, we are not asserting that Manning Marable is a liar. We do not make such a claim. Nor do we direct any ill will or disrespect toward Marable or his publisher, Viking Press. Instead, this book is purposely titled and published because of our intent to provide a necessary correction of Manning Marable's *Malcolm X*.

W. Paul Coates
Publisher, Black Classic Press

JARED A. BALL

An Introduction to a Lie

> *We are living in a time when image-making has become a science. Someone can create a certain image and then use that image to twist your mind and lead you right up a blind path.*[1]
>
> (Malcolm X)

Our honor was threefold after receiving a call from W. Paul Coates asking us to compile a book of critical responses to Manning Marable's *Malcolm X: A Life of Reinvention.* The first honor, of course, was being invited to work with Black Classic Press, a truly legendary publishing house. The second honor was that Todd Steven Burroughs, my coeditor, and I had both become involved early on in the debate that arose soon after the publication of Marable's book, which, unfortunately, was coupled with his untimely death. The third honor was that Paul's offer gave us an opportunity to take up what we believe is our generational duty: to accept responsibility, at minimum, for editorially defending and extending the legacy of Malcolm X and the ideas with which Malcolm most seriously grappled. The unenviable alternative, as we saw it, was to quietly accept or worse to openly support Marable's false reinvention of the man and his ideas.

More than merely viewing Marable's reinvention of Malcolm as false, we have, beginning with our choice of book title, unapologetically laid down our claim that it is a lie. Marable's book, we contend, is the carefully constructed and intentional political reshaping of a man who was as important a conduit for and exemplar of African American politics as the world has ever seen. As each of our chapter contributors point out, Malcolm X's political importance, beyond that of the man himself, compels both a need of those in power to distort his memory and our need to respond vigorously to such attacks.

Margo Arnold, for example, maintains that Malcolm is recognized as a revolutionary by what she calls our "Black Radical Collective Consciousness," and that Marable's book has given members of that collective "the blues." She claims that it is that revolutionary consciousness—the consciousness that first produced Malcolm X—which demands a collective rebuttal to attempts such as Marable's to deny him and, in turn, to deny all Black people his legacy.

That is why we, the editors and contributors to this volume of critical essays, charge that Manning Marable and Viking Press have produced what is, for them, a *politically necessary version* of Malcolm X and his governing radical ideas. By so doing, we argue their final product serves as an attempt to discredit a Black radical tradition—specifically, Black Nationalism—and to set Malcolm up, by the book's end, as some sort of "race-neutral," multicultural, mainstream-leaning, liberal Democrat.

This conclusion—and Marable's seemingly infinite flaws of scholarship, citation, and basic accuracy—has led contributor William Strickland to suggest in his essay that *Malcolm X: A Life of Reinvention* "disqualifies itself as a work of historical scholarship." Similarly, Marable's multiple blunders cause contributor Raymond Winbush to describe *A Life of Reinvention* as "speculative non-fiction" at best and leads contributor Patricia Reid-Merritt to ask, and investigate, just "who was Manning Marable" and what must have been the "perceived social and personal benefits" of his "*deliberately* producing a controversial book which casts doubts on the motives, character and sincerity of one of the most revered figures of the Black freedom movement" (emphasis mine). As contributor Greg Thomas concludes, what Marable has produced is not a book at all but rather an "operation or a maneuver."

Compare the dangerous reinvention imposed upon Malcolm X by Marable to what a number of other contributors to this collection suggest is better described as Malcolm's radical evolution. With nuance and intellectual sleight-of-hand, several of our contributors maintain that Marable's work serves to diminish the threat that Malcolm posed to the state and to its long- and still-standing hostility toward political radicals. None other than Mumia Abu-Jamal, for example, refers to *A Life of Reinvention* as "tragic," in large part for its total omission of any serious discussion of the role played in Malcolm's demise by the US Government's infamous Counter-Intelligence Program (COINTELPRO). Abu-Jamal has contributed a revision of his earlier views about the Marable book in an essay written for this volume. As he writes in that essay:

> Why an historian of Marable's standing and expertise neither utilizes nor references works which provide us with an inside (i.e., political and functional) view of the role of the FBI and, indeed, the State, in its relationship with Black nationalist and/or Black liberation organizations...is, to say the least, troubling. For his failure to give this contextual framework—which [may have] required, perhaps, half a chapter to set forth—normalizes the FBI as just another "law enforcement agency," and misrepresents both their historic, contemporary and continuing role in American society as essentially, race police—or discrete defenders of white supremacy.

Abu-Jamal further suggests that Marable's inept portrayal of Malcolm sets forth a course for interpreting the present moment as well. He contends that as people around the world are once again revisiting social-movement building and could, in that process, potentially reengage radical politics, a figure like Malcolm X demands a more liberalizing reinvention. Likewise, as increasing numbers begin to question the absence of real change in the American political system and social order (such as was presumably associated with the election of the first Black President), and as they more clearly recognize the worsening inequalities in this country, the kinds of analyses presented by a radical figure such as Malcolm X must also suffer renewed reinventions.[2]

A LIE OF REINVENTION

The contributors to this volume maintain that it is the persistence of exploitation in the United States and the world that makes the ideas that produced Malcolm X—and the ideas produced by him—as relevant today as they were in his time. Collectively, we ask: In what world do we live where ideas such as revolutionary nationalism, pan-Africanism, anti-imperialism, and the rights of the oppressed to struggle by any means are somehow irrelevant? Increases in mass incarceration, continuing political imprisonment, and worsening conditions of employment, poverty, access to health care, and quality education have, in 2012, as much a need for Malcolm X's analysis and suggested responses as ever.

Indeed, it could be argued (and is, by several contributors included herein) that a fundamental turning away from the politics of resistance and revolution has left African America with the kinds of persistent inequality associated with incomplete freedom movements. The suppression of Malcolm X as he really was—politically, ideologically, and programmatically—has been equaled in the contemporary era only by the suppression of his politics within the circles of those claiming to carry on his legacy. The continuity of oppression from Malcolm's time to now requires *both* the initial physical assassination of the man and the subsequent re-assassination of his ideas. In truth, those assassinations are what make today's inequality possible. They are merely the necessary first steps. The danger represented by Malcolm X and his ideas is today as persistent as the oppression he sought to destroy in his time. It is in this context that the editors and contributors to this book argue that the lie of reinvention has been applied to Malcolm X by Manning Marable.

Reinvention conveys a sense of starting anew and totally redefining one's position, place, or purpose. In the context of the anti-Black-radical, anti-left politics of Marable's book and the "post-racial," Obama-era setting of its publication, this reinvention obviously attempts to place Malcolm X in the ancestral lineage of a modern world falsely defined as advanced, civil, or simply better than before. Given the massive body of knowledge produced by and about Malcolm X that clearly identifies an increasingly radical and threatening political trajectory, this reinvention could not have happened unconsciously.

Hence, the lie. The science of image making that Malcolm X spoke of so many years ago has since undergone a process similar to the conditions that particular science is meant to obscure. The manipulation of consciousness or public opinion, which Malcolm understood perfectly as being necessary to hide or justify worsening conditions, continues now at levels commensurate with the kinds of worsening inequality we see in the world today.

The editors' journey toward what has become this particular project began nearly two years ago as long-time friends and colleagues, now both at Morgan State University. We were among the many excited anticipants awaiting Manning Marable's "masterpiece" and a welcome excuse to re-discuss Malcolm in a contemporary historical sense. Not since the early 1990s had either of us felt the kind of mass swell from below that could push, even demand, the return of Malcolm X to popular consciousness. We felt Marable deserved full credit for his contribution to that effort, but between his untimely death and some early warning signs about the nature of his forthcoming book—not the least of which was an early and scathing critique from Karl Evanzz—we became more than a little concerned.

Beginning only a few short days after the release of Marable's book, we co-hosted a series of radio programs on the work.[3] We consulted media critic Richard Prince and his most essential online column, "Journal-isms," for the latest news on and responses to the book. Later, we were able, finally, to delve deeply into the text itself. To our great disappointment, more than the simple warnings we had received were confirmed. Malcolm X was indeed present, fully developed, in the book's pages, but his story had been re-told and recast from the many books and other sources that Marable simultaneously borrowed from and dismissed. More troubling was that we found the ideas, the analyses, the fire that Malcolm brought to the scene all gone—worse still, they were attacked and vilified.

Marable's "definitive masterpiece" was to us a mere tombstone: a 600-page eulogy that attempted to lay permanently to rest the Malcolm X that we knew and revered. Indeed, it aimed to bury the very ideas that produced Malcolm X and those he made his own, our own. The book attacked the very ideas that made Malcolm X and all Black people then, and now, dangerous. The book you are now reading vis-à-vis Marable's is fitting in that it does in far fewer words what his book does so little of: it appropriately re-politicizes both Marable's subject and his ideology.

As several contributors to this volume point out, the continuity of the state's need to marginalize the "real" Malcolm X requires that mainstream accounts of the man appear exactly as they do in Marable's book. Marable's need to reconcile today with a living, breathing Malcolm X forces him to draw impossible conclusions rather than to note, more accurately, that there could be no today as it is without first destroying Malcolm the man and subsequently destroying, in perpetuity, both the ideas that made the man and those that he transformed into the governing ideas of the most radical elements in this society. So powerful were Malcolm X's contributions to the radical movements that emerged after his assassination that many of that movement's adherents had to be themselves assassinated, imprisoned, or exiled to this very day.

In their respective essays, Kali Akuno and Kamau Franklin, who are each members of the Malcolm X Grassroots Movement, take particular note of an issue that Akuno describes as *A Life of Reinvention*'s "ideological polemic... [the] general focus of [which] is Black nationalism, and Black revolutionary nationalism in particular." Franklin's own brief role as legal counsel for one of Malcolm X's accused killers highlights an important difference in historical interpretation that emerges between what he calls "movement" and "non-movement" people and a cause of great concern over what has become a tradition of struggle over the post-assassination interpretation and application of Malcolm's ideas. According to Franklin, "[It is] impossible to ignore Malcolm's positions on Black political struggle. His ideas became the new mainstream political thinking of the movement's new Black Power direction, and thus began the fight for the political ideas of Malcolm X." Franklin contends that if Marable's attempt to engage in this fight is to criticize and ultimately supplant Alex Haley's 1965 book on Malcolm with his own newly accepted "definitive" epic, then it is tantamount to an "ivory tower assassination attempt." As both Akuno and Franklin clarify, however, whatever flaws existed in Haley's book or the intent behind Haley's involvement, it unquestionably encourages what Marable's does not—namely, "radical organization against the state."

Franklin's critique of Marable's class position and state function as an elite academic working with an elite publishing house is echoed by several contributors to this volume, notably William Strickland, Raymond Winbush, Amiri Baraka, and Margo Arnold. Strickland, for one, maintains that the goal of Marable and his editor(s) at Viking Press (a subsidiary of Penguin Group, one of the six largest publishers in the world) was to craft a version of Malcolm X that would appeal to the "broadest audience possible." Were we to apply the Propaganda Model of Noam Chomsky and Edward Herman to Marable's book, as does Winbush to a certain extent, it becomes difficult to deny Marable and Viking that success. Indeed, what they have done, quite to the point of Chomsky and Herman, is to produce an ideological media product that represents the political perspectives and worldviews of those who rule.

Consider, for example, not only the nomination of *A Life of Reinvention* for a National Book Award or it subsequently being bestowed the Pulitzer Prize for history, but also the accolades offered it by so many in the establishment media world. Among the latter is that of Wendy Wolf, a Viking Press editor who, to promote the book, engages in an aspect of "psychological warfare" often euphemistically referred to as "public relations." Wolf dubs *A Life of Reinvention* a "comprehensive biography," asserting that she is somehow qualified, apparently by association with the flawless Marable himself, to claim with confidence that, "little serious, popular work on Malcolm's life has been published in the years since [Alex Haley's *Autobiography of Malcolm X*]."[4] Wolf continues her seemingly Marable-inspired dismissal of previous works on Malcolm (from which Marable borrowed extensively) as not only silly but also as mere "idolatry" that does little more than lead to the erection of "barriers to true understanding."[5]

To this, we could easily add the full ensemble of establishment press praises of Marable's book. The accolades were indeed remarkable and plentiful. The *Washington Post*, for example, hailed it as a "work of art." The *New York Times* called it "prodigiously researched," proclaiming that "[Marable] artfully strips away the layers and layers of myth that have been lacquered onto his subject's life—first by Malcolm himself in that famous memoir, and later by both supporters and opponents after his assassination in 1965 at the age of 39." *The Atlantic* called the book "a comprehensive portrait." To the *San Francisco Chronicle*, it was a "masterpiece." *Newsday* dubbed it "prodigious," and even *The Nation* defined it as a "definitive biography."[6] As Bill Strickland explains, such praise can only come from a book on Malcolm X that first develops an "historical narrative subordinated to the marketing strategy" of an elite publisher.

Raymond Winbush and Rosemari Mealy allege in their essays that part of the flawed narrative Marable developed about Malcolm X is the inexplicable omission of the voices of the women with whom Malcolm X lived and organized. They denounce the ultimately miniscule number of women interviewed for a volume of such magnitude and from a scholar of Marable's ample resources and time. They question how, given the twenty years Marable is reputed to have worked on *A Life of Reinvention*, he could not have interviewed or presented substantive commentary from such principle members of Malcolm's life. Malcolm's wife Betty Shabazz, for example, appears in the book largely as backdrop and as the subject of unsubstantiated rumors of infidelity. Winbush points out that Shabazz lived in the same city and navigated the same academic professional world as Marable until her death in 1997. Thus, Marable's failure to conduct an interview or oral history with her, writes Winbush, is "similar to a person living in Atlanta while doing a biography of Martin Luther King, Jr., and not interviewing Coretta Scott King living just five miles away."

This matter is addressed in greater detail by Greg Thomas in his essay, suggesting that Malcolm X's sister, Ella Little Collins, seems to exist for Marable only as a target of relentless demonization. Collins too lived until the mid-1990s (she died in 1996), so, like Shabazz, he contends that she could easily have been involved in and interviewed for Marable's project. Thomas goes on to question the inappropriateness of Marable's several unsubstantiated inquiries into Malcolm X's sex life by asking an essential question: what is revealed about the observer by the questions he asks of his subject? He further describes Marable's work as part of a "counterrevolutionary backlash" that "reduces sexuality to a matter of accusation." Moreover, contrary to all the supported, documented evidence, he explains that Marable concocted an entirely baseless distortion of Malcolm as one who viewed all women as "unreliable."

In his subsequent analysis of Marable's class-biased interpretation of Malcolm X, Thomas, like Margo Arnold in her essay, later positions the author of *A Life of Reinvention* as a "sponsored representative" of Columbia University and Penguin Group, the parent company of Viking Press. He contends that this elite stratum of society has an innate need to engage in the type of political destabilization that demands the mischaracterization of radical figures like Malcolm X and countless others.

A. Peter Bailey, as one of the few persons Marable interviewed for the book who had first-hand experience working with Malcolm, adds more depth to that discussion in his essay for this volume. Bailey maintains, for example, that the distortions in Marable's book are so numerous as to make him even "less determined to trust other scholars." He goes on to detail several instances where comments he made during his interview were forcibly bent to fit Marable's biases, so much so that he claims the published remarks bear "no relationship" to what he actually said.

For Sundiata Keita Cha-Jua the shortcomings in Marable's research result in part from his flawed interpretive framework and methodology. Cha-Jua argues convincingly that Marable's preference for a narrative literary style and his failure to adopt an approach rooted in the transdisciplinary nature of Black Studies are the work's major problems. These, suggests Cha-Jua, are also ideological choices that are themselves rooted in a hostility toward Black Nationalism and which inhibit Marable's ability to appropriately define and describe the thought and action of a Malcolm X. By juxtaposing the work of another scholar, Marika Sherwood, against that of Marable in their respective uses of Malcolm X's recently released travel notebooks,[7] Cha-Jua demonstrates the impact of Marable's flawed interpretive framework. The differences in interpretation, contends Cha-Jua, are political and expose serious problems with Marable's interpretation of events—specifically his charges of adultery.

Contributor Eugene Puryear also has similar issues with Marable's approach that he describes as "reformist vs. revolutionary tendencies." For Puryear and Cha-Jua, this is about the politics of the observer imposing himself on and thereby distorting the subject. For instance, Cha-Jua notes that once figures like Malcolm X, his older sister Ella Little Collins (herself a powerful, pioneering Black nationalist entrepreneur and leader), and Herman Ferguson (a founding member of the Organization of Afro-American Unity whose Republic of New Afrika affiliation and work is never mentioned by Marable), are taken out of their "sociohistorical and discursive contexts," Marable's "diagnoses" of Malcolm X—from his psychological state to his political consciousness—become questionable. Marable thus becomes incapable, in their view, of interpreting Malcolm, whose legacy, though perhaps imperfectly defined, is to them clear enough.

Another glaring example of Marable's struggle to diagnose Malcolm's real politics is his consistent inability to confront directly his subject's final mass organizational political act: the establishment of the Organization of Afro-American Unity (OAAU). In concert with his dismissal of virtually all the work about Malcolm X produced in the 1990s and his diminishment of the political content of that work, Marable dismisses and diminishes the expressed goals of the OAAU as well as its potential and continued impact. Unlike the 1991 book, *Malcolm X: The Man and His Times*, edited by Malcolm's friend, colleague, and OAAU cofounder, the late John Henrik Clarke, or the 1999 publication by William Sales, *From Civil Rights to Black Liberation: Malcolm X and the Organization of Afro-American Unity*,[8] Marable says little about the OAAU's history or its "Statement of Basic Aims and Objectives." In so doing, the organization becomes barely more than background material for Marable's cobbled-together and softened conclusions about Malcolm's ultimate political worldview.

This important omission, though it does little to advance the importance of Malcolm's analysis in the twenty-first century, is an essential feature of establishment publications in a post-9/11 and post-Obama political climate. The OAAU had to suffer diminution at Marable's hand in order for him to conclude that Malcolm X "would certainly have condemned the [al-Qaeda] terrorist attacks on September 11, 2001,"[9] or that Malcolm would have "anticipated that the black electorate could potentially be the balance of power in a divided white republic"[10] and the election of Barack Obama in 2008. It had to be dismissed in order for Marable to make assertions about Malcolm's "race-neutral concepts of Pan-Africanism" and his purported desire to "reject violence for its own sake" so that his "gentle humanism and antiracism could...become a platform for a new kind of radical, global ethnic politics."[11]

Having thus provided readers with what are clearly his own preferred politics, Marable can and does neatly pose Malcolm X and al-Qaeda as polar political opposites, of necessity cleaning up the radical Muslim for broad publication in a post-9/11 world. He then turns Malcolm's own analysis against him by ascribing it to the previously dubbed "condemned terrorists" whom Marable feels likewise compelled to turn into political straw men. Marable then relates again how al-Qaeda appropriated Malcolm and used his language to designate Obama as a "race-traitor," a "hypocrite," and, along with Colin Powell and Condoleeza Rice, "house negroes."[12] Whether or not these descriptions are accurate or have any validity at all can by then never even be considered, once rendered as the views of the condemned. Thus, by default, Obama, Powell, Rice, and the Black politics they represent stand anew alongside Malcolm X as equally opposing al-Qaeda. Marable therefore cleanses the contemporary by distorting the past and leaves only his own preferred reading of Malcolm as ever-maturing and apart from such hostile radicalism.

Furthermore, although Marable selectively quotes from the OAAU's objectives, careful to include its positive reference to the U.S. Constitution and Declaration of Independence,[13] he cautiously avoids mention of how those references were included to protect the OAAU's support of the right of every American citizen to bear arms, namely: "A man with a rifle or a club can only be stopped by a person who defends himself with a rifle or a club."[14] William Sales, in comments made while a participant on one of our radio program discussions of Marable's book, added to this point, reminding us that Ho Chi Minh also quoted from the Declaration of Independence in his 1945 declaration of Vietnamese sovereignty and that this certainly did not mean that Minh looked upon the United States uncritically.[15]

Similarly, and unlike Sales, Marable makes soft political use of his interview with Max Stanford in an attempt to refashion Malcolm's stance on armed struggle. Stanford was a cofounder of the Revolutionary Action Movement (RAM), a militant political organization and the only one that Malcolm X joined before his trip to Mecca in 1964. But despite his important organizational relationship with Malcolm X, it is not Stanford's politics that draws Marable's attention. In fact, Marable's mention of Stanford is mostly to support his speculations about Malcolm's "emotional state."[16] Sales' work, on the other hand, describes more fully the OAAU and its historic burgeoning relationship with RAM, according Stanford's contributions more appropriate meaning. Marable additionally fails to include Stanford's comments, as recounted by Sales, that the OAAU "was to be the broad front organization and RAM the underground Black Liberation Front of the U.S.A.."; nor does

Marable mention that the original name of the OAAU was to be the Afro-American Freedom Fighters—that is, before Malcolm was encouraged to change that name to a less overtly guerrilla warfare-inspired one, hence supporting the notion of the OAAU as RAM's "front."[17]

Marable also carefully avoids discussion of the OAAU's formally stated position on voting, a statement that clearly suggests an Obama presidency would be demonstrably antithetical to Malcolm's position on the matter. Marable, shortening the full statement, quotes from it as follows, writing that "the [OAAU] also promised to mobilize the entire African-American community 'block by block to make the community aware of its power and potential.'"[18] The complete statement, however, reads thus: "...we [the OAAU] will start immediately a voter-registration drive to make an *Independent voter*; we propose to support and/or organize political clubs, to run Independent candidates for office, and to support any Afro-American already in office who answers to and is responsible to the Afro-American community."[19]

Although Sales, among many others, was not interviewed by Marable, he pointed out several other contradictions between Malcolm's views on the vote during our radio program. He also took issue with Marable's description of those views as part of an overall attempt to situate Barack Obama within Malcolm's quite different and radical approach to electoral politics. Among the contradictions, Sales asserted that Malcolm more likely "anticipated" Obama's refusal to address the specific concerns of Black people. As further evidence of the differences between Malcolm and Obama, he noted the latter's preferred focus on the middle class as opposed to the worsening crisis of the poor (particularly the Black poor). He also noted the President's record-breaking Wall Street backing, his aggressive Zionism, support of U.S./Western imperialism through his backing of AFRICOM (the U.S. Africa Command), and his use of NATO to attack Libya—thus following, rather than breaking, an established pattern of U.S. military aggression and violent intervention in African governance.[20] On these bases alone, the political use and description of Malcolm X by al-Qaeda, contrasting him against establishment Black figures and politicians, is, despite Marable's dismissal of this use as turning Malcolm X into a "fiery symbol of ethnic violence and religious hatred," actually more accurate than Marable's own.[21]

Eugene Puryear offers a strong response to Marable's nuanced but constant attacks on Marxist-Leninist politics in his contributed essay. Puryear's defense of the meaning behind Malcolm's "The Ballot or the Bullet" speech is particularly convincing. As he points out, Marable selectively quotes from that speech, almost consistently critiques it without proper context, and, of course, never examines it in full. He further maintains that Marable construes the speech as proof of Malcolm's movement away from nationalist politics and of Malcolm's renewed hope in America's electoral system. Puryear additionally asserts that Marable draws a falsely connected political lineage, one that runs from Malcolm X directly to Barack Obama.

According to Puryear, Malcolm's message in "The Ballot or the Bullet" speech was similar to V. I. Lenin's view of voting, not as a trend toward pragmatism but as part of a revolutionary strategy. Like Kali Akuno and Kamau Franklin, Puryear suggests that although Malcolm may not have left us with a "unified system of thought" or a universal field theory of revolution, he did—contrary to Marable's reinvented Malcolm—"leave a clear spirit of resistance, militancy and defiance."

We credit Karl Evanzz—author, Malcolm X researcher, and contributor to this volume—not only with helping us to launch our own critique of Marable's work but also for engaging us via a radio interview in an important discussion on the nature of Marable's and his own source material. During that interview, the transcript of which we have included in this volume, we noted, as do most of the contributors to this book, that Marable, although he dismisses virtually all of the 1990s scholarship on Malcolm, uses that same body of work, with limited referencing, as the basis for his biographical data on Malcolm X and for his description of Malcolm's assassination. Indeed, to this last point, Evanzz responded that little of Marable's discussion of Malcolm's assassination troubled him because it was taken largely from his own work, or, as Evanzz explained, "[Marable] is just quoting me and Zak Kondo."[22]

Evanzz also characterized Marable, on the radio then and subsequently in his essay republished here, as a "fraudulent" scholar. He faults Marable specifically for giving Nation of Islam Minister Louis Farrakhan a virtual pass for his involvement in Malcolm X's assassination (a point also made by Franklin). He further cites Marable's baseless character assassination of Malcolm's father and his marginalization of the role played by Malcolm's older sister Ella in Malcolm's life, along with Marable's belittling of the Garvey movement and his inappropriate use of Malcolm's nephew Rodnell Collins as a source for the allegations about his subject's homosexuality. The latter Evanzz identifies as a mistake he himself once made decades ago, and one that he intends to correct in a forthcoming reissue of his earlier work on Malcolm's assassination.[23]

We also felt it important to include Amiri Baraka's essay on Marable's Malcolm X in this volume. In it, Baraka asks a fundamental question: "What was the consciousness that produced this work?" That inquiry leads to an equally important exploration of the history of the White Left, not as an ideological grounding for an analysis of Malcolm X's philosophy and ideas, but as an exploration into the mind and politics of Manning Marable. Baraka asserts that Marable's logic emanates from that of a life-long institutional academic (not a "movement" person) whose Democratic Socialist perspective is debilitatingly anti-Marxist-Leninist. As a result, he maintains, Marable was wholly incapable of interpreting Malcolm X's Black nationalism, pan-Africanism, or anti-colonialism/imperialism.

In a recent "debate" between Baraka and Michael Eric Dyson,[24] Baraka demonstrated that the particular history of progressive European politics—specifically, the history of Marxism, Leninism, socialism, and communism—remains largely unfamiliar to many of Marable's defenders. As adroitly as Baraka exposed Dyson's inexpertise with these radical White traditions, he herein exposes Marable's ineptness in this regard and holds it up, importantly, for investigation. During the radio discussion with Baraka, Dyson imprudently attempted to dismiss Baraka's efforts to explain the essential differences between revolutionary Marxism and social democracy as being grounded in the ideas of "dead White guys." This, of course, was not then, nor is it in these pages, Baraka's point. Rather, it was, and is, to save the history and image of once-threatening radical ideas, which may again threaten established power if they are not so consistently distorted.

Margo Arnold's critique offers what may stand as powerful insight into these and other issues related to Marable's perspective. Her examination of the concept of a Black Radical Collective Consciousness includes an examination—or rather, a juxtapositioning—of Marable, the elite academic, and the formation of his interpretative ideas. She accomplishes this in the manner of historiographer Edward Carr, who, she notes, "warned that belief in hard-core historical facts independent of the interpretation of the historian is a preposterous fallacy that is hard to eradicate." Thus, while exposing the necessary history about the relationship of Marable's "home" and funding institution (Columbia University) and the Harlem community—most specifically, the struggle around the preservation of the Audubon Ballroom, best known as the site where Malcolm X was assassinated—she exposes Marable's book as a work commissioned by a hostile entity. By so doing, she implicitly calls into question Marable's anti-radical motives, positing that his book exemplifies the worst of what Malcolm warned against: leadership and spokespeople propped up by "dollarism." Like others in this volume, Arnold concludes that *A Life of Reinvention* is ultimately a "fraudulent and demeaning text."

Chris Tinson's penultimate essay challenges Marable on a number of similar assumptions, railing specifically against Marable's posthumous liberalizing of Malcolm X. Tinson too juxtaposes a number of Marable's conclusions, particularly those that intentionally misinterpret Malcolm's views on electoral politics, with the nationalism of Harold

Cruse's warnings against all forms of integration, radical or conservative. Tinson contends that Marable's primary thrust in *A Life of Reinvention* was to alleviate his intended audience's concerns about how Malcolm X might be read today. He also claims that Marable sought to position Malcolm within a continuum whose conclusion is that of the vote as proof of the American political system's potential for radical change. Only in that way, Tinson concludes, could Marable present Barack Obama as an extension of Malcolm X's radical analysis. He reminds us necessarily (as did Malcolm) that support for a particular politician is not support for the overall political system, stressing that Malcolm routinely described the United States as fundamentally an imperial colonizing power that is, as yet, incapable of democracy. He further points out that, to Malcolm, electoral politics, by definition, could never be the sole or even the most heavily emphasized strategy for liberation. As Tinson concludes, Marable "read [Malcolm] in reverse" by projecting all of his shifts in ideology as both immature and trending toward the liberal. By questioning Marable's own analytic lens Tinson encourages us to challenge any attempt to depict changes in Malcolm X as either linear or liberal in trajectory.

In the coda to this volume, coeditor Todd Steven Burroughs uses his experience at a related panel event to contextualize the struggle against the liberalization of Malcolm X and his radical ideas. Burroughs challenges readers of Marable's *Malcolm X* to recognize how that author and his academic protégés are weakening the discussion of Black (and actually all) political struggle through what he and Greg Thomas describe as a process of branding. Both Burroughs and Thomas are correct in that once Malcolm X is branded in association with Marable, Columbia University, and Penguin/Viking Press, it/they become "absolutely unquestionable." Indeed, the simple fact of the book's branded status—contrary to the claims made by its defenders—extinguishes debate, further study, and (they hope) contemporary and future political organization around the ideas expressed by Malcolm X.

The branding that Burroughs and Thomas describe is a political act of obfuscation, one meant to distance an image or product from the reality of its origin or its political, economic, and social function. But their metaphorical reference has also become literal, as evidenced by the as-yet-unsuccessful attempts to engage defenders of Marable's *Malcolm X* in principled and public debate. Thus, as Burroughs uses an actual panel experience to highlight his point on the matter, so too might the absence of many other such panels—those that never were or apparently never will be—support the point as well. For example, we extended an early summer 2011 invitation to Zaheer Ali and other members of Marable's Malcolm X Project research team to appear on my radio show, to respond to questions that were to be provided weeks in advance. That invitation has never been answered. Similarly, several panels to which I was invited to debate Ali on the veracity of Marable's book have been cancelled or rescheduled without Ali's participation. As of the writing of this introduction, no such public debate has occurred with any other of Marable's critics.

The privilege granted by the power of branding is also one of evasion, elusion, and equivocation, such that, like the frightened boxer who avoids serious challenges to retain a fraudulently claimed belt, the establishment-sanctioned brand—Manning Marable's Malcolm X—"wins" by default. Left thus unchallenged, Marable's Malcolm silences and subdues Malcolm X and his truly revolutionary ideas—the ideas that made, and make him still, our "Black shining prince."[25] That is why we, the editors and contributors to this volume, collectively claim that the Marable-brand Malcolm is a self-negating testament against the man himself and why we have endeavored so mightily to be the negation of the negation. The amassed errors, distortions, omissions, and re-interpretations that accumulate to the lie that is Marable's *Malcolm X: A Life of Reinvention* need to be exposed as such.

Jared A. Ball
2012

ENDNOTES

1 John Henrik Clarke, ed., "Communication and Reality," in *Malcolm X: The Man and His Times* (Trenton, NJ: Africa World Press), 1990, 307-308. This quote is excerpted from a speech Malcolm gave to members of the Domestic Peace Corps on December 12, 1964.

2 Please see the latest *State of the Dream* report (for 2012) from the United for a Fair Economy (UFE) collective. This organization's research suggests that although the United States will soon witness racial shifts that will position White people as "minorities," persistent racial wealth divides, income gaps, Black mass incarceration, and inadequate access to housing will create conditions that mirror South African *apartheid* by 2042. Accessed February 25, 2012, http://faireconomy.org/dream/2012/executive_summary.

3 Our radio program, then called "The Legacy Edition of We Ourselves," airs most Fridays now under the name, "The Super Funky Soul Power Hour" on WPFW 89.3 FM Pacifica Radio in Washington, D.C. (The program is audio-archived online at http://www.voxunion.com/category/coupradio.)

4 See Wolf's interview with the National Book Foundation, 2011, archived online: http://www.nationalbook.org/nba2011_nf_marable_interv.html.

5 Ibid.

6 "Praise," from the publisher's website, archived online at: http://us.penguingroup.com/nf/Book/BookDisplay/0,,9780670022205,00.html?sym=REV.

7 Marika Sherwood, *Malcolm X Visits Abroad*. London: Tsehai Publishers, 2011.

8 John Henrik Clarke, ed., *Malcolm X: The Man and His Times* (Trenton, NJ: Africa World Press, 1991); William W. Sales, Jr., *From Civil Rights to Black Liberation: Malcolm X and the Organization of Afro-American Unity* (Boston: South End Press, 1999).

9 Marable, 487.

10 Ibid., 484.

11 Ibid., 487.

12 Ibid., 485-87.

13 Ibid, 350-51.

14 Clarke, *Malcolm X: The Man and His Times*, 337.

15 Interview with William Sales on "The Legacy Edition of We Ourselves," WPFW 89.3 FM Pacifica Radio, Washington, DC, June 3, 2011. Archived online at http://www.voxunion.com/malcolm-x-and-the-oaauafro-american-freedom-fighters/.

16 Marable, 355.

17 Sales, *From Civil Rights to Black Liberation*, 105-106.

18 Marable, 351.

19 Clarke, *Malcolm X: The Man and His Times*, 339, emphasis added.

20 Interview with William Sales.**

21 Marable, 487.

22 Interview with Karl Evanzz, on "The Legacy Edition of We Ourselves," April 15, 2011. Archived online at http://www.voxunion.com/malcolm-x-his-ideas-and-his-killers-w-karl-evanzz-and-zak-kondo.

23 Interview with Karl Evanzz, April 15, 2011.**

24 Interview on *Democracy Now!*, May 19, 2011. Archived online at http://www.democracynow.org/2011/5/19/manning_marables_controversial_new_biography_refuels.

25 Ossie Davis, "Eulogy for Malcolm X," February 27, 1965. Accessed March 1, 2012, http://www.hartford-hwp.com/archives/45a/071.html.

**A transcript of this interview also appears in this volume.

PATRICIA REID-MERRITT

Malcolm X: What Measure of a Man?—Assessing the Personal Growth and Social Transformation of Malcolm X From an African-Centered Social Work Perspective

El-Hajj Malik El-Shabazz and Manning Marable, two African American men of undoubtedly unequal historical significance, share one undeniable thing in common: Neither one is here to defend himself.

INTRODUCTION

Much has been said about the final scholarly contribution of Columbia University professor Manning Marable. Published just a few days following his untimely death, his book, *Malcolm X: A Life of Reinvention*, was favorably received by several leading Black intellectuals.[1] Henry Louis Gates, for one, hailed it as "the definitive biography of this outrageously misrepresented figure."[2] Cornel West praised it as the "definitive treatment of the greatest black radical voice and figure of the mid-twentieth century."[3] Michael Eric Dyson claimed that the book offered "a brilliant portrait of Malcolm" that "vividly captures the complicated outlines of black life at a critical juncture in American history."[4]

Other leading Black intellectuals expressed concerns about the book. According to Maulana Karenga, "Marable's reinvention of Malcolm is too often portrayed in negative and diminishing ways, depriving Malcolm of one of his most definitive characteristics, an audacious agency reflective of the awesome history and expansive humanity of his people."[5] Amiri Baraka viewed Marable's book as one weakened by "consistent attempts to 'reduce' Malcolm's known qualities and status with many largely unsubstantiated injections."[6] Abdul Alkalimat noted that some major conjectures in *A Life of Reinvention* led him to view the book as an egregious attempt at a scholarly work, one that "comes up short for lack of evidence."[7]

Social work is steeped in an understanding of the human condition and of how individuals, families, groups, and communities strive to develop their maximum human potential.[8] A fundamental tenet of the social work profession is to understand the human need and capacity for positive growth and social change. Assisting others to master the ability to dip into their deep reservoirs of inner strength and transform themselves into productive, contributing members of families and communities is one of the underlying goals of the social work profession. For the African-centered social work professional, the ability to assess the personal growth and social transformation of individuals and their communities is deeply rooted in the African experience. As such, the impact of history, cultural heritage, and social milieu cannot be dismissed.[9] It is within such a framework, one grounded in the belief that the essence of life is about change and transformation, that I will examine Manning Marable's assessment of the life of Malcolm X and of Malcolm's contribution to the struggle for Black freedom, equality, and human dignity.

MANNING WHO?

On the surface, *Malcolm X: A Life of Reinvention* evinces a major scholarly undertaking befitting of those individuals whose life works are tied to the academy. Its impressive number of pages (594), nearly 500 notes, and hundreds of reference sources cause readers to pause and consider the mammoth amount of effort devoted to the preparation of this work. However, sheer volume alone does not automatically equate to great scholarly work. One must raise questions about the nature and quality of the research and about the author's motives, social location, and political orientation.

In this particular assessment of Marable's Malcolm X book, one must also ask questions about the perceived social and personal benefits of deliberately producing a controversial book that casts doubts on the motives, character, and sincerity of one of the most revered figures of the Black freedom movement. In that light, who was Manning Marable, and what compelled him to engage in such an endeavor?

William Manning Marable was born in 1950 in the American Midwest. He was a child of the 1960s, raised on images of the Civil Rights and Black Power struggles that gripped the nation. Like many of us from that generation, Marable heard the cries for freedom and social justice and sought ways to participate in the movement for social change. Coming of age during America's socially tumultuous Civil Rights era set us apart from the previous generation and allowed us to question, without restriction, all claims of definitive social truths put forward by the status quo, both Black and White.

It was in this socially charged environment that Marable developed his keen sense of intellectual curiosity about issues affecting the African world community and his fascination with one of the leading voices of the Black freedom movement: Malcolm X. According to Marable: "The origins of [*A Life of Reinvention*] date back to the winter of 1969, my freshman year at Earlham College in Indiana, when I first read *The Autobiography of Malcolm X*. Malcolm had become the icon of the Black Power movement, and I eagerly devoured the edited volumes of his speeches and interviews."[10] Marable further states that he, like others, initially accepted the *Autobiography*, which Malcolm co-wrote with Alex Haley, as a statement of truth, but over the next several decades began to question "numerous inconsistencies, errors, and fictive characters at odds with Malcolm's actual life history."[11]

Marable's transformative journey in the academic community, from his first exposure to Malcolm X to the publication of his own book on

Malcolm, altered and further shaped his worldview. A trained historian, he developed a professional career as an educator, public speaker, and advocate for social democracy, citizen participation, and progressive social ideals. He spent several decades in the field of Black Studies and played a leading role in establishing a Black Studies presence at Columbia University. Marable was also an outspoken social critic who promoted both popular and unpopular causes. He was a vocal critic of racially based and culturally conscious theories of Black social and political development, castigating these as inept theoretical constructs that did not provide "critical study of historical realities" leading to a larger movement toward social change.[12]

Marable's view of the world was framed primarily by his belief that a true democratic process trumped all other efforts for social and political unity.[13] This view did not hold true for Malcolm X, whose social orientation and commitment to a political platform rested on a belief in undeniable Blackness—that is, a vision of racial unity among all African people.[14] For Marable, however, Malcolm's ideal could never be viewed as a viable, socially galvanizing political option.

According to Marable, the major purpose of his book on Malcolm X was to shed light on what he believed to be the untold, problematic, and hidden, true-life story of the man, purportedly by utilizing new historical records heretofore unavailable or inaccessible to other scholars and researchers. Given Marable's sociopolitical orientation, however, and the way in which he presents this scholarship in the book, it also seems clear that Marable's intent was to shape a new view of Malcolm X—one that conformed to his own perspectives. And although he criticizes Alex Haley's 1965 work on Malcolm X as one in which the author presumably "had an agenda of his own,"[15] it appears that Manning too is guilty of the same charge.

WHAT MEASURE OF A MAN?

There is little doubt that *A Life of Reinvention* raises questions about the genuine character of Malcolm X and the life Malcolm chose to live. In so many ways, Marable's re-telling of Malcolm X's life is an example of an epic tragedy, one that clearly demonstrates the destructive characteristics of individuals, social institutions, and society. The major difficulty with Marable's work is its author's analysis, interpretation, and presentation of material he believes to be factual. Throughout the book, he utilizes a consistently problematic framework to portray Malcolm X as a consciously conniving, slick character weighed down by a heavy element of sleaze. The approach apparently favored by Marable is that of character assassination, which he wields repeatedly to diminish the image of Malcolm X.

Marable would have his readers believe that the socially undesirable characteristics that Malcolm X developed in his early life as "Detroit Red" remained a permanent part of his personality. He further avers that Malcolm X was a "hustler/trickster" who managed to capture the imagination of Black America[16]; a chronic liar who embellished the truths of his early beginnings; and a crook—but not a big crook, just a little one.[17] Marable also portrays Malcolm X as a disloyal friend and confidant[18]; a confused misogynist[19]; a poor father, husband, and sexual partner[20]; and a closet homosexual who sold sexual favors to a wealthy White man.[21] Marable makes many additional disturbing claims about the depth of Malcolm X's religious and political convictions: that Malcolm conspired with the Ku Klux Klan[22]; supported the southern segregationist Republican, Barry Goldwater[23]; and evidenced two-faced support and resentment of Martin Luther King Jr., and other Black civil rights leaders.[24]

Although a clear record, one acknowledged by Malcolm, exists of his troubling earlier life experiences as a pimp, thief, drug dealer, and ex-convict,[25] other claims put forth in *A Life of Reinvention* are unsubstantiated. Relying mostly on insinuations, innuendo, and undocumented proofs, Marable, in an apparent effort to tarnish Malcolm X's reputation, raises a number of unjustifiable questions about Malcolm's personal, ethical, and moral character. On numerous occasions, he makes claims about Malcolm's character, only to acknowledge the lack of evidence to support his suspicions. He does so by deliberately focusing on sensitive issues that would likely provoke concern, particularly in the African American community.

For example, with regard to claims about Malcolm X's sexual desires and infidelity, Marable notes, "It is impossible to know whether the minister rekindled sexual intimacies with his longtime love [Evelyn Williams], or if Islamic sanctions against premarital sex affected their behavior."[26] If such speculation is "impossible to know," why then is it necessary for Marable to include it? He also states that years after Malcolm's death, Nation of Islam Minister Louis Farrakhan "insisted that Malcolm continued to be deeply in love with Evelyn Williams," but later admits that the only person expressing this claim was Minister Farrakhan.[27]

Marable's references to Malcolm X's sexual orientation must be viewed as direct attacks on Malcolm's manhood, which Marable believed the Black community had embraced as the ultimate symbol of the strong, masculine, defiant image of a Black man. For example, when offering insights to Malcolm's supposedly secret sex life, Marable writes the following: "Based on circumstantial but strong evidence, Malcolm was probably describing his own homosexual encounters . . ."[28] The use of the terms *circumstantial* and *probably* to support a claim of "strong evidence" is a definitive example of an oxymoron. Facts can only be based on undeniable truths, and in this instance, Marable's "evidence" is obviously lacking. Moreover, as Clarence Lang,[29] Baraka,[30] and Alkalimat[31] have noted, in those areas throughout the book for which Marable does not have specific details, he appears more than willing to speculate. Lang contends that Marable "often overreaches his evidence, does not rely enough on primary documents, and draws too many conclusions from inferences and speculation."[32]

Regarding Alex Haley's critically acclaimed work on Malcolm X, Marable makes the following claim, noting that, "Haley was not above enhancing the material when discussing it with his editors, partly because of the story's real commercial possibilities."[33] Does not Marable embellish his own Malcolm tale for the same possible commercial benefits, given that most of the discussion about the content and direction of the book was between him and his editor, who undoubtedly was seeking to publish a commercially successful product? And finally, although Marable's efforts toward presenting a revisionist history of Malcolm X are disturbing enough on their own, they raise an even larger question: Why is Marable's line of inquiry relevant to explorations of the role and contribution that Malcolm X made to the struggle for Black freedom?

THE UNDENIABLE X

One of the more interesting and ironic outcomes of *A Life of Reinvention* is the wealth of information it has brought forth about the undeniable social and historical significance of Malcolm X. According to Marable: "[Malcolm] was a truly historic figure in the sense that, more than any of his contemporaries, he embodied the spirit, vitality, and political mood of an entire population—namely, Black, urban, mid-twentieth-century America."[34] As a cultural and political icon, Marable contends that Malcolm X "gave millions of younger African Americans newfound confidence. These expressions were at the foundation of what in 1966 became Black Power, and Malcolm was its fountainhead."[35] Marable includes Bayard Rustin's assessment of Malcolm in support of his claim, repeating Rustin's claim that "[Malcolm's] contribution was substantial. He brought hope and a measure of dignity to thousands of despairing ghetto Negroes."[36] To this, Marable adds his own view: "Even when I have disagreed with [Malcolm], I deeply admire the strength and integrity of his character, and the love he obviously felt toward the African-American people and their culture."[37]

Unfortunately, having acknowledged these accolades in the introduction and different sections of his book, Marable proceeds to kick dirt on a dead man's grave. Yet, if, as he believed, the publication of his book would lead to an altered view of Malcolm, the man—that is, as one of a man with diminished admirable human qualities and character—then ultimately Marable failed. He failed by attempting to give greater weight to Malcolm's real or imagined human frailties than to the man's tremendous strengths.

The retelling of Malcolm's life story reveals that throughout his brief life, Malcolm exhibited an exceptional ability to grow, develop, and transform himself into a mature and admirable human being who lived a purposeful life. He was a tremendous survivor, well honed in the social and cultural techniques needed to thrive in a racist social environment. He was also a thoughtful and mature man who possessed undeniable power and influence, and he was clearly an articulate and inspirational leader of his people.

American racism produced Malcolm X, both as a political and religious being, yet Malcolm engaged in day-to-day struggle to claim his right to self-determination. In his fight to affirm the inherent dignity, value, and worth of the Black race, he never wavered. He was, indeed, an exceptional individual who achieved extraordinary accomplishments during extraordinary times, from the internal building of the Nation of Islam to the establishment of the Organization of Afro-American Unity. When he was born in 1925, Malcolm was just another poor Negro boy in the segregated Midwest with limited social opportunity, but he became an internationally acclaimed and recognized advocate for social justice.

In assessing the growth and personal transformation of Malcolm X, one must emphasize, even if Marable does not, his enormous reservoir of inner strength that allowed him to devote his life to the struggle for Black freedom. Malcolm did not play the game of social "reinvention," as Marable contends; rather, he was actively engaged in the ongoing human process of growth, development, and social change. And he succeeded.

Marable's efforts to provide a new interpretation of Malcolm X cannot diminish the magnitude of Malcolm's historic impact. From an African-centered social work perspective, all that Malcolm X was able to achieve in his lifetime far outweighs any real or perceived questions about his possible human weaknesses. His enormous strength, courage, social accomplishments, and achievements should be the focus of his historical record and legacy.

It is also important to note that, within Marable's framework, few of the individuals or organizations that helped to shape the focus and direction of the book escape unscathed by his critical pen. Equally disconcerting and unfavorable claims about the undesirable personal and social characteristics of the Nation of Islam; Elijah Muhammad; the Fruit of Islam; Malcolm's sister Ella Little Collins; and, perhaps most tragically, Malcolm's widow, Betty Shabazz, whom Marable repeatedly portrays as the socially and religiously convenient wife, life partner, and mother of Malcolm's six children. Pertaining to these significant persons and organizations in Malcolm X's life, Marable readily admits "gossip" as the main source of his data.[38]

GIVING VOICE TO BETTY

Not surprisingly, Marable's portrayal of Betty Dean Sanders Shabazz, who will forever be known as Malcolm's wife and widow, is less than flattering. He repeatedly posits, for example, that notions romanticizing a loving relationship between Malcolm and Betty were part of the popular folklore that developed after Malcolm's death. Marable's misrepresentation of Betty and his misguided ideas about her relationship with her husband must be addressed, for Betty was a central figure in Malcolm's life.

Betty Dean was born in 1934 in Detroit, Michigan, and raised by foster parents. After experiencing numerous incidents of southern-style, Jim Crow racism in Alabama while attending Tuskegee Institute, she moved to New York City, where she trained to be a nurse. It was there that she met Malcolm and became involved with the Nation of Islam.[39] Utilizing second- and third-party sources, Marable describes Betty's relationship and marriage with Malcolm as challenging, stressful, and personally and emotionally unfulfilling for both. He further portrays Betty in the image of a pathetic Black woman, trapped by conflicting social, personal, and religious values. From personal experience, I recall her quite differently.

I first met Betty at a small café called the Red Bull in Nairobi, Kenya, in 1985. We both had traveled back to the Motherland to attend the Third World Conference on Women. Six other African American women and I were joining Betty for an informal lunch at the café, and we were all nervous. After all, we would be sitting with the widow of the icon of the Black Power movement, Betty Shabazz! Betty, on the other hand, was calm and joyful, and she engaged the small gathering of nervous sisters quite easily.

We were barely finished with our soup before she started talking about her love for Malcolm. We listened eagerly. She was a bit playful and coquettish, teasing us with stories about her relationship with her late husband. Without warning, she began to talk about their shared intimacies in a way that made us all blush. At one point, a young sister even blurted out, "That's just too much information for me to know about my hero!"

The next day, I had the pleasure of arranging an informal reception for Betty at the home of Omar and Sabrina Muhammad, a prominent Muslim family in the Nairobi community. The Muhammads were overwhelmed and delighted at the thought of hosting a gathering for the widow of Malcolm X. Betty and I shared a ride to and from their home in a rented limousine. In that brief period of time, she continued to discuss her love for Malcolm and, again, without warning, began sharing stories about how their intimate life resulted in six female children. She also explained why she was no longer a Muslim and, as Marable correctly describes, the anger and frustration she felt about the lack of support that she received for herself and her family from the Muslim community following the death of her husband. In my view, Betty portrayed herself as an independent woman, one who had pulled herself up by her own bootstraps to survive and provide for herself and her six daughters. When we arrived at the Muhammads' home, Betty was welcomed—or more accurately, aggressively embraced—by all present. She reveled in the attention they showered on her.

I saw Betty on several occasions after our return from Kenya, mostly from afar. My most memorable contact with her was a conversation we had in 1987 while she was visiting Philadelphia. I was struggling with the burden of my daughter's battle with typhoid fever and Betty offered wise and comforting advice. She reminded me of the many life challenges, particularly those of motherhood, that all women face and assured me that loving care and the marvels of modern medicine would pull my daughter through adversity.

The Betty Shabazz I knew was a genuine woman with little patience for pretense. She was intelligent, confident, witty, and assertive. She was also a woman of indomitable strength. Marable, however, presents a different view.

Basing his assertions on what he himself describes as "gossip," Marable portrays Betty as a manipulative, conniving individual who was trapped in a loveless marriage of convenience, deprived of both commitment and devotion.[40] Lacking solid proof, he airs a number of other pernicious claims about Malcolm and Betty. He alleges, for example, that both husband and wife, but more specifically the wife, engaged in adultery.[41] He further concludes that Malcolm X's willingness to devote himself to the cause of Black liberation and to dedicate himself to the unrelenting public appearance schedule that resulted from his immense popularity is proof that Malcolm did not embrace his role as a husband and father.[42]

But even Marable is forced to acknowledge the contradictions inherent in what he assumes to be true versus the definitive truth as spoken by Betty. He notes, for example, that Betty "would always insist that Malcolm had pursued her 'persistently and correctly,'" during their courtship[43] and that she personally described her marriage as "hectic, beautiful, and unforgettable—the greatest thing in my life."[44] Despite Betty's claims, Marable concludes the following: "In reality, the twenty-three-year-old [Betty] was poorly prepared for married life."[45] The sheer arrogance of his conclusion begs the question: How is anyone to know who is or is not "prepared" for marriage, and who is Marable to judge?

In *Lackawana Blues*, a play and movie based on the life of playwright and actor Reuben Santiago-Hudson, Mama, the central character, delivers a very memorable line as she attempts to explain to the young Rueben the complex relationship between herself and her young lover. As she proclaims: "There's no explaining some things that are between a man and a woman."[46] I believe that this will and should remain true for the private life of Malcolm and Betty.

Marable further notes that, following the death of her husband, Betty Shabazz enrolled in a doctoral program in education at the University of Massachusetts, Amherst. She received her PhD three years later and went on to serve as an academic administrator at Medgar Evers College in Brooklyn, New York. There, Betty gained a solid reputation as a noted educator and social advocate, particularly around issues related to public health. Of her independent work, however, Marable's view is, again, less than flattering. As he writes, Betty became only "a *sort of* [emphasis mine] celebrity among black middle-class and professional groups."[47]

Like her husband, who preceded her in death, Betty is no longer here to give voice to her own defense. She died in June 1997, from severe burns that she received from a fire set in her home by one of her grandsons. Regardless of the perceived or real difficulties and challenges that Betty faced during her life with Malcolm, she too was able to transform herself into a purposeful, productive individual. Marable aside, she too deserves to be remembered for her most admirable traits and her important contributions to the life and legacy of Malcolm X and the movement for Black liberation.

CONCLUSION

In its entirety, it may be difficult to set aside *Malcolm X: A Life of Reinvention* with the hope that it will not be embraced by a new generation of students, historians, scholars, and youthful revolutionary-minded enthusiasts. The work has already received tremendous exposure in the press and academic community and, in all probability, it will be part of the public discourse in Black America for many years to come. As even Amiri Baraka, one of the book's staunchest critics, maintains, the best thing about its publication is the renewed interest and heightened level of discussion it has generated about Malcolm throughout the worldwide African community.[48]

However, *A Life of Reinvention* cannot be permitted to become the definitive last word on the life and times of Malcolm X. New readers, both young and old, who seek to learn more about the iconic cultural figure must look pass the flimsy and unsubstantiated aspects of the work—past even those aspects that Maulana Karenga describes as "salacious"[49]—and seek out the valuable lessons presented. Although Marable repeatedly casts doubt on the perceived impeccable character of his primary subject, his book builds an incredibly strong case for viewing Malcolm X as one of most charismatic, effective, and admired Black leaders of the twentieth century. It also provides readers with numerous opportunities to move beyond the negative assessments of Malcolm and focus on the positive.

Marable's reinvention of Malcolm X's life as one cast in the framework of a slickster hell-bent on getting something from or getting over on somebody is perhaps this epic work's greatest misrepresentation. In truth, the facts and evidence of Malcolm's life offer instead an example of a constantly growing and transforming social being who engaged in a lifetime of struggle to develop the best fit between himself, his values, his beliefs, and his social environment. Thus, when Marable concludes that Malcolm, "through his powerful language . . . inspired blacks to see themselves not as victims, but possessing the agency to transform themselves and their lives,"[50] he is right on point. When he writes that "Malcolm encouraged blacks to celebrate their culture"[51] and that his "spiritual journey was linked to his black consciousness"[52] and the love of his people, readers of *A Life of Reinvention* acknowledge that Marable was capable of capturing the real life story of Malcolm X without bias or envy.

Yet, all must proceed cautiously in the continuous investigation, critique, and development of new scholarship around the historically significant period known as the Black Freedom Movement. As those of us who are scholars and researchers strive to offer new insights and interpretations of the challenges and achievements of that era and its most notable figures, we must be mindful of our responsibility to provide an accurate, detailed account of the past that is both grounded in historical truth and dignity and reflective of an African-centered view of the world. It is now our responsibility to preserve our historical legacy.

ENDNOTES

1 Manning Marable, *Malcolm X: A Life of Reinvention.* New York: Viking Press, 2011.

2 Henry Louis Gates Jr., endorsement (back cover) for *Malcolm X: A Life of Reinvention.* New York: Viking Press, 2011.

3 Cornel West, endorsement (back cover) for *Malcolm X: A Life of Reinvention.* New York: Viking Press, 2011.

4 Michael Eric Dyson, endorsement (back cover) for *Malcolm X: A Life of Reinvention.* New York: Viking Press, 2011.

5 Maulana Karenga, "Pursuing Pathology by Another Name," *The Los Angeles Sentinel*, April 21, 2011, http://www.lasentinel.net/Reinventing-Malcolm-with-Marable-Part-III.html.

6 Amiri Baraka, comment on *The Pan-African News Wire*, "On Manning Marable's Malcolm X Book," May 10, 2011, http://panafricannews.blogspot.com/2011/05/amiri-baraka-on-manning-marable-malcolm_10.html.*

7 Abdul Alkalimat, "Rethinking Malcolm: What was Marable Thinking?" *The San Francisco Bay View*, July 8, 2011, http://sfbayview.com/2011/rethinking-malcolm-what-was-marable-thinking.

8 Patricia Reid-Merritt, *Righteous Self-Determination: The Black Social Work Movement in America*. Baltimore: Black Classic Press, 2010.

9 Ibid.

10 Marable, *Malcolm X: A Life of Reinvention*, 489.

11 Ibid.

12 *Manning Marable, Beyond Black and White: Transforming African American Politics* (New York: Verso, 1996), 192.

13 Ibid.

14 See the "Malcolm X Papers," housed at New York Public Library's Schomburg Center for Research in Black Culture.

15 Marable, *Malcolm X: A Life of Reinvention*, 9.

16 Ibid., 11, 74.

17 Ibid., 51.

18 Ibid., 67.

19 Ibid., 36, 116.

20 Ibid., 150.

21 Ibid., 66.

22 Ibid., 13, 178–79, 180.

23 Ibid., 352, 367.

24 Ibid., 252, 264–65.

25 Malcolm X, *The Autobiography of Malcolm X as Told to Alex Haley*. New York: Grove Press, 1965.

26 Marable, *Malcolm X: A Life of Reinvention*, 140–41.

27 Ibid., 266.

28 Ibid., 66.

29 *Solidarity: A Socialist, Feminist, Anti-Racist Organization*, "Book Review: Manning Marable and Malcolm X: The Power of Biography" (by Clarence Lang), http://www.solidarity-us.org/node/3358.

30 Baraka, "On Manning Marable's Malcolm X Book."*

31 Alkalimat, "Rethinking Malcolm."

32 Lang, "Manning Marable and Malcolm X."

33 Marable, *Malcolm X: A Life of Reinvention*, 331.

34 Ibid., 13.

35 Ibid., 480.

36 Ibid., 466.

37 Ibid., 14.

38 Ibid., 379, 388.

39 Wikipedia, "Betty Shabazz," http://en.wikipedia.org/wiki/Betty_Shabazz.

40 Marable, Chapter 5, "Brother, a Minister *Has* to Be Married," 130–54; see also 145–50, 164, 180–81.

41 Ibid., 266, 379–81; 385–86, 393–94, 427.

42 Ibid., 217, 222, 379–82.

43 Ibid., 145.

44 Ibid., 147.

45 Ibid.

46 Reuben Santiago-Hudson, *Lackawana Blues*, HBO Movie Special, 2005.

47 Marable, *Malcolm X: A Life of Reinvention*, 472.

48 Baraka, "On Manning Marable's Malcolm X Book."*

49 Karenga, "Pursuing Pathology."

50 Marable, *Malcolm X: A Life of Reinvention*, 481.

51 Ibid.

52 Ibid.

*This essay also appears in this volume.

MUMIA ABU-JAMAL

Manning's Malcolm—& Ours (2.0)

Abu-Jamal's initial statement about and response to Malcolm X: A Life of Reinvention *has been widely disseminated. In this essay, he offers a "2.0" version—a revised, closer look and a far more critical reflection.*

It is a measure of the power of Malcolm X's memory that it still evokes both controversy and passion almost half a century after his passing into death and martyrdom. Master historian Manning Marable's recent contribution, *Malcolm X: A Life of Reinvention*, which has sparked both such strong reactions, merely confirms that observation.

At nearly six hundred pages in length, it has the dubious distinction of being both Marable's masterwork and tragic in its shortcomings. Tragic, too, was the untimely passing of Marable, who made his transition mere days before the work hit stores. There is something both eerie and poignant about reading, in the book's acknowledgements, Marable's discussion of his "full recovery" from a double lung transplant and his "successful surgery" (to address complications caused by sarcoidosis) just days after his passing.[1] That very real sense of tragedy, however, does not mitigate the work, which suffers from serious and undeniable maladies.

Every student of history knows that one lives or dies according to one's primary or secondary sources and, indeed, one's interpretation of the same. In a work of *A Life of Reinvention*'s length, about a figure so central to twentieth-century African American identity, it is disturbing to read about charges of Malcolm's alleged homosexuality with little or no substantiation save sheer speculation and rumor.[2] Marable, utilizing page notes as opposed to footnotes, offers absolutely nothing to support his view. Although former US Secretary of Defense Donald Rumsfeld infamously and repeatedly noted (referring to Iraq's suspected weapons of mass destruction) that "absence of evidence is not evidence of absence," for a historian, such a lapse seems unforgivable. This is especially so in Marable's case because he was a master historian in the sense that he "made" other historians via his exalted role at Columbia University.

Betty Shabazz receives similar treatment through Marable's use of rumor and innuendo to discuss her alleged affair with Charles 37X Kenyatta. Though it is difficult to prove such activities, given the nature of human sexual behavior, it is also true that over great periods of time (in this case, almost fifty years), tongues loosen. In that respect as well, Marable seems to go for the sensational rather than for that which he can substantiate.

Marable's uncovering of the internal letters between Alex Haley and his editors is likewise revealing. In some ways, those letters are startling in their tone, for they expose what seems like a fundamental betrayal of the "subject" (Malcolm X) by an author (Haley) who regards his subject with more than a hint of condescension and, perhaps, even contempt. This revelation brings a sparkle to Marable's work, for it shows its readers the unwritten (in the text, that is) rules that shaped, formed, and finalized what has become a classic work, *The Autobiography of Malcolm X*, which has reached millions at home and abroad.

What is perhaps most disturbing about Marable's so-called magnum opus is his signal failure to grapple with the impact and reality of COINTELPRO—especially the Federal Bureau of Investigation's covert and often illegal Counter-Intelligence Program—on the lives of Malcolm and his followers. This infamous program is not even referenced formally in the book's index! Indeed, Marable seems to treat the FBI and police files that he (and his researchers) perused as simple governmental documents—that is, as ones that should be accorded trust unless shown otherwise.

In this writer's mind, Marable's shortcomings on that score evince a level of naiveté that is nothing short of stunning, for they highlight the class and experiential differences between those who have merely read or theorized about Black liberation struggles and those who have lived and participated in such movements. To accept the FBI's documents without question flies in the face of both scholarly practice and firsthand accounts by agents who worked in the field. It further shows, with crystalline clarity, the class divide between a bourgeois, Ivy League historian and the many hundreds of thousands who labored in the fields of the Black liberation struggle and who faced the full might of the state for doing so.

Marable's failure to address the psychological aspects of perpetual surveillance on individuals and movements leaves his readers in the dark about how those who must operate under such conditions actually perform in their social, organizational, and personal roles. An honest account of this de-facto war against dissent provides understanding of the pervasive paranoia that suffused movements of the 1960s.

Why a historian of Marable's standing and expertise neither utilizes nor references works that would have provided an inside—or at least a political and functional—view of the role of the FBI (and, indeed, the state) in its relationship with Black nationalist and/or Black liberation organizations is beyond me. Numerous sources are available, including reports on the findings of the 1976 US Senate Subcommittee hearings (popularly known as the Church Committee hearings) on the topic, the latter of which are, to say the least, troubling.[3] For his failure to provide this critical contextual framework—which may have required perhaps half a chapter to set forth—Marable, by default, normalizes the FBI, presenting it as just another law enforcement agency. He also misrepresents the FBI's and other agencies' historic, contemporary, and continuing role in American society as essentially the "race police" or discrete defenders of White supremacy. This serious omission, especially for people who would be drawn to *A Life of Reinvention* due largely to their familiarity with the name "Malcolm X," does a disservice to younger readers who were not alive during the 1960s. Marable and his book leave those audiences woefully uninformed.

That said, for Marable to have tackled the book's theme and its subject at all took considerable courage of a sort that is not often seen in academia. His failures, to be sure, limit the scope of the work, yet his successes elevate it. *A Life of Reinvention* acutely captures the sense of frustration, betrayal, and—yes—paranoia that must have suffused Malcolm's consciousness when he saw the forces arrayed against him by many of the men he personally recruited to the Nation of Islam. The book also captures the "air" of the time, juxtaposing the lazy, taciturn 1950s against the explosive, bombastic 1960s. Marable paints Malcolm as a smart, determined, and quite able man who, for all of his considerable gifts, had (as do we all) significant deficits.

And true to the book's subtitle, one must conclude that Malcolm was indeed a creative master of constant reinvention—evolving from hustler and convict to minister, activist, exile, and revolutionary organizer in ways similar to those of his contemporary in leadership: that incipient socialist, Martin Luther King Jr.

Although some reviewers and activists have taken issue with the notion of reinvention as posed in Marable's book, the question remains: Who does not change when confronted with a fast-changing world? Is a man of thirty-five the same man he was at twenty-one? One certainly hopes not.

Despite the continuing agitation roiling throughout New York, Philadelphia, and other cities where Malcolm lived, labored, and ministered, Marable succeeds in making Malcolm and Betty appear more "human" and thus more accessible to us all in the present era. Through Marable's book, Malcolm and Betty are better able to inspire us to similar reinventions and to enrich our lives with their sacrifices and splendid examples.

ENDNOTES

1 Manning Marable, *Malcolm X: A Life of Reinvention* (New York, Viking Press, 2011), 493.

2 Ibid., 66, 78.

3 See, for example, US Congress, *Senate Select Committee to Study Governmental Operations with Respect to Intelligence Activities* (Final report, 94th Congress, 2nd Session, Books I–VI, *et al.*), Washington, DC: US Government Printing Office, 1976; Ward Churchill and Jim Vander Wall, *The COINTELPRO Papers: Documents from the FBI's Secret Wars Against Dissent in the United States,* Cambridge, MA: South End Press, 1990/1992; and Frank Donner, *The Age of Surveillance: The Aims and Methods of America's Political Intelligence System,* New York: Vintage, 1981.

KALI AKUNO

A Work of Negation: A Critical Review of Manning Marable's *Malcolm X: A Life of Reinvention*[1]

In his effort to twist and distort the meaning of Malcolm X's life into one more palatable to the liberal, multicultural, social democratic forces who supported his work, Manning Marable has missed the mark. His inverse portrait of Malcolm in his final years, as that of a pragmatic liberal humanist, is polemical and dismissive—a mere assemblage of minutia rather than a palpable biography. Moreover, it overlooks the essence of Malcolm's revolutionary nationalist and Pan-Africanist agendas as embodied in the goals and objectives of the organization he founded before his death: the OAAU, or Organization of Afro-American Unity.

Manning Marable's *Malcolm X: A Life of Reinvention* must be seen for what it is: an ideological polemic. The general focus of this polemic is Black Nationalism and revolutionary Black Nationalism in particular. Marable's critical focus and fixation on Malcolm X as the quintessential point of reference for Black Nationalists since his cold-blooded assassination in 1965 is a means to socially advance a line of reasoning against this broad political philosophy and social movement by turning its iconic figurehead on his head. The objective of this inversion is to prove, in no less than 594 pages, that those who adhere to and seek to advance some variant of a Black Nationalist program not only have it all wrong, but in fact are distorting what Malcolm himself stood for at the end of his days.

A LIE OF REINVENTION

As Marable would have it, at the time of his assassination, Malcolm X had all but abandoned Black Nationalism to become a pragmatic, liberal humanist with social democratic political leanings. As several critics have already pointed out, this character bears a striking resemblance to Marable himself. Paraphrasing Patrick Moynihan, although Marable is unquestionably entitled to his own opinion, he is not entitled to his own facts. And the fact stands that the document that most clearly reflects Malcolm X's political philosophy and programmatic orientation at the time of his death is the program of the Organization of Afro-American Unity (OAAU).

The OAAU's was without question a revolutionary nationalist program. It was modeled on the anti-imperialist program of the Organization of African Unity (OAU) advanced by the Casablanca block of the Union in the early 1960s. The Casablanca Group included several progressive states that were offering political, financial, and military aid to the revolutionary, anticolonial struggles then raging on the continent of Africa, particularly in the Portuguese-held colonies and southern Africa. Chief among the Casablanca states were Kwame Nkrumah's Ghana, Sekou Toure's Guinea, and Gamal Abdel-Nassar's Egypt—all of whose leaders Malcolm X had long known and admired. This closeness is evidenced by Malcolm's constant references to the 1955 Afro-Asian or Bandung Conference, even prior to his departure from the Nation of Islam (NOI); and to the Non-Aligned Movement, to which he was relating concretely at the time of his death. Marable consistently tries to tiptoe around these and other clearly known facts, and, where he cannot, he insists on trying to twist their meaning into something more temperate and palatable to the liberal, nonracial or multicultural, social democratic movement and program he was seeking to advance.

Nowhere is this thrust by Marable more painfully evident than on pages 484 through 486 of his book. The selection that perhaps best illustrates Marable's disdain for Black Nationalism, and his narrow interpretation of it, is found on page 485, where he states:

> The unrealized dimension of Malcolm's racial vision was that of Black nationalism. A political ideology that originated before the Civil War, Black nationalism was based on the assumption that racial pluralism leading to assimilation was impossible in the United States. So cynical were many nationalists about the incapacity of whites to overcome their own racism that they occasionally negotiated with white terrorist groups like the Ku Klux Klan, in the mistaken belief that they were more honest about their racial attitudes than liberals. Yet as Malcolm's international experiences became more varied and extensive, his social vision expanded. He became less intolerant and more open to multiethnic and interfaith coalitions. By the final months of his life, he resisted identification as a "Black nationalist," seeking ideological shelter under the race-neutral concepts of Pan-Africanism and Third World revolution.

Marable rehashes the old liberal line against Black Nationalism—that it is a largely rejected strain of Black politics that periodically re-emerges like a phoenix during times of heightened oppression against Black people. Like many of his predecessors who held and advanced this line, Marable has a hard time grasping the fact that since the inception of the genocidal White-settler project that is the United States, there have been large numbers of African people who have not been in the least mystified by the material and ideological trappings of their would-be masters. Moreover, these Africans have sought at various times and in various ways to establish their own independent states or safe havens on American soil or they have sought repatriation back to Africa. Uncompromising self-determination and sovereignty has always been the fundamental objective of this tendency of the Black Liberation movement. Marable's statements assume that structurally the United States is qualitatively less White supremacist in nature now than it was in the nineteenth century. Though some of the formal trappings of White supremacy have changed (and changed considerably, as in the case of the elimination of de jure apartheid), the fundamental essentials of the racist political economy in the US remain the same. One must also keep in mind that although history never repeats itself exactly, there are plenty of signs that the "second Reconstruction" has exhausted itself with the election of President Obama and is in the process of being reversed, much as the first Reconstruction was reversed between the late 1870s and 1890s.

Neither Pan-Africanism, Third World Internationalism, nor Tri-Continentalism was ever "race-neutral." All of these social movements were and are crystal clear in their assertions that one of their primary enemies has been and remains White supremacy, be it in the guise of European and American colonial occupation or imperialist exploitation. Malcolm X's deepening embrace of Pan-Africanism and Third World Internationalism was never a rejection or retreat from Black Nationalism. If anything, as it pertains to Malcolm's adoption of these ideologies and movements, the base of his contemporary US influences alone—which run the gamut from Paul Robeson, W. E. B. Du Bois, Queen Mother Moore, Robert F. Williams, C. L. R. James, Vicki Garvin, Carlos Cooks, Elombe Brath, Harold Cruse, John Henrik Clarke, and Gaidi and Imari Obadele, to name but a few—indicate, more than anything, that Malcolm was actually embracing the more revolutionary and internationalist currents of the Black Liberation movement as he evolved in political consciousness. (The myth, perpetuated by Marable's book and by others, that it was solely Malcolm's international travel that advanced his politics in this vein must also be totally debunked.) These revolutionary currents were brutally repressed in the 1940s and 1950s by the US government and largely sidelined by the liberal, petit bourgeois "leadership" of the social movement now labeled the Civil Rights movement. This leadership made a conscious choice to abandon the economic demands and human rights framework advanced by the Black Liberation movement in the 1930s and 1940s, so as not to be castigated or associated with Communism or with the revolutionary nationalist movements opposed by US imperialism during the high tide of the Cold War.

In light of these facts, it becomes clear that Marable's distortions in *Malcolm X: A Life of Reinvention* are more than just mere twists of fact. His book should be read as a product of the political and ideological struggles of its own time and historical context, just as much as it should be read and interpreted as a product of a singular consciousness. More accurately, the book is the product of a team consciousness, since it is obvious that more than one hand was responsible for some sections of the work.

It is the contemporary weaknesses of the Black Liberation movement as a whole, and of its Black Nationalist wings more specifically—buttressed by imperialism's hegemonic cooptation of Afrocentrism and other liberal variants of multiculturalism into the "postracial" politics of American nationalism that define the so-called "Age of Obama"—that co-enabled the production of this work. Nowhere is this more evident than on page 486, where Marable suggests the following: "If legal racial segregation was permanently in America's past, Malcolm's vision today would have to radically redefine self-determination and the meaning of Black power in a political environment that appeared to many to be 'post-racial.'"

Here again, Marable displays his narrow understanding of Black Nationalism. In the above leapfrogging statement, he again fails to address the more than forty years of Black nations' internal struggle over the question of self-determination. What is negated in this statement is not only an explanation of the political and military defeat of the Black Liberation movement in the 1970s and 1980s. Also negated is the Black petit bourgeoisie's broad betrayal of the Black Liberation movement by virtue of the conscious, deliberate, and consistent choices it has made since the 1970s to incorporate itself into the American imperialist project. Given the resulting vacuum, and in alliance with the Democratic Party, the Black petit bourgeoisie has assumed an unrelenting hegemonic stranglehold over Black politics, removing it from the streets, the schools, and the shops to ensure that the peoples' political engagement would be safely confined to narrow electoral channels. The liberal Black petit bourgeois program and cultural orientation willfully subjects and subordinates the interests of Black people to the interests of the American imperialist project, essentially to ensure that its own position within that project is secured and consolidated. The postracial political climate that Marable speaks of in *A Life of Reinvention* is not some neutral phenomenon that somehow spontaneously emerged. It is the outcome of this struggle—an outcome with clear winners and losers—the primary loser being the Black working class.

Since its qualitative fragmentation (particularly after the collapse of the National Black Political Convention and the dissolution of the African Liberation Support Committee in the mid-1970s) and repression-induced retreat in the 1970s, the Black Liberation movement has been largely unable to address the deteriorating conditions of the Black working class. These worsening conditions, produced by the capitalists' globalizing counter-offensive to the gains won by Black workers and the working class as a whole from the 1930s to the 1960s, have helped to fundamentally block that movement from enacting a comprehensive and independent political program to advance the goal of Black self-determination. One of the primary results of this defeat has been a steady capitalist-, individualist-, and careerist-orientated ideological drift in the Black community. That drift mirrors the growing class fragmentation of the Black nation into haves (and have accesses) and have-nots. The haves occupy the hegemonic center, and through the hegemonic block that they have constructed within the Black nation, they have advanced a program that creates space for the general acceptance of Black cultural and physical inclusion within the imperialist project (just so long as that space does not threaten the settler order at home and the never-ending expanse of capital globally). The have-nots, due to their lack of a strong and viable alternative, have been and are increasingly excluded from labor markets, warehoused in prisons, and contained in isolated urban ghettos or ex-urbanian cantonments longing for economic justice and self-determination.

Marable spent a considerable portion of his political and academic life contemplating what could and should be a viable political alternative for the have-nots. As one of his defining political projects, he was unwavering in his resistance to the advance of conservative and reactionary Black Nationalist politics. Yet, he often displayed in his works and political engagements a somewhat narrow understanding of the complexity of Black Nationalism, which often led him to short-change revolutionary nationalism and its promise and potential as an alternative. It is clear from reading *A Life of Reinvention* that Marable was not just casting Black Nationalism narrowly unintentionally; rather, that he was committed to seeing that no version or tendency of this phenomenon be projected as an alternative.

As hard as *A Life of Reinvention* tries to negate the propagation of this ideological and political alternative by its attempted inversion of the political life and legacy of Malcolm X, it largely fails. And it fails because as much as Malcolm X was constantly pushing himself and being pushed by his peers to grow politically, his commitment to the self-determination of African people in the United States and throughout the world was unwavering. No assemblage of minutia can twist this historical fact.

ENDNOTES

1 This essay originally appeared in the August 12, 2011, edition of *Left Turn* magazine and has been minimally copyedited for republication in this volume; it is reprinted here with permission of the author. The views expressed in this article are those of the author and do not reflect the official positions of either the Malcolm X Grassroots Movement (MXMG), of which the author is the National Coordinator, or the US Human Rights Network (USHRN), of which he is the Director of Education, Training, and Field Work. Email feedback to: kaliakuno@gmail.com.

KAMAU FRANKLIN

An Ivory-Tower Assassination of Malcolm X[1]

This author's personal familiarity with the Black Power and Black liberation movements of the 1960s and 1970s, including his brief role as an attorney for one of Malcolm X's accused killers, provides a critical context for the examination of Manning Marable's A Life of Reinvention. *He concludes by asserting that Marable sought in his book to remake Malcolm X in his own image—and was richly rewarded for doing so—rather than to provide an accurate retelling of Malcolm's life.*

I am pleased by some of the ongoing debate surrounding Manning Marable's recent biography *Malcolm X: A Life of Reinvention*, particularly the immediate responses offered to the book by two early Malcolm X biographers, Karl Evanzz and Zak Kondo.[2] One reason we should pay close attention to these two authors is that they both previously published most of the information regarding Malcolm's assassination—information that Marable retells and uses without proper credit. Evanzz and Kondo offered blistering critiques of Marable's numerous research shortcomings and of his ideological conclusions about Malcolm's supposed path. They also aim to defend Malcolm's legacy, as Karl Evanzz put it, as "a Black Panther of a Man."

Marable's reinvention of Malcolm X into the embodiment of his own ideological viewpoints amounts to what I call an ivory-tower assassination attempt on Malcolm X's meaning as an ideological force for Black self-determination. More specifically, it is an attempt to assassinate Malcolm's own self-expressed self-concept as a Black nationalist freedom fighter.[3] The real killers of Malcolm X have been known for forty years. Talmadge Hayer was the only gunman captured at the Audubon Ballroom after the shooting. He later signed an affidavit revealing the names of his true accomplices. A few years ago, I briefly served as the attorney for Kahlil Islam (*aka* Thomas 15X Johnson), one of the wrongly convicted assassins who sought to overturn his conviction in the case and clear his name. The other convicted assassin is Muhammad Abdul Aziz, then known as Norman 3X Butler. If Marable's book helps with the effort to have the case of Malcolm X's assassination reopened, have the only other known living assassin (William Bradley, formerly known as Willie X, now known as Al-Mustafa Shabazz and living in Newark, New Jersey) brought to justice, and launch a full investigation of the role of various police agencies in Malcolm's death, it will have served some useful purpose, but I can see no other.

Instead, Marable's work is the latest attempt to remake or reinvent Malcolm X and turn him into a political football for political and moneyed interests. In Marable's narrative, Malcolm is transformed into a race-neutral Pan-Africanist, which is itself a contradiction in terms.[4] According to Marable, that Malcolm helped pave the way for a moderate Democrat to become the first Black president of the United States.[5] Marable further claims that the 2001 United Nations-sponsored World Conference Against Racism held in Durban, South Africa, was a fulfillment of Malcolm X's new international vision.[6] A noble conference, indeed, but the fulfillment of anyone's vision of sustained change in international relationships between the West and the nations of Latin America, Africa, the Middle East, and Asia? That seems a highly dubious claim. No one can point to a change in the political or economic conditions of Black people in the United States (or internationally) based on the happenings at the Durban conference or in the election of the first Black president. Marable is clearly speculating given his lack of evidence. Therefore, his assertions can only be interpreted as an attempt to reinvent Malcolm in order to fulfill his own vision.

Another shortcoming is that Marable does in his biography what he accuses others of: he mainstreams Malcolm X into the embodiment of acceptable liberal-left ideas on social justice. For example, he asserts that Malcolm X was led in his personal journey toward becoming a man of peace and that Malcolm was moving away from violence as both a political and self-defense strategy.[7] He further suggests that Malcolm's reaction to acts of terrorism, including those of September 11, 2001, would have been one of disdain and disapproval.[8] Although many would be eager to suggest that Malcolm X was opposed to violence that kills innocent civilians, Marable makes no distinction between Malcolm's known views on revolutionary violence in the cause of liberation struggles and so-called terrorist acts.

Malcolm was a supporter of the Algerian, Congolese, Cuban, Kenyan, Palestinian, South African, and Vietnamese struggles, to name but a few. He did not shy away from supporting wars for independence and the violent bloody struggles against oppressors. This included his support for Third World peoples and Black people in the United States defending themselves against American invaders or White racists within this country's borders.[9] As Malcolm himself stated in his autobiography, he believed in justice, not simple peace.[10] Marable casually attempts to suggest that Malcolm X gave up on the idea of establishing rifle clubs for Black people,[11] despite the fact that the need for such groups was a basic position of the Organization of Afro-American Unity (OAAU), the organization Malcolm X formed after leaving the Nation of Islam.[12] In 1964, Malcolm told an audience of Black Methodists that he would get results whether it took a political party or an army.[13] Marable's safe, watered-down views about where Malcolm X was headed reflect a classic liberal stance adopted to reposition leaders who, while often embraced by the Black masses as true leaders, remain otherwise unacceptable to whites and disconnected intellectuals.

Marable does this while attempting to titillate his audience with innuendoes (perhaps to increase book sales?) and to position his biography as "the go-to book" on Malcolm X, replacing Haley's *Autobiography*.

Unfortunately, again, none of this is new; it is the latest in a continued tug-of-war about the meaning of Malcolm X to the Black liberation struggle and Malcolm X's place in the pantheon of influential figures in that struggle. Marable now joins others who have jostled to interpret Malcolm's words in ways that benefit their own ideological outlook. Whether the task at hand has been to humanize or scandalize Malcolm X or to direct him to the left or center, our would-be interpreters usually overplay their hand to reveal their own true objectives. Marable is no exception.

BREITMAN, MARABLE, AND PERRY: THREE BLIND MICE

After Malcolm X's assassination, many Black leaders attempted to play down his significance to the Black freedom struggle. Their push was to move past Malcolm X and to portray him as a man who contributed little to the liberation movements of Black people. Examples range from that of a conservative like Carl Rowan, who at the time was the Director of the United States Information Agency and dismissed positive international coverage of Malcolm X as something that had to be corrected by his agency.[14] They also included left-liberals like Bayard Rustin, a Civil Rights Movement competitor for the souls of Black folk, who said at the time of Malcolm's death that, "We must resist the temptation to idealize Malcolm X, to elevate charisma to greatness."[15] However, Malcolm's ideas, as published in the *Autobiography*, along with his many taped and reprinted speeches, make it impossible to ignore his positions on Black political struggle. His ideas became the new mainstream political thinking of the movement's new Black Power direction, and thus began the fight for the political ideas of Malcolm X.

Many perspectives have been offered on what might have been next for the un-assassinated Malcolm X. Where was he heading ideologically, and what were his political plans? Should his image be raised high or should it be torn down? Given Malcolm's increased posthumous popularity, these questions became important to movement people who wanted to identify with him or claim some part of him. For nonradical and non-movement people, interpreting Malcolm was seen as lucrative in the short term and important in de-politicizing potential recruits to militant movement activities. Depending on the writers' personal interests with respect to controlling the public discourse and on their status as allies, professed friends, or detractors of Malcolm's, every conversation on Malcolm X since his death has been aimed at telling Black people what we should believe in about him and about the movement he personified. Laying claim to having insight into the mantle of the fiery leader of Black self-determination cannot be undervalued.

In *A Life of Reinvention*, Manning Marable, in some sense, marries the goals, if not the complete ideas, of two of the most important re-interpreters of Malcolm X: George Breitman and Bruce Perry. Both men published their books during times of substantial interest in Malcolm X and his ideas. In his 1967 book, *The Last Year of Malcolm X: The Evolution of a Revolutionary*, Breitman attempts to inform us of Malcolm's stroll toward socialism during the time of the Black Power Movement. Perry, in his 1991 book, *Malcolm: The Life of the Man Who Changed Black America*, gives us a psychological profile of a Malcolm X who is apparently wrought with demons that only Perry could see, approximately thirty years after his death. Yet, Perry's book was perfectly timed as a response to the hip-hop-inspired reemergence of interest in Malcolm X in the late 1980s and 1990s.

Breitman, a lifelong leading member of various communist and socialist organizations, made a very fluid attempt to broaden the ideas of Malcolm X postmortem. [16] Breitman was given particular credit by the Socialist Workers Party for helping to edit and publish Malcolm X's speeches. Prior to his assassination, Malcolm, who had ties to the White left through his several appearances at the Militant Labor Forum, had been approached about having his speeches published, but no actual agreement was ever reached. Breitman's edited volume, *Malcolm X Speaks*, was first published in 1965, without much commentary included, because Breitman and an unidentified member of Muslim

Mosque, Inc. were at odds about Breitman's view of where Malcolm was headed.[17] The book was stripped of Breitman's views, but the need for another publication became imminent.

The resources of the White left were instrumental in popularizing Malcolm's ideas, but the people who controlled those resources felt that Malcolm's ideas needed re-interpretation. Those close to Malcolm, however, did not see the intellectual changes these forces claimed he was undergoing. According to Breitman, Malcolm "had not had the opportunity to put the parts together" of his own thinking.[18] Breitman thus insisted that Malcolm would have wanted to change many things in the *Autobiography*, including the last chapter, entitled "1965." Breitman casually cast away the ideas mentioned in that chapter as a product of Malcolm's earlier thinking and not to be confused with what Breitman tells us was Malcolm's later thinking. [19] Breitman was also the first to propose that the *Autobiography* was more Haley's invention than a representation of who Malcolm was and was becoming.[20]

Breitman's commentary does not make Malcolm as palatable for today's intellectual left mainstream as Marable attempts to do. Breitman instead positions Malcolm as someone the White communist left can savor as a potential convert. He picks individual statements by Malcolm and extrapolates from them their "true" meaning, which, of course, tends to be close to his own Socialist/Communist leanings. Marable borrows and infuses this same technique throughout his book. Indeed, he picks up so much steam using this approach that so by the end of his tale, in the Epilogue, we are left with a Malcolm who sounds more in tune with Marable's Democratic Socialist politics than anything anyone who actually worked with Malcolm could remember.

Malcolm's speeches have been duly credited, along with the *Autobiography*, for spreading Malcolm's message to a wider audience after his assassination. Malcolm's words have since been studied and digested, regurgitated, and studied again by everyday people from would-be civil rights workers to Socialists and Communist radicals. The resulting debate has included a healthy dose of "What would Malcolm do?"—as any good discussion about ideology, theory, movements, or leadership should include. However, Breitman is circumspect at best in revealing his own ideological leanings in his books on Malcolm, views that clearly influenced his telling of who Malcolm X was becoming at the time of his death. Breitman's interpretation suited Breitman's politics. In his telling, Malcolm was turning toward socialism and away from nationalism. This was the first major attempt to pull Malcolm X away from his core beliefs as a nationalist.

One of the most notable comments in *The Last Year of Malcolm X* was Breitman's statement that "Malcolm was pro-Socialist in the last year of his life but not yet a Marxist."[21] It's the "yet" that grabs me about this. First, Breitman assumes that the path from socialism to Marxism was, for Malcolm, a natural course and the one on which he was traveling. Although I agree with Breitman that Malcolm clearly was entering a phase in which he was expressing anti-capitalist views. However, as Malcolm himself explained several times, he had also entered a phase in which he was "attempting to turn a corner" with regard to how he was viewed. During that phase, Malcolm also cautioned, adopting new labels was to be avoided.[22]

One label that Breitman and others have attempted to remove from Malcolm is that of nationalist. Even when they carefully couch their views in the reality of Malcolm's own words, organizational life, and work, they cannot completely relegate Malcolm's nationalism to the past. For example, as it became difficult for Black civil rights leaders to speak negatively about Malcolm directly to the Black community, it also became difficult for "political" writers who claimed to genuinely respect Malcolm to push him into the integrationist camp. Whether that camp be Breitman's left Marxism, Marable's right Marxism, or radical humanism (as Marable calls it),[23] a more valid "full-scale study" of Malcolm X could have been realized by both Breitman and Marable if they laid out for their readers their own political views on the way forward for the Black community and America. It seems, however, that the hidden nature of capturing a dead icon and re-inventing him is too tempting for some writers to withstand.[24] Breitman and Marable both struggle throughout their respective interpretations to deal with Malcolm's own use of the word "nationalism" as well as Malcolm's ideas on separation, both mental and physical.

Malcolm's often contradictory public search to define himself nationally and internationally during his final months allows his speeches and interviews to be culled in many ways by many different groups regarding the future direction of his ideas. What is most interesting, however, is that Malcolm's inner circle of fellow organizers and workers are the most discounted in others' efforts to decipher the direction in which Malcolm X was heading. Their own internal disagreements aside, the views of Malcolm's confidants seem not to support Breitman's or now Marable's carefully worded accounts. This leaves at least this reader wondering if Malcolm X was on his way to fill out an application to be a part of the next International symposium or to be a leading member of the Left Forum.

Neither Breitman nor Marable ever worked with Malcolm X, as did John Henrik Clarke, Herman Ferguson, Max Stanford, the Obedele brothers of Detroit, and Father Albert Cleage, among others. Yet somehow, those who worked very closely with Malcolm are treated by and large as people to be doubted when discussing Malcolm's changing political analysis. It is almost as if some mass hypnotic state made them unable, in their personal, day-to-day contact with Malcolm X, to see what only outsiders like Breitman and Marable could. Both assert that their studies of the man and his ideas take precedent over the interpretations of Malcolm's political and personal comrades, many of whom dispute Marable and Breitman's presumptions of Malcolm's future left or right turns.

John Henrik Clarke, who helped write part of the Organization of Afro-American Unity's charter, worked closely with Malcolm until his assassination. He and others helped to push back against the attacks on Malcolm's legacy with regard to his involvement in the Black liberation movement. In the Introduction to his book, *Malcolm X: The Man and*

His Times, Clarke states that after Malcolm returned from his international trips, he was willing to work with anyone who was sincere. Clarke makes clear, however, that this did not mean Malcolm would let those persons join his organization because of his overall lack of trust for White liberals and for the American left took precedent.[25] Other colleagues of Malcolm's such as Reverend Cleage spoke more directly to the point after Malcolm's assassination, claiming that Malcolm X was fighting not for a radicalized integration but for Black liberation and power.[26] Cleage further suggested that we as Black people would "lose" Malcolm if we allowed the myths unfolding at the time of his death to take hold as the truth.

Bruce Perry is a less-interesting biographer of Malcolm than either Breitman or Marable. Never active in the movement himself, he enters the picture as a voyeur whose interest is in decoding Malcolm's supposed psychological state because by the early 1990s, the media's efforts to deconstruct iconic figures and topics as a means of drawing audiences were in full bloom. Perry, like Marable, early on informs readers of his 1992 book, *Malcolm: The Life of the Man Who Changed Black America*, that others have gotten it all wrong about Malcolm X's life story and that he can correct those inaccuracies.[27] Perry further claims that his research reveals the real Malcolm X—the one that no one knew, not even Malcolm himself.[28] What he provides, however, is simply conjecture and a vision of Malcolm that is unrecognizable to those who knew him. Perhaps Marable, seeing the value of such titillation, decided to walk a sloppy line down a similar path. Not surprisingly, the only two books on Malcolm X that I can remember receiving both in-depth and positive reviews from the *New York Times* in my lifetime were Marable's and Perry's.

Like Marable, Perry uses secondary sources to support his claims about Malcolm's street hustling days and his sexuality.[29] Marable, however, claims that this method "humanizes" Malcolm, whereas Perry claims to use it to deconstruct him. Whereas Perry seemed more interested in offering a pseudo-psychological profile for a new take on Malcolm, Marable appears more interested in the increased book sales such speculation can bring. Indeed, many of the documented conclusions that Marable claims drove Alex Haley to want to reinvent Malcolm X for purposes of higher book sales can be subscribed equally to Marable and his methods.

Perry's attempt to reinvent Malcolm—from a bold unyielding critic of White supremacy in the United States to a confused, self-hating man haunted by his childhood and not really angry about racism, discrimination, or White supremacy—is not a place that Marable chose to go.[30] Instead, Marable's biography offers a "two-fer"—a dual attempt to transform Malcolm from a powerful Black nationalist to a more academy-friendly, race-neutral, social justice activist and to humanize him with titillation and conjecture.

TITILLATION AND CONJECTURE

Marable and his defenders attempt to justify his chosen Malcolm X focus by creating a straw man argument. In our reverence of Malcolm X as a leader of his people, they contend, Malcolm's followers have also idealized him. I contend, in response, that *this is an attempt to give cover to whatever assertion Marable makes.* Marable's defenders claim that everyone else has put Malcolm on a pedestal and that Marable has only attempted to make him appear more "human." I beg to disagree.

I suggest that most people who care to read about Malcolm consider him to be a man who was searching for the right answers and who stood tall against government, media and political enemies with grace, charm, and a fiery spirit. It is the directness of his argument and his eloquence that makes Malcolm X stand head-and-shoulders above most of his contemporaries. When I hear a Malcolm X speech today, he seems just as dangerous in his tone and accuracy as he did in the 1960s. The attraction to Malcolm, however, is not in his perfection; it is in his daring. Far from believing that Malcolm was perfect, most people are drawn by what they believe he was doing right. They see him as a source of inspiration for his organizing and for his conduct. He took himself, his work, and the freedom of his people seriously. That is the most human thing a person can do.

Did Malcolm make mistakes? Of course he did. Having a thorough discussion about these mistakes or positions would have been a much more fascinating topic for people interested in movement building than some of the conjectures offered in Marable's book.

Some of the more humanizing aspects that Marable could easily have explored include the following:

- why Malcolm continually allowed himself to be sidetracked and drawn into fight with the Nation of Islam after leaving that organization—that no-win situation distracted him from his work and increased hostilities on both sides;
- why Malcolm believed that Elijah Muhammad or any human being was more than human and in fact divine—indeed, Islam may have offered him a spiritual path out of the muck and mire of drugs and street life, but it also blinded him from drawing needed conclusions earlier and led to his downfall;
- why Malcolm failed to develop the membership base of the Organization of Afro-American Unity (a path I believe he was on before his death, given those he was recruiting to that effort, including Maya Angelou)—he had too many people around him who were not organizers but loyalists;
- why Malcolm made so many openly contradictory statements on the way forward for Black people in America and the world; for example, although publicly he would say he was willing to work with a wide array of groups, he was continuously bashing those groups—not a very good way to create unity;
- how Malcolm's documented sexism and homophobia stopped him from trusting half of his potential constituency for far too long and

led to some of the hyper-masculine attitudes of those who took up his mantle.[31]

All these topics and others are worth serious exploration. Yet, instead of doing so, Marable seemed more eager to engage in the rampant media speculation of our times, hunting for possible scintillating tidbits that pundits would be sure to pick up on and that would drive up the sales of his book.

Endemic in Marable's tale on Malcolm is his offering of unproven and or poorly sourced stories, presumably only for their titillation value, and the many speculative conclusions he draws throughout the book regarding what Malcolm may have been thinking. Marable also spends far too much time making some not-so-clever assertions about Malcolm's hustler days and his marriage to and life with wife Betty Shabazz. *A Life of Reinvention* is so thick with clauses like "most likely," "strong circumstantial evidence," "appears to be," "perhaps," "may have," and "hard to determine, but" that it is maddening. In my own unscientific counting, Marable uses such speculative terms to describe events in Malcolm's life on more than fifty occasions. He also uses declarative statements on the same topics to present them as unvarnished truth to be taken as fact.

Some speculation and author insight is, of course, part of the nature of biography. However, the carefree way that Marable approaches it gives much cause for alarm. Marable was too credible an author and scholar for this to be an accident. This is particularly troubling when statements Marable attributes in his book to Minister Louis Farrakhan of the Nation of Islam go unchallenged, for the most part, without any speculation into the Minister's own motives. Some other and similarly infuriating statements include the following:

- Page 22: Without offering an explanation or any evidence (even in his footnote), Marable casually accuses Amy Jacques Garvey of murder, saying she may have been involved in the assassination of a Reverend Eason, a Garvey rival.

- Page 52: Marable claims Malcolm was eager to be known as "Detroit Red," again without providing any source to justify why Malcolm was "eager" to be called that as opposed to it just being a given nickname.
- Page 61: Marable states that because the young Malcolm X (then Malcolm Little, a.k.a. Detroit Red) was a cocaine user, he could not have engineered the number of successful burglaries he told Alex Haley about without being discovered. Growing up in Brooklyn, New York, I knew plenty of drug users who robbed and did not get caught. I also knew many who did get caught. To suggest something is exaggerated because one was not caught is pure speculation.
- Page 66 (and 78): Marable mentions "uncertain particulars" about Malcolm's description of a relationship one of this crime associates had with wealthy Boston bachelor Paul Lennon that he elevates to "circumstantial but strong" evidence that Malcolm "probably" was talking about an encounter he himself had with Lennon. Later on that page, this presumption becomes "apparent" until, by page 78, Lennon is called Malcolm's "homosexual lover." If Marable had stopped at pure speculation, it may have been fine, but his ratcheting up of this relationship from possible to declarative seems meant more to attract readers than to retell Malcolm's history.
- Page 133: Marable misrepresents Malcolm's famous "The Ballot or the Bullet" speech, downgrading it from a threat of revolution if Black demands were not met immediately to a call for a bloodless revolution for democratic rights.
- Page 151: Marable speculates that "perhaps" Malcolm "kept" Betty Shabazz pregnant as a way to keep her under control. This is stated as if the ability to time or prevent pregnancies was freely available in the late 1950s and early 1960s. It was not.

- Page 233: Without corroborating evidence, Marable accepts Minister Farrakhan's assertion that he talked Malcolm out of leaving Betty when Malcolm's marriage was on the rocks.

- Page 243: Without questioning Farrakhan's motives, Marable accepts Farrakhan's assertion that he pleaded with Malcolm to understand that having enforcers within the Nation of Islam (NOI) was morally wrong, with Malcolm responding that murder might be necessary to set an example. Does Marable not see that it may have been convenient for Farrakhan to portray himself as sheltered and naïve about the NOI's enforcement policies when, to this day, questions linger about Farrakhan's role in Malcolm's death?

- Page 334: Marable states that Malcolm gave up his call for "Negroes to form rifle clubs," yet he never provides any citation to confirm the precise moment this happened. (Why not? Because it obviously *did* not.)

- Page 335: Marable expresses puzzlement about why Malcolm would not bad-mouth the NOI when he had secretly recorded the FBI attempting to "flip" him (Malcolm) into an agent. In what is to me a comical conclusion, Marable reasons that Malcolm was making the recording for use in his civil case against the NOI over the ownership of his house, as if the FBI could be called to testify. This is contradictory to a more straightforward conclusion that Malcolm X was not inclined to give the FBI any additional insights into the reasons behind his split with the NOI and that he was committed to being a revolutionary and not a snitch for the state.

- Page 368: Marable questions Malcolm's anti-Israeli views as only being stated in the interest of his allies without any factual information to back it up. Could it be, as Malcolm stated over and over again, that Malcolm's opposition was a result of his viewing Israel as a settler state that, like the United States, oppressed its indigenous population?

- Page 380: Marable writes that Betty Shabazz may have had an affair, but that "the actual extent of [her] relationship is difficult to discern." By page 393, however, Marable states that Malcolm, around the time of his November 1964 return to the United States from Africa, has not only learned of the "romantic relationship" but "skillfully diffuses" it. Marable continues that Malcolm seemingly was so successful at this diffusion that by January 1965 Betty was pregnant again with twins. Marable offers no discussion about how a person with Malcolm's temperament, lifelong patriarch that he was, might react to finding out that his wife is having an affair with one of his chief lieutenants.
- Page 394 (and 451): Marable suggests that it "appears" that Malcolm started an affair with an eighteen-year-old girl. He writes that little is known about her or their relationship except that it "appears" to have continued until Malcolm's death. By page 451, Marable declares that Malcolm was "secretly involved with her." Again, no footnotes are given and no evidence provided for either statement.
- Page 478: Marable states that the evidence suggests that Farrakhan had no direct link to Malcolm's assassination; he does not, however, bring up Farrakhan's several contradictory statements about Malcolm's assassination. For example, he neglects to cite Farrakhan's 1993 statement on the topic:

> "We [the NOI] don't give a damn about no white man law if you attack what we love. And frankly, it ain't none of your business. What do you got to say about it? Did you teach Malcolm? Did you make Malcolm? Did you clean up Malcolm? Did you put Malcolm out before the world? Was Malcolm your traitor or ours? And if we dealt with him like a nation deals with a traitor, what the hell business is it of yours? You just shut your mouth and stay out of it."[32]

Somehow, this very public statement on the killing of Malcolm X must have escaped Marable's reach. Instead, he accepts Farrakhan's assertions of innocence without any of the pondering or conjecture that is so rampant throughout the rest of the book on other matters. How is Farrakhan served by accepting his word without laying out other possibilities of Farrakhan being involved?

This is just a small sampling of the ways the Marable book retells Malcolm's history. When coupled with the author's personal ideas about how these historical events should be viewed and his penchant for reinvention, these examples become all the more troubling.

THE MEANING OF THE AUTOBIOGRAPHY

No other book in the last one hundred years (maybe not since *The Communist Manifesto*) has had as instant an impact on its readers and subsequently on the movements to which they ascribe as *The Autobiography of Malcolm X as Told to Alex Haley*. I have never met anyone who has said that after reading that book, they went out and joined a conservative, pro-capitalist group. Marable claims, however, that the book's "ghostwriter", Alex Haley, as "liberal Republican,"[33] attempted to subdue the radical nationalist thoughts of Malcolm X and the influence of Malcolm's ideas on his readers and to emphasize the tragedies of racial segregation.[34] If that is true, then Haley failed miserably in that task.

Like many young Black people, when I first read *The Autobiography of Malcolm X*, I could not put it down. I read and reread parts of it not only for their interesting characterizations of Malcolm X's life but, more importantly, because that book spoke to me in a way that opened my eyes to the real history of White supremacy and to the ideas of Black nationalism as the way to counter that history. *The Autobiography of Malcolm X* made me want to learn more about Malcolm X and the struggle for Black liberation.

After reading Haley's book, I started reading with a purpose—for the first time in my life. I then set out on a quest for knowledge that, for once, was not for the purpose of getting a degree or passing a test or even simply passing the time. Instead, I sought to understand the world around me and to act on that acquired knowledge. I began to read and listen to Malcolm's speeches. That led me to search out books on capitalism, imperialism, African history, and the history of Africans in America.

My response to *The Autobiography of Malcolm X* was not a unique or isolated experience. Indeed, the book is so popular in the Black community that it commonly is referred to as simply "*The Autobiography*." Many people trace their political awakening or putting the pieces of dissonant notes to their personal song together to their reading of *The Autobiography*. At one point, it was almost a rite of passage if one sought to become a political person, particularly for young brothers from the streets, like me, and for working-class sisters. The book inspired us to find out more about the political and economic structures in our community and about how White supremacy affected our communities from both the inside and out. For the last forty-five years, *The Autobiography*'s influence on the minds of any person attempting to understand the struggle of Africans in the United States has been a great one.

The ideas, platform, and work of Malcolm X, all of which virtually jumped off the pages of *The Autobiography*, left a path for others to follow in the 1960s and 1970s and informed the Black Power and Black nationalist movements. *The Autobiography*, along with *Malcolm X Speaks*, helped shape and directly inform a developing ideological framework for those latter movements. No other figure in modern history can be credited with pollinating such radical movements and with the realigning of political positions in the African American community.

Everyone who came after Malcolm X in the Black power struggle, in leftist movements in the United States, and in anti-imperialist movements of other oppressed groups internationally all included Malcolm as a prominent influential revolutionary figure. In word and deed, those individuals and groups have paid widespread homage to Malcolm, each claiming to be carrying on the legacy of his work. However, acknowledging Malcolm does not constitute putting him on a pedestal. It is merely the logical conclusion of an analysis of the scope and impact of his words and work.

Young revolutionaries and the movements of their time have all named Malcolm as the igniter of their flames, including Amari Obedele, Assata Shakur, Bobby Seale, H. Rap Brown, Huey Newton, Kathleen Cleaver, Eldridge Cleaver, Nahanda Abiodun, Stokely Carmichael, the Revolutionary Action Movement, the Black Panther Party, the Republic of New Afrika, and others. Even the FBI, in one of its most revealing memos about its counter-insurgency campaign against the Black liberation movement, clearly stated, in their terms, the need to "prevent the rise of a messiah who could unify and electrify the militant Black nationalist movement."[35] Most likely, Malcolm X was such a messiah, in the FBI's view. He is certainly the martyr of that movement today.

In Marable's attempt to dislodge *The Autobiography* as *the* book of choice on Malcolm X and replace it with his own, he begins by asserting that *The Autobiography* is more a product of Alex Haley than it is of Malcolm X.[36] He draws contradictory conclusions, on one hand blaming Haley for the unpublished chapters that did not get into the book, while later acknowledging that it was Malcolm who did not want those chapters published in the first place.[37] Marable also points to the success of *The Autobiography* as the source of later efforts to make Malcolm a multicultural American icon even though, as Marable knew full well and restated later in the book, Malcolm's metamorphosis from angry Black militant to multicultural American icon took place two decades after *The Autobiography* was published.

Marable maintained that the mainstreaming of Malcolm X was a phenomenon of the culture and success of 1980s and 1990s mass marketing and repackaging.[38] He notes that hip-hop artists began to adopt Malcolm as an image of masculinity, as someone who spoke truth to power and seemed uncompromising, as someone who suited their own hopeful images of themselves. Artists as diverse as Public Enemy and Big Daddy Kane in the hip-hop world made mention of Malcolm X in their lyrics and interviews. Such revolutionary rap became the "in" thing for hip-hop, and it actually helped sales. More artists, some sincere and some not, began to invoke Malcolm X as a marketing tool. Then the ultimate Black marketer of his day, filmmaker Spike Lee—who used race to market himself in a fashion similar to that of his contemporary, pop singer Madonna (who used sex because it was good for business)—got involved. In Lee's Malcolm X movie, Malcolm retained some of his innate militancy, but his status as an American icon was firmly branded by the imagery of the American flag being burned into an "X." This image could then be purchased on a cap for $19.99 in a Spike Lee store. The branding of Malcolm X reached its zenith when Malcolm's image was put on a postage stamp. Marable recounts other such efforts to capitalize on the Malcolm X brand, but fails to prove, as he asserts, that *The Autobiography* was responsible for it, or how.[39]

One of the ongoing themes in Marable's tale is that *The Autobiography* is historical fiction. Besides asserting it to be true, Marable does little to prove it. He leaves out, for example, any discussion that might explain his reasoning that the destruction of Black liberation movement by local police and federal authorities in the late 1960s and 1970s was an intervening act that moved Malcolm and the reading of *The Autobiography* from an act of dissent to merely an interesting read without any potential consequences. However, after the movements that challenged and posed threats to U.S. institutions were defeated through government infiltration and government-sponsored infighting such as that which led to the death of Malcolm X and others, Black leaders settled into a comfortable dance with the Democratic Party. The reemergence of Malcolm in the late 1980s was thus far less threatening to the state. To suggest, as Marable does in *A Life of Reinvention*, that *The Autobiography* played the seminal role in mainstreaming Malcolm seems more of an attempt to de-legitimize Haley's book as a source of history than to thoroughly critique the historical period in which *The Autobiography* was first published. Interestingly enough, however, Marable cites *The Autobiography* as a source more than any other reference for documenting aspects of Malcolm X life.

A LIE OF REINVENTION

Throughout his book, Marable documents Haley's drive for publication and financial benefit by presenting and discussing that author's own correspondence. Though this may highlight Haley's greed, it does little to illuminate what Marable contends was Haley's ascribed purpose—namely, to de-emphasize Malcolm's political views. Marable also suggests that Haley's choice of M. S. Handler as the writer of *The Autobiography*'s Introduction was probably to give the book some liberal "cover." This is probably true, but it seems very similar to Marable's decision to include the endorsements of the three-headed monster of the established Black intellectual elite—Cornel West, Henry Louis Gates, and Michael Eric Dyson—on the back cover of his own book to widen the appeal of his book as *the* definitive academic text on Malcolm's life.

MARABLE'S EPILOGUE

If Marable's book becomes the new lens through which present and future generations learn about Malcolm X, then the Malcolm those generations will come to know will have lost some of his street swag, indomitable spirit, and political compass. Marable's new construction of Malcolm takes the man from the streets and mutes his passionate Black nationalism, reinventing him as a "race-neutral" kind of guy.[40] To be certain, Marable received a pretty good paycheck from his sponsors in the ivory tower to present his readers with a Malcolm whom he sees as somehow connected to our current President and to portray the election of Barack Obama as part of Malcolm's political legacy.[41] No one whom I have spoken to or heard speak who worked with Malcolm in his last days has ever made a similar claim, but given the posthumous acclaim heaped upon Marable and his book, it seems safe today to attempt to turn Malcolm into someone who can be safely embraced by middle-class, college-educated people of all races. Although Marable at times cannot sufficiently suppress Malcolm's views nor Malcolm's role with regard to the building of a militant, Black-nationalist political group,[42] he succeeds in shifting the paradigm by claiming that Malcolm, in his last days, was separating himself, albeit slowly, from the

Black nationalist agenda.[43] (This objective is contradicted later in the book when Marable admits that Malcolm continuously stated that his first priority was to Black people in America, clearly a nationalist sentiment.[44]) Notwithstanding, Marable muses throughout his book that Black nationalism provided Malcolm with only a limited vocabulary as he searched for a framework beyond race.[45] He consistently attempts to strip away Malcolm's racial allegiance to Black people by somehow mistaking the fact that a Black nationalist like Malcolm could also be an a Pan-Africanist and a budding internationalist without contradiction.

In *A Life of Reinvention,* Marable hoped to give us a Malcolm X who is more of an antiracist social-justice seeker than either a Black nationalist, a Pan-Africanist, or an internationalist. That is not Malcolm's legacy. That is the legacy of overpaid, ivory-tower radicals who have never refused a paycheck from their White institutions; who have never sided with Black nationalists because most of their liberal friends (and bosses) would disown them. It is the legacy of those who have never perceived a different direction or more viable political strategy for Black people beyond putting more pressure on the Democratic Party; who have never pushed back against the forces of the state and its attack on Black liberation politics thru its COINTELPRO operations. It is the legacy of those who left us a denatured "movement" whose authority lies squarely in the hands of liberal-to-moderate forces of all races who are intent on steering Black people toward mainstream-voting, nonprofit-poverty-pimp organizations and useless public punditry.

Marable, whose own politics always had an anti-Black nationalist bent, was a founder of the Black Radical Congress (BRC) in the 1990s. His inability to restrain his non-radical impulses led to a split in the group, but Marable continued to call meetings of his faction of the BRC, literally serving hors d'oeuvres and wine while "organizing" the masses. His sad attempt to reinvent Malcolm in his last published manuscript is a reflection of such stubbornness and backwardness, so much so that by the end of the book Malcolm's extrapolated views–that is, what he would believe if he was around today–are (surprise, surprise!)

far closer to Marable's views and ideological beliefs than anything Malcolm could ever have conceived.

When biographers replace their subjects' ideology with their own ideological wish list, they are no longer scholars but propagandists who are merely speaking through their subjects. Obama as part of Malcolm's legacy—really? Malcolm supporting the bombing of Africa? I don't think so. Malcolm as supporting the continued embargo of Cuba and the expansion of free-trade zones throughout the developing world? Again, not. Malcolm may not have become a socialist before he died, but he was clearly an anti-capitalist.

Would Malcolm really have backed reliance on the two-party system to solve the problems of African people in the United States? Come on, now—Malcolm spoke about Black *self-determination*, not integration. That is why Malcolm worked openly and actively to improve the collective lives of Black people, devise closer links to Africa, and bring the United States government up on charges before the United Nations. His intent, as he himself said, was not to bring the case to the criminal (i.e., civil rights), but to bring the criminal to court (i.e., human rights).

This was our Malcolm, the real one. Marable's attempt to "kill" him twice by making him more "human," then to re-package Malcolm's ideas into his own version of a "mature" person, is disdainful at best and shameful at worst.

ENDNOTES

1 Though much of the this essay's content duplicates that of an earlier version that was published online, the copyediting process has resulted in a number of textual changes to enhance the clarity and organization of the author's ideas and to conform the citation style to that of this volume.

2 Karl Evanzz wrote *The Judas Factor: The Plot to Kill Malcolm X* (New York: Thunder's Mouth Press, 1993) and Zak A. Kondo, with coauthor Nia N. Kondo, wrote Conspiracys (*Conspiracies): Unraveling the Assassination of Malcolm X* (Washington, DC: Nubia Press, 1993).

3 Malcolm X, "The Ballot or the Bullet," speech delivered April 12, 1964, Detroit, Michigan.

4 Manning Marable, *Malcolm X: A Life of Reinvention* (New York: Viking Press, 2011), 485.

5 Ibid., 484.

6 Ibid., 485.

7 Ibid., 487.

8 Ibid., 487.

9 Malcolm X, "The Ballot or the Bullet"; see also the Organization of Afro-American Unity (OAAU), *Program of the Organization of Afro-American Unity*, specifically the sections entitled "Statement of Basic Aims and Objectives" and "The Basic Unity Program" both of which emphasize the right to self defense and rifle clubs (http://www.malcolm-x.org/docs/gen_oaau.htm); Malcolm X, *The Autobiography of Malcolm X, as Told to Alex Haley* (New York: Penguin), 417.

10 Malcolm X, *The Autobiography of Malcolm X, as Told to Alex Haley* (New York: Penguin, 2010), 366.

11 Marable, 334.

12 OAAU, *Program of the Organization of Afro-American Unity*, specifically the sections entitled "Statement of Basic Aims and Objectives" and "The Basic Unity Program" both of which emphasize the right to self defense and rifle clubs (http://www.malcolm-x.org/docs/gen_oaau.htm)

13 Russell Rickford, *Betty Shabazz, Surviving Malcolm X: A Journey of Strength From Wife to Widow to Heroine* (Naperville, IL: Sourcebooks), 172.

14 Malcolm X, 446, 447.

15 George Breitman, *The Last Year of Malcolm X: The Evolution of a Revolutionary* (New York: Pathfinder Books, 1970), 83.

16 Naomi Allen and Sarah Lovell, eds., *A Tribute to George Breitman: Writer, Organizer, Revolutionary* (New York: Fourth Internationalist Tendency, 1987).

17 Breitman, 2.

18 Ibid.

19 Ibid., 5.

20 Ibid., 5.

21 Breitman, 50, 51.

22 Malcolm X, 375.

23 Marable, 334.

24 I (the author), for example, am a member of an organization called the Malcolm X Grassroots Movement, and my personal political views are Revolutionary New Afrikan Nationalism.

25 John Henrik Clarke, *Malcolm X: The Man and His Times* (Trenton, NJ: Africa World Press, 1991), xxii.

26 Cleage, "Myths About Malcolm X," speech delivered in Detroit, Michigan, February 24, 1967.

27 Bruce Perry, *Malcolm: The Life of the Man Who Changed Black America* (Barrytown, NY: Station Hill Press, 1992), x.

28 Ibid., x.

29 Ibid., x, 77, 82, 83.

30 Ibid., x.

31 Clarke, *Malcolm X and His Times,* 182. In private conversations, Malcolm was known to make homophobic comments such as calling Bayard Rustin "nothing but a homo" in the conversation he secretly taped with the FBI.

32 Louis Farrakhan, speech delivered at NOI Saviors Day celebration, 1993.

33 Marable, 9.

34 Ibid.

35 What Really Happened, "Actual FBI COINTELPRO Documents: COINTELPRO Revisited—Spying & Disruption," see section on "Counterintelligence Program: Black Nationalist-Hate Groups, Internal Security," http://whatreallyhappened.com/RANCHO/POLITICS/COINTELPRO/COINTELPRO-FBI.docs.html.

36 Marable, 9.

37 Ibid.

38 Ibid., 8-9.

39 Ibid., 9.

40 Ibid., 333.

41 Ibid., 484.

42 Ibid., 350.

43 Ibid., 365.

44 Ibid., 368.

45 Ibid., 384.

WILLIAM L. (BILL) STRICKLAND

Remembering Malcolm: A Personal Critique of Manning Marable's Non-Definitive Biography of Malcolm X

At the outset, I want to "make it plain"[1] *that my critique of Manning Marable's* Malcolm X: A Life of Reinvention *is political, historical, and personal—personal because I was born in Boston and grew up in the same Roxbury that Malcolm once called home though he was, of course, a generation older.*

PART I: MALCOLM, ROXBURY, AND ME

I first met Malcolm when I was a youngster in Roxbury because he was a good friend of my cousin, Leslie Edman, who I thought, in my elementary school days, was the coolest cat in the world because girls would call him long distance from faraway, exotic places like New York City. I also knew Gene Walcott—before Malcolm recruited him into the Nation of Islam—and he became Louis X. Indeed, in those days Gene Walcott was Boston's and New England's own version of Harry Belafonte, playing the violin and performing calypso music on his ukulele under his stage name: "The Charmer." Now the world knows him as Minister Louis Farrakhan.

I especially remember Malcolm though because he and Leslie were members of a neighborhood sports club called the Panthers. They wore these shiny black jackets embossed with the orange emblem of a black panther (long before the Oakland Black Panthers). So when Malcolm came to my aunt and uncle's house on Hubert Street to pick up Leslie and be off to whatever devilment they were up to, his jacket made an impression that has stuck with me over the years. But I would move away from Lower Roxbury after the third grade; away from Hubert Street, Marble Street, and Shawmut Avenue where Gene Walcott lived, to "The Hill" in Upper Roxbury.[2] And time-wise, I would finish high school and military service and be in college before I met Malcolm again.

That was in the early 1960s when Malcolm came to Harvard to speak. After the talk, I introduced myself, brought up our Roxbury connection, and told him that I was Leslie Edman's cousin. After that, we stayed in touch, crossing paths purposefully—and coincidentally. I invited him, for example, to speak at an extracurricular seminar in Eliot House, and I arranged interviews for him on Harvard's radio station when he was in Cambridge. I also would attend meetings at Louis X's Temple No. 11 on Intervale Street when I knew that Malcolm was going to be the guest minister because, aside from Malcolm, fate had also intervened to pique my interest in the Nation.

What had happened was that I had been accepted as an undergraduate in a graduate seminar in sociology taught by one of the preeminent sociologists of the day, Gordon Allport, the author of *The Nature of Prejudice*.[3] And who was in that seminar? Why, C. Eric Lincoln, who had just published his groundbreaking book on the Nation of Islam, *The Black Muslims in America*.[4] Also enrolled was Atlanta's Whitney Young, who was being prepped to go to New York and become head of the National Urban League. So the race question was all around me, motivating me to write my seminar paper on the Nation and to visit the mosque whenever I could.

To this day, I don't know what Malcolm saw in me, but we became friends. He even came to my house on Cobden Street on occasion. And whenever I had a break from school and went down to New York, I would drop by the Nation's restaurant on 116th Street to see if Malcolm was in town. But despite our various interactions, he never tried to convert me. So though I never joined the Nation, it was Malcolm's political perspective that I imbibed—and that guides me still—because in the same way that Karl Marx is the fundamental critic of capitalism and Frantz Fanon is the fundamental critic of colonialism, Malcolm X is the fundamental critic of American racism.

MALCOLM, THE MOVEMENT, AND ME

Like many others in college at the time, I answered the call of the Movement and formally joined the Boston chapter of the Northern Student Movement (NSM), which had been organized by a young White undergraduate at Yale named Peter Countryman. Peter, inspired by the southern student sit-ins, had mobilized northern students to aid the southern movement in general and SNCC, the southern Student Non-Violent Coordinating Committee, in particular.[5]

Combining protest against northern discrimination with its original focus of tutoring children in urban black communities, NSM had offices in New York, Detroit, Chicago, Baltimore, Hartford, and Boston. But the more the NSMers tried to combat the failures of the public school system, the more they began to feel that the problem of education was just one of the many afflictions of a basically unjust system. So, taking a leaf from SNCC's book, they elevated their game to community organizing; trying, *a la* the SNCC mantra, to empower people to empower themselves.[6]

At this stage of NSM's development, Peter Countryman decided to go back to school and asked me to become NSM's executive director. I agreed and left Boston and Roxbury to move to New York to NSM's national office on Morningside Drive near Columbia and above Central Park...and Harlem. Later, the office would move to 514 West 126th Street, to the same block, I would soon learn, where one of Malcolm's most devoted followers, the Japanese American, Yuri Kochiyama, lived. So the gods had put Malcolm and me back in touch once more.

Living now in New York, I would see Malcolm fairly often because he would preside on 125th Street, making critical commentary on national and international events and on the errors he believed the civil rights movement and its leaders were making, and, of course, extolling Elijah Muhammad's worldview. In those days, one didn't need television news, all one had to do was stroll over to 125th Street, and tune in on "the X."[7]

After Malcolm left the Nation in March 1964, we were in even closer contact because NSM had begun working more closely with SNCC and I went to Mississippi to help the MFDP, the Mississippi Freedom Democratic Party, with its Congressional Challenge.[8] Coming back from Mississippi in June, I bumped into Malcolm in Lincoln Center not too long after he had returned from Africa. He told me that he was forming a new organization and having planning meetings that he asked me to participate in. I said "sure" and went as a student representative to what turned out to be Malcolm's secular political organization: the Organization of Afro-American Unity, the OAAU. But after successfully kicking off the OAAU, Malcolm left in July for Africa again, not returning until around Thanksgiving.

In the meantime, NSM had deepened its involvement with the MFDP and its Congressional Challenge to focus on three targeted White Mississippi Congressmen who had won their Congressional seats by depriving Black Mississippians of their right to vote, a violation of the Fourteenth and Fifteenth Amendments. In protest, the MFDP had nominated Mrs. Annie Devine, Mrs. Victoria Gray, and Mrs. Fannie Lou Hamer to challenge for those three Congressional seats when Congress reconvened in January.

NSM rallied its supporters in all their cities to support the Challenge[9] and an overall Northern Coordinating Committee was established in New York, which I co-chaired. Naturally, I immediately sought Malcolm's support. Thus, when a delegation from Mississippi came to Harlem in December, Malcolm not only spoke to the youth, he also hosted a meeting with Mrs. Hamer and me that Christmas week at the Williams Institutional Church to publicize the MFDP's Challenge. Exactly two months later, he was killed.

ATLANTA, THE INSTITUTE OF THE BLACK WORLD, AND THE SEARCH FOR "AN ADEQUATE THEORY OF EMANCIPATION"[10]

After Martin Luther King's assassination in 1968, Coretta Scott King asked Dr. Vincent Harding, the stellar Black historian and one of Martin's closest friends, to take the helm of the new Martin Luther King, Jr. Memorial Center.

Vincent was teaching at Spelman at the time, but he agreed to become director of the Center. He also proposed to establish, as one element of the Center, a project that he and his colleague, Stephen Henderson, chair of Morehouse's English Department, had been brainstorming about for some time: a Black think tank that would analyze the lessons of the movement that had just ended; research the longitudinal history of the Black struggle; and propose policies, agendas, and programs that might help advance the next stage of struggle. It was to be called The Institute of the Black World (IBW). To staff it, Vincent reached out to scholars and activists from near and far to join him in Atlanta as senior research fellows.

In education, Chester Davis came from Sir George Williams in Canada. Lerone Bennett, Jr., took leave from *Ebony* magazine to teach history along with another native Chicagoan, Sterling Stuckey. Joyce Ladner, a SNCC alumna, came from St. Louis; and Steve Henderson and Gerald McWorter (now Abdul Alkalimat) joined IBW while retaining their teaching positions at Morehouse and Spelman, respectively. And I, flattered by Vincent's invitation, left New York to teach and analyze politics.

IBW was a critical learning experience for me in ways too numerous to count. One of the most important was that, through researching movement history and talking to Vincent about Martin, I gained an appreciation for Dr. King that I had never had before, since, as a confirmed Malcolmite, when I and my high school buddies would see Martin on television saying things like, "If any blood is to be spilled, let it be ours," we would look at one another and ask, "What's wrong with this silly mother....?" But discovering later that the FBI and other government agencies had the same animus toward Martin that they had toward Malcolm caused me to regard Martin more sympathetically. It soon became evident, however, that the politics of IBW and those of some of the key advisors of the Center were not compatible, so IBW broke with the King Center to follow its own independent path.

Ironically, the IBW (1969-1983) lasted as long as Martin's own movement life from Montgomery to Memphis (1955-1968)—even though we had to overcome the inevitable fallout from funding sources when we no longer had the benediction of a Martin affiliation. Thus, we had to try and fend for ourselves.

One strategy we agreed upon was to reduce payroll, so several of us took teaching jobs away from Atlanta but commuted regularly to continue contributing to IBW's mission. Chet Davis, for example, went to the University of Massachusetts, Amherst; while Bobby Hill, the Jamaican Garvey scholar who had joined IBW's staff, went to Dartmouth. Vincent went to the Quaker school in Pennsylvania, Pendle Hill; while I followed Chet to Amherst and UMass.

And who was at UMass studying for her doctorate in education? Betty Shabazz, Malcolm's widow.

AMHERST, MALCOLM, AND ME

I did not know Betty Shabazz personally, though I had spoken to her on occasion when I called their house in Queens to speak to Malcolm. Of course, I naturally sought her out, and we talked a few times because she had moved to Mount Vernon, New York, and was commuting weekly to Amherst. But when we talked, she did not seem terribly interested in writing about Malcolm herself or being interviewed about her life with Malcolm. And when I asked her if there were any unpublished documents, she mentioned, "Yes, there were some things in the garage." But she never volunteered anything further. So I concluded that if I was truly interested in doing what I could to advocate how central I believed Malcolm's thought and analysis was to illuminating and advancing the Black struggle, I could not depend solely on other voices.

So I wrote about Malcolm for *Présence Africaine*; *The Village Voice*; and sundry other newspapers, magazines, and journals. Then the gods intervened again, sending Jan Carew, the Guyanese writer/playwright to Hampshire College in 1977; and Tanzanian revolutionary, Abdul Rahman Babu, to Amherst College in the early 1980s.[11] Both were living witnesses to Malcolm's thought and persona abroad, in London and Africa, respectively, in the last few months of his life. Now the gods had brought us each, sequentially, to Amherst.

I recount these smidgens of my personal relationship with Malcolm so that readers will understand my "Malcolm bias" and the lens through which I view—and fundamentally disapprove of—Manning Marable's solipsistic creation.

PART TWO: MANNING MARABLE'S NON-DEFINITIVE BIOGRAPHY

The problems with Manning's biography of Malcolm X[12] are many and multiple. They range from historical gaffes and endless nonsequiturs to key historical omissions; from patchwork analysis pieced together from the works of others without accurate attribution—and sometimes with no attribution at all—to selective and questionable sources. But most of all, the work disqualifies itself as a work of historical scholarship since it is consistently riven with allegations and statements based on speculation alone. (I invite readers to read—or reread—the book with pen and notebook at hand to keep count of the frequency of qualifiers in the text such as "may have," "could have," "probably," "likely," "if," *ad infinitum*.)

And then there are the facile character assassinations of Malcolm, Betty Shabazz, Alex Haley *et al.*, justified, we are told, as "humanizing" Malcolm's story. Malcolm, for example, is accused, among other things—and *en passant*—of adultery, homosexuality, sexual inadequacy, misogyny, anti-Semitism, and being purposefully manipulative about the facts of his life (i.e., "Malcolm deliberately exaggerated," p. 260; "[Malcolm] packaged himself...[like] a great method actor," p. 10; etc., etc.

NOT RIOTS, BUT REBELLIONS: MALCOLM AND THE MASSES CONFRONT THE AMERICAN POLICE STATE

Manning's interpretation of Malcolm's life as "reinvention" had given me my original sense of unease because reinvention suggests a designed twisting of the truth and self-glorifying motives. I wondered why, for instance, Manning did not use more neutral language such as "transformation" or "development," or "growth," or "evolution." But utilizing that kind of language would derail a central theme of the book, which is to portray Malcolm as both hero and anti-hero, to de-iconize him. Thus, in the very first pages of the book, Manning accuses Malcolm of being "controversial" and of making "provocative" statements. I wondered, of course, "controversial" and "provocative" to whom because Malcolm enthralled most folk who heard him.

As evidence for his accusation, Manning cites an interview that Malcolm gave to a *New York Times* reporter in March of 1964, in which Malcolm said:

> The whites had better understand this while there is still time. The Negroes at the mass level are ready to act. *There will be more violence than ever this year* [emphasis mine].[13]

Manning then frames Malcolm's observation by quoting the New York City Police Commissioner who castigates Malcolm as:

> another self-proclaimed leader [who] openly advocates bloodshed and armed revolt and sneers at the sincere effort of reasonable men to resolve the problem of equal rights by proper, peaceful, and legitimate means.[14]

And what happened four months later in the summer of 1964? In July, Harlem erupted over the police killing of fifteen-year-old James

Powell, the second Black youth shot by New York City cops that month.[15]

Nor was Harlem the only Black community to erupt that summer. Rebellions also occurred in Jacksonville, Florida; Rochester, New York; Philadelphia, Pennsylvania; and Paterson, Elizabeth, and Jersey City, New Jersey.[16] All of these 1964 rebellions, which America misleadingly called "race riots," were in response to some real or perceived racist conduct by the police of those cities. But instead of citing these rebellions as proof of the accuracy of Malcolm's March prediction, Manning mentions them not at all, thus lending undeserved credibility to the police commissioner's condemnation of Malcolm. I was incredulous at this omission because one feature of the Harlem rebellion was the masses calling on Malcolm, who was in Africa at the time, to come home and lead them. So the police commissioner's "self-proclaimed leader" was precisely the leader Harlem turned to in its summer uprising.

Neglecting these rebellions, which continued to erupt until July 1968[17] is to neglect their ties to Malcolm's own earlier protests against police racism in Harlem in 1957 and 1958; and to his later desire to confront the Los Angeles police who invaded the NOI Mosque there in 1962, assaulted mosque members willy-nilly, and killed Malcolm's transplanted Roxbury comrade Ronald Stokes. Only Elijah Muhammad's prohibition kept Malcolm and other Black Muslims from descending on Los Angeles to avenge Stokes' death.[18]

So from 1964 to 1968, with the exception of the firestorm of Black rebellions that swept the country after Martin's assassination in Memphis that April, Black folk nationwide rose up against racist police rule, emulating Malcolm's pioneering protests of the 1950s. Consequently, Manning's failure to identify Malcolm's historical link to these subsequent mass protests against the police—the occupying military force over Black America—is an analytical shortcoming that significantly undermines his stated aim of clarifying Malcolm's real political-theoretical contribution to the Black struggle (i.e., rejecting America's identity as a democratic Republic and linking it to South Africa as a racist state).

MALCOLM'S (AND MARTIN'S) ASSASSINATION REVISITED

In recapitulating the events of Malcolm's assassination in the Audubon Ballroom on February 21, 1965, Manning, once again, leaves out crucial details. He laboriously identifies the members of Malcolm's security detail, giving their names, where they were stationed, their usual routines, and alleged deviations from those routines that he, Manning, hints is suspicious. Except that there was one bodyguard, Gene Roberts, famously depicted in the photo of the group trying to minister to the fallen Malcolm on the Audubon stage, whom Manning does not mention at all!

This omission is not only incomprehensible, it is historically—and politically—inexcusable since Gene Roberts, as Manning tells the reader belatedly,[19] was an undercover police agent. Roberts is *trés* significant in evaluating the role of the police that day because after Malcolm's previous meeting at the Audubon on February 15, Roberts had told his police superiors that he had observed what he believed to be "a dry run on Malcolm's life."[20] He said that there had been…

> a commotion [and that he had seen]...this young fella come down the middle aisle and slip into about the second or third row and take a seat. He was wearing a blue suit, white shirt and a red bow tie, which is basically the uniform for the Nation of Islam. I remember seeing a couple of people there that I hadn't seen before...and I mentioned their names.[21]

Roberts said that the reaction of his superiors to his warning was, "We'll take care of it...And that was that."[22]

Well, we now know how they "took care of it." That, despite Malcolm's house having been bombed on February 14 and their own agent reporting a potential death threat on February 15. On February 21, a minuscule police presence was carefully stationed in an irrelevant part of the building, but not inside the ballroom, while the vast majority of police were stashed across the street, conveniently and safely away from the meeting itself. Of course, when questioned about it later, the police claimed that someone in Malcolm's "entourage" had made the request that they absent themselves. They did not volunteer, of course, the fact that Malcolm's so-called entourage was heavily infiltrated with police spies.

This tragicomedy is remarkably similar to one that would take place three years later on April 4, 1968, when the Memphis police reduced Dr. King's security detail from the usual ten or more officers to two and then pulled the head of the detail, Black detective Ed Redditt, from his assignment at the Lorraine Motel and ordered him back to police headquarters. There, in a meeting with the chief of police, the sheriff, and members of the Highway Patrol, Army Intelligence, National Guard, and Secret Service, Redditt was told that "*word has come from Washington that there is a contract out on his life* and that he must go home immediately [emphasis mine]."[23] (Are we to assume that James Earl Ray had such good connections?) Redditt deferred, however, volunteering to stay on the job despite the alleged threat on his life, but to no avail. The chief of police ordered him home and sent him there, accompanied by Memphis police officers, who camped in his house "to safeguard him." (And of course to ensure that he did not go back to the Lorraine on his own.)[24]

The Memphis scenario at the Lorraine Motel was a virtual replica of the Audubon scenario in New York in 1965 in that the Memphis police, like the New York police, also alleged that someone in Dr. King's entourage had told them they would not be needed because a local Black street gang, the Memphis Invaders, would handle security. Although it has never been conclusively proven that it was members of the Memphis Invaders, or provocateurs pretending to be Invaders, who precipitated the violence of the first King march in Memphis on March 28—violence that prompted Dr. King to return to Memphis to prove that nonviolence could work—it has been verified that police agents had infiltrated the Invaders. Indeed, one of those agents, Marrell McCollough, like Gene Roberts in New York, is captured in the photograph depicting King's aides huddled around his body on the balcony outside his Lorraine Motel room.[25]

It is thus quite extraordinary that a scholar of Manning's reputation should inform his readers of the inherent contradictions of the official explanation of the assassination of Malcolm X but not expound on the bigger picture that emerges when one witnesses the same dishonest "cover story" trampling on the truth of King's assassination. But the shape of that "big picture" did surface, if ever so briefly, some thirty years after King's assassination when, unbeknownst to the American people, and scrupulously ignored or misreported by the national media, the official version of the King slaying was rejected on December 8, 1999, by a Memphis jury of six Blacks and six Whites, who concluded that King was assassinated by "*a conspiracy* involving Loyd Jowers and others, *including government agencies* [emphasis mine]."[26]

One would have thought that such a verdict would have been front-page news in every newspaper in America and the lead story on all the television news shows. But with the exception of one reporter from the local Memphis paper, only foreign media covered the trial. In addition, the startling headline: "Memphis Jury Sees Conspiracy in Martin Luther King's Death," was treated as only one of several stories reported on page twenty-three of the *New York Times*![27]

Unaccountably, Manning fails to mention this exposé, even after accusing both the FBI and the NYPD of having "advance knowledge" of the plot to kill Malcolm. He also hypothesizes "that the New York District Attorney's office may have cared more about protecting the identities of undercover police officers and informants than arresting the real killers."[28] His lapse may be due to the fact that he seems to accept the sanctioned version of King's death, equating it with that of Medgar Evers, because he writes that both were "gunned down by lone white supremacists."[29]

But be that as it may, we know that Malcolm was not only targeted by the FBI, BOSS (Bureau of Special Services), and the NYPD but also by the CIA, the State Department, the Secret Service—and god knows who else. We also know that J. Edgar Hoover, after King's "I Have a Dream" speech at the March on Washington, said that, "We must mark him now...as the most dangerous Negro of the future in this nation from the standpoint of Communism, the Negro, and national security."[30]

So what are we to call these forces arrayed against Malcolm, Martin, and the movement as a whole? Well, Malcolm often reminded us what to call them when opening his meetings at his myth-shattering jocular best. He would greet the audience with, "Hello, brothers and sisters... and friends and enemies." Then, while folk were still chuckling, he would ask: "You know that you have enemies, don't you? You wouldn't be here if some 'enemy' hadn't brought you here."

This was the iconoclastic Malcolm with a different vision than the civil rights leaders of his day because, unlike most of them, Malcolm did not proceed on the assumption that America was capable of racially reforming its institutions and culture on its own. That is why he proposed the two-pronged strategy of internationally charging the United States of genocide at the United Nations on the one hand, and the national strategy of "the Ballot or the Bullet" on the other.

MALCOLM "DECONSTRUCTS" AMERICA

Malcolm was such a spellbinding orator that the fact that he was also a political theoretician is little appreciated, but he was. He advocated, for example, that instead of pursuing the diversionary goal of integration, Black people ought to control their own communities economically and politically and fight to exercise their Fifteenth Amendment right to vote nationwide. Then they could extricate themselves from the hypocritical grasp of the two-party system and be an independent political power in their own right. But if America was unwilling to "do the right thing," voting-wise and otherwise, Malcolm advised Blacks to emulate the revolutionary struggles of Africa, Vietnam, Cuba, Algeria, *et al.* and fight for their liberation too, i.e., "the Ballot or the Bullet."

Accordingly, the larger context lacking in Manning's biography of Malcolm is its failure to sufficiently explicate that Malcolm was much more than America's supposedly most angry Black man. Rather, Malcolm was America's most quintessential racial critic, the person who exposed the inadequacy of defining "the racial problem" in terms of "prejudice," "discrimination," "southern segregation," *et al.* In fact, he used to say: "Stop talking about 'the South.' When you cross the Canadian border, you're in the South."[31]

Ergo, the critical question that America needed to ask itself was not whether Malcolm was its most angry Black man or "a hater," but why tens of thousands of Black men and women, given their own racial experience in this land, were so willing to accept Elijah Muhammad's depiction of the White man as "the devil." I suspect that would have been Malcolm's sixty-four-thousand dollar question.

So whereas Aretha breathed life into our cultural souls, Malcolm resurrected our political minds—and souls. Because it was Malcolm who told us that we were victims of a national and historical SYSTEM. And he gave that system a name that clarified our consciousness a thousandfold: he called it racism. And in so doing, he not only redefined our struggle, he also redefined America.

PART THREE: ON THE METHODOLOGY OF MERCANTILISM, CHARACTER DENIGRATION, AND WRITING A BIOGRAPHY FULL OF HOLES

"REINVENTION" ÜBER ALLES

It is awkward to criticize someone whom one knew fairly well who is now not able to defend himself. Some may even consider it in bad taste—or worse. Though understanding those feelings, I have two rejoinders. First, speaking well of the dead is a standard that Manning did not adhere to himself. Second, our task as scholars and researchers is to seek the truth of our history rather than bend it to our subjective will.

For the lessons to be drawn from the history—for our own time and for the future—are infinitely more important than the arbitrary musings of any one individual. In fact, as one example of the arbitrary nature of Manning's hegemonic trope, his theory of Malcolm's "reinvention" of self, let us take the concept and apply it to his own life. To wit: In the thirty-odd years of Manning's academic career (1974-2011), he taught at at least eleven different colleges and universities. Two were Black (Fisk and Tuskegee), the rest were White institutions. Moreover, his academic identity at those institutions was many and varied. He began as an associate or full professor of political science. Then in his next locales, he morphed into a professor of economics or history or sociology. After that he was, at the same university, a professor of history, political science and sociology, all in one. In the latter stage of his academic journey, Manning chaired a Black Studies department, then took his last post at Columbia as director of the Institute for Research in African American Studies. Thus, Manning traveled from east coast to west coast; from Massachusetts and upstate New York to California; thence to the South, from Alabama and Tennessee, and from there to the Midwest, Ohio, and Indiana. He then crossed the Mississippi to Colorado before finally returning to the East and taking root at Columbia University.[32]

This is quite a unique travel record since one assumes that Manning received offers of tenure at some, if not most, of the universities where he taught. So why did he leave so many, so often? Was it wanderlust? Or was it the tempting, status-raising offers he received from an academy that coveted him as a young, rising Black star?

And who and what did Manning leave behind as he vacated one position after another? One might even ask: Did he leave all of these places voluntarily or was there some hidden history, personal or professional, behind all these uprootings? My point here is twofold: to demonstrate how neatly Manning, by raising questions from left—or right—field about his life, might be garbed in the cloak of self-reinvention himself. It also shows how easy it is for practically anyone to be tarred-and-feathered by that approach, a particular example of which is the most problematic conjecture in the book: Malcolm's alleged homosexuality.

A LIE OF REINVENTION

The index for Manning's book contains two citations regarding Malcolm and "homosexual encounters." In the first, Manning tells his readers that the fictional character, Rudy, in the *Autobiography*, the one who allegedly sprinkled talcum powder over an "undressed" White man named Paul Lennon was actually Malcolm himself. As he writes: "*Based on circumstantial but strong evidence*, Malcolm was *probably* describing his own homosexual encounters with Paul Lennon [emphasis mine]."[33] But where is this "strong evidence"? Manning does not cite it, but he invokes his relentless tendency to "probablytize" history.

A little later in that same paragraph, still riding the Detroit Red horse, Manning writes, "But in his Detroit Red life, he [Malcolm] participated in prostitution, marijuana sales, cocaine sessions, numbers running, the occasional robbery and *apparently* paid homosexual encounters [emphasis mine]."[34] Though he changes the adverb from "probably" to "apparently," the aspersion does not change. Then, having established Malcolm's homosexual history to his own satisfaction, Manning writes about it as a given fact in his next chapter: "...Malcolm-Detroit Red, Satan, hustler, one time pimp, drug addict and drug dealer, *homosexual lover*, ladies man, numbers racketeer, burglar, Jack Carlton, and convicted thief...[emphasis mine]."[35] Manning thus becomes his own authority, quoting himself as his evidentiary source! (I am certain that other contributors to this volume will have something to say about the homosexual issue raised by Manning, so let us focus now on another example, which, I think, is the most revealing about where this book is really coming from: Manning's case against Alex Haley and the *Autobiography of Malcolm X*.[36])

ON MAKING A CASE FOR ONESELF

There is a persistent theme in Manning's biography of Malcolm X: that Alex Haley, a Black Republican and integrationist, was fundamentally opposed to Black Nationalism and therefore slyly shaped the *Autobiography* to be more in tune with his own ideology than with Malcolm's. As Manning writes:

> *Few of the book's reviewers appreciated that it was actually a joint endeavor—and particularly that Alex Haley...had an agenda of his own. A liberal Republican, Haley held the Nation of Islam's racial separatism and religious extremism in contempt....In many ways, the published book is more Haley's than the author's because Malcolm died in February, 1965, he had no opportunity to revise major elements of what would become known as his political testament* [emphasis mine].[37]

To begin with, Manning's statement that most of the reviewers of the *Autobiography* did not realize "it was...a joint endeavor," defies logic since the title of the *Autobiography,* in big, bold letters, reads: *The Autobiography of Malcolm X AS TOLD TO ALEX HALEY*! There is also the small matter of the seventy-three-page "Epilogue" by Haley at the end of the book. So one assumes that book reviewers, who are allegedly literate, are able to put two and two together and conclude that the book was "a joint endeavor"—but Manning doesn't seem to think so.

Then there's his issue of Haley being a Black Republican. Well, let's see if we can make sense of that fact... Haley was from Tennessee, and Tennessee happens to have been the birthplace of the Ku Klux Klan, whose political party, to which the White Leagues, the Knights of the White Camellia, and other White terrorists belonged, was the party that overthrew Reconstruction: the Democratic Party. Therefore, every Southern Black man voting after the passage of the Fourteenth and Fifteenth Amendments, who was not harassed, intimidated, or murdered, and who had freedom of choice to vote, was a Republican. Indeed, Frederick Douglass once said: "The Republican party is the ship. All else is open sea."[38]

But we need not linger with the horror stories of the nineteenth century to establish the strength of the Klan in the Democratic Party because fifty years after Reconstruction, the Klan was so strong that in 1924, at the Democratic National Convention in New York City, it nominated its own candidate for president, a New York lawyer named William McAdoo.[39] McAdoo had been born in Georgia, reared in Tennessee, and moved to New York at the age of twenty-nine in 1892. Thirty-two years later at Madison Square Garden, the Democratic Party held the longest political convention in American political history. Deadlocked Democratic delegates cast one hundred-and-two ballots over sixteen days before they could elect a compromise candidate over McAdoo, the Klan's nominee. Although they had lost the first prize, the Klan had already consolidated its power in Oregon, Texas, California, Georgia, Oklahoma, Kansas, Indiana, and the South. It had elected a senator from Texas and "as many as seventy-five members of the U.S. House of Representatives."[40]

So what party should a southern Black man like Haley belong to, especially in the years 1963-1965 when the *Autobiography* was being written and when the Democratic Party in Alabama and Mississippi was proudly flying a flag depicting a picture of a white rooster with the caption, "White Supremacy"? Being a Black Republican, as Haley was in those movement years, is therefore not the same as being a Black Republican in the era of Clarence Thomas, Ronald Reagan, Bush Sr., or Bush Jr. and Cheney, *et al.* That is a distinction that seems to have eluded Manning entirely.

Manning's other points seem equally in limbo. He implies, for instance, that Haley inserted ideas of his own into the text but offers no proof. He also claims that Malcolm had no time to revise the *Autobiography* because he was killed in February and the book was published six months later (even though Haley claimed that Malcolm reviewed all the chapters and that they worked together in December and January "incorporating his new views into the final chapters of the *Autobiography*..."[41]). In fact, on February 14, a week before Malcolm's death, Haley told his agent, Paul Reynolds, that the book was practically finished; that he was "winding up Malcolm X's book.... *You'll have it prior to March*...[emphasis mine]."[42] That is to say, within two weeks! So if Haley wrote something after March, what was it and where is it?

Most tellingly, Manning's insinuations about Haley masterminding and undermining Malcolm's message in the book is contradicted by Haley's own admission that just the opposite was happening in his collaboration with Malcolm on the *Autobiography*, that it was profoundly affecting *him*. Accordingly, he told his agent and editors that "...he was at the point at which the process of writing the *Autobiography* was *changing him*" and when "'*the material begins to direct you and command you into what must be done with it*' [emphasis mine]."[43]

But casting a shadow over Haley's and the *Autobiography*'s integrity is only one scene in a script that disparages the work of all previous writers, researchers, and biographers of Malcolm X. According to Manning, "the historical Malcolm, the man with all his strengths and flaws was being strangled by the iconic legend that had been constructed around him. In reading nearly all the literature about Malcolm produced in the 1990s, I was struck by its shallow character and lack of original sources..."[44] The solution to this perceived historical deficiency was, to Manning, self-evident: like the cavalry in the classic American westerns, he felt compelled to ride to the rescue.

But significantly, Manning was no Lone Ranger riding to the rescue by himself. Factually, a more appropriate image is to see him as the overseer of a large research plantation stretching back over two decades, manned—and womanned—by countless staff. That is what distinguishes Manning's project from nearly all other Malcolm researchers and historians: he had financial and institutional resources others did not have. He had numerous staff over the years that others did not have. He worked over a time span others did not enjoy. Remember Manning developed his research perspective over a twenty-year time period, while Haley and Malcolm wrote the *Autobiography* in just two years.

More importantly, the *Autobiography* was a two-person collaboration in which Malcolm was the ultimate decision maker as to what went into the book. Manning, on the other hand, acknowledges that he worked closely with one Viking editor "*in the development of each chapter*" [and] "...communicated almost daily...for nearly eighteen months... [with other editors to discuss] *various versions of chapters, in the effort to reach the broadest possible audience* [emphasis mine]."[45] Thus, Manning's biography was a collective effort crafted, under the publisher's aegis, "to reach the broadest possible audience," which is to say that the historical narrative appears to have been subordinated to the marketing strategy, depriving readers of comprehending not only how Malcolm inspired untold thousands but also how prophetically his political analysis, insights, and conclusions about America's fundamental racial failings became the movement's own; and how the incessant betrayals by government and society led even the once hopeful and idealistic Martin Luther King, Jr., to deplore a society crippled by its "materialism, militarism, and *racism*" and to conclude the following, six months before his own assassination:

> I have found out all that I have been doing in trying to correct this *system* in America has been in vain....I am trying to get to the roots of it to see just what ought to be done.... *The whole thing will have to be done away with* [emphasis mine].[46]

Malcolm couldn't have said it better.

ENDNOTES

1 *Malcolm X: Make It Plain* is the title of the 1993 Public Broadcasting System (PBS) documentary on Malcolm X and the title of the companion book by William Strickland, edited by Cheryll Y. Greene and published by Viking Press in 1994.

2 "The Hill" in Upper Roxbury was a mixed community of Black, Jewish, and Irish Americans. It had previously been primarily a Jewish neighborhood, called "The Hill" because Warren Street ascended upward gradually from Dudley Street, Roxbury's mercantile center, to Humboldt Avenue, the main upper thoroughfare, to end finally on Seaver Street, face-to-face with Franklin Park and its then-famous zoo.

3 Gordon W. Allport, *The Nature of Prejudice*. New York: Basic Books, 1979.

4 C. Eric Lincoln, *The Black Muslims in America*. Boston: Beacon Press, 1961.

5 Charles E. Cobb, Jr., *On the Road to Freedom: A Guided Tour of the Civil Rights Trail* (Chapel Hill, NC: Algonquin Books, 2008), 44.

6 Ibid.

7 William Strickland, "Malcolm: The Last Real Social Critic," *The Village Voice*, February 26, 1985, 15.

8 Stokely Carmichael, with Ekwueme Michael Thelwell, *Ready for Revolution: The Life and Struggles of Stokely Carmichael* (New York: Scribner, 2003), 356-357. In fall 1963, Mississippi Blacks, denied their right to vote, held a "Freedom Vote," organized by the Council of Federated Organizations (COFO), an alliance among CORE, SNCC, and the Mississippi NAACP. Over 80,000 Blacks voted in that election, and out of that vote emerged the MFDP and, the following year, the MFDP's Congressional Challenge.

9 Carmichael, *Ready for Revolution*, 419-420. On January 4, 1965, the three Mississippi Congressmen were prevented from taking their seats until a resolution made by Congressman William Fitts Ryan of New York, challenging their seating, could be voted upon. Sixty Congressmen rose to support Ryan's "fairness" resolution. And when the vote was taken, the MFDP received 149 votes or thirty-five percent of the Congress, but it was not enough. The resolution failed by 71 votes.

10 J. H. O'Dell, "Colonialism and the Negro American Experience," *Freedomways*, 4 (1966), 299. Jack O'Dell, who originally worked with Martin Luther King and was "redbaited" by J. Edgar Hoover, was one of my important political mentors. In the essay he wrote decades ago, he said, "This problem of definitions, the problem of an adequate theory of emancipation, becomes crucial to the success of our Freedom movement." Jack explicated everything I was feeling at the time—and feel still.

11 Jan Carew met Malcolm in February 1965, when Malcolm went to London to speak at the London School of Economics. He interviewed Malcolm the day after that, on February 12, and, motivated by that interview, subsequently interviewed Malcolm's brother Wilfred and others. Those interviews, and further research, culminated in Carew's 1994 book on Malcolm, *Ghosts in Our Blood: With Malcolm X in Africa, England, and the Caribbean* (Chicago: Lawrence Hill, 1994). Babu was a key leader in the 1964 revolution in Zanzibar that led to the new independent state of Tanzania. Malcolm met him in Africa in fall 1964, when he was seeking the support of African nations in his project to bring the United States before the United Nations for violations of Black people's human rights. Late in December, when Babu came to America to represent his country at the United Nations, he attended Malcolm's OAAU meeting at the Audubon Ballroom.

12 Manning Marable, *Malcolm X: A Life of Reinvention*. New York: Viking Press, 2011.

13 Ibid., 3.

14 Ibid.

15 Karl Evanzz, *The Judas Factor: The Plot to Kill Malcolm X* (New York: Thunder's Mouth Press, 1992), 251.

16 National Advisory Commission on Civil Disorders, *U.S. Riot Commission Report: Report of the National Advisory Commission on Civil Disorders.* New York: Bantam, 1968.

17 Louis H. Masotti and Jerome R. Corsi, *Shoot-out in Cleveland: Black Militants and the Police; A Report to the National Commission on the Causes and Prevention of Violence.* New York: Bantam, 1969.

18 Evanzz, *The Judas Factor*, 117-21.

19 Marable, 422.

20 Strickland, *Make It Plain*, 202.

21 Ibid.

22 Ibid.

23 Mark Lane and Dick Gregory, *Code Name Zorro: The Murder of Martin Luther King, Jr.* (Englewood Cliffs, NJ: Prentice Hall, 1977), 131.

24 Ibid., 132-33.

25 William F. Pepper, *Orders to Kill: The Truth Behind the Murder of Martin Luther King* (New York: Carrol & Graf, 1995), 254-55.

26 Loyd Jowers, a former Memphis policeman, was the owner of a bar and grill next to James Earl Ray's rooming house and across the street from the Lorraine Motel where Martin Luther King was shot. In 1993, on Sam Donaldson's television show, *Prime Time Live*, Jowers claimed that he had participated in a plot to kill King. Consequently, in 1999, the King family took Jowers to court and the jury found him guilty of the two charges put to them by the Shelby County judge: (a) "Did Loyd Jowers participate in the conspiracy to do harm to Martin Luther King?" and (b) "Do you also find that others, including government agencies, were parties to this conspiracy as alleged by the defendant?" Two-and-a-half hours later, the jury answered in the affirmative on both counts.

27 Emily Yellin, "Memphis Jury Sees Conspiracy in Martin Luther King's Death," *New York Times*, December 9, 1999, 23.

28 Marable, 13.

29 Ibid.

30 Kenneth O'Reilly, *Racial Matters: The FBI's Secret File on Black America, 1960-1972* (New York: The Free Press, 1989), 130.

31 Strickland and Greene, *Make It Plain*, 3.

32 Carolyn B. D. Smith, "Manning Marable," *Answers.com*, http://www.answers.com/topic/manning-marable.

33 Marable, 66.

34 Ibid.

35 Ibid., 78.

36 Malcolm X, *The Autobiography of Malcolm X as Told to Alex Haley*. New York: Grove Press, 1965.

37 Marable, 9.

38 In the 1880s, after the Republican Party's capitulation to the Democrats and the overthrow of Reconstruction, Richard T. Greener, the first Black graduate of Harvard, proposed to Douglass that Blacks become an independent political force. The quote was Douglass's response.

39 Robert K. Murray, *The 103rd Ballot* (New York: Harper & Row, 1976), 87-88.

40 Ibid., 19.

41 Marable, 402.

42 Ibid., 403.

43 Ibid., 261.

44 Ibid., 490.

45 Ibid., 492.

46 Strickland and Greene, *Make It Plain*, 165.

RAYMOND A. WINBUSH

Speculative Nonfiction: Manning Marable's ***Malcolm X***

Is an award-winning biography worthy of the genre when it lacks primary source material? Raymond Winbush doesn't think so. He asserts that A Life of Reinvention *relies heavily on speculation and conjecture to fill in the gaps of thinking and reflecting on Malcolm's life when Marable should have done the hard digging expected of historians and biographers—including conducting hundreds of oral history interviews instead of just sixteen. Winbush further maintains that Marable's lack of groundbreaking research is disguised by piles of footnotes that ultimately reveal "really nothing new" about Malcolm.*

TWO STUDENTS MEET MALCOLM

About two months after an American bullet blew off the head of Martin Luther King Jr., on a Memphis balcony, I read *The Autobiography of Malcolm X*. I had just won a scholarship to Harvard University from my undergraduate alma mater, Oakwood University, and, along with hundreds of other American African students from historically Black colleges and universities across the country, I was "bussed" by The Ford Foundation to visit Harvard, Yale, and Columbia. The program was designed to stimulate our interest in going to graduate school. Besides me, the class included a young George Curry, who would eventually become a nationally known journalist; a young Pearl Cleage, who would go on to write powerful novels and plays about African women; and a young Harold Vann, who would change his name to Khallid Muhammad and become one of the most outspoken members of the reinvigorated Nation of Islam under Minister Louis Farrakhan.

Part of the curriculum at Harvard that summer was to read books about the times in which we were living, and Malcolm's *Autobiography* and Franz Fanon's *Wretched of the Earth* were considered must-reads for my generation. A Jewish professor teaching African American studies at nearby Brandeis University assigned the *Autobiography* to us. He was obsessively compulsive about not uttering a word that might prove offensive either about Malcolm or Martin, because Martin's assassination had just occurred and Malcolm's had taken place just over three years prior. I suppose his volunteering to teach the class was an early effort to bridge the diversity gap during a period when racial tensions were running high, especially among Black students on the nation's college campuses, who were asserting themselves by joining and supporting the Black Panther Party, the Student Nonviolent Coordinating Committee, and (for those who felt more comfortable joining or working with nearly all-White groups) the Students for a Democratic Society.

Grove Press was the hot press of the day. It published books considered extremely controversial during the 1960s, among them D. H. Lawrence's *Lady Chatterley's Lover*, Henry Miller's *Tropic of Cancer*, Frantz Fanon's *The Wretched of the Earth*, William Burroughs's *Naked Lunch*, and Samuel Beckett's *Waiting for Godot*, to name a few. I remember seeing quite a few raised eyebrows on my friends' faces when Malcolm's *Autobiography* was published by a house that had been sued several times for obscenity because of the racy titles in its catalogue. The fact that Malcolm's collaborator on the *Autobiography*, Alex Haley, was also a primary interviewer for *Playboy* magazine, contributed to even further speculation about why the morally conservative Malcolm X would have allowed his life to be exposed to the world by a publishing house known for its risqué output.

Regardless, I *devoured* the book. Our somewhat timid Jewish professor told us that we needed to read it within a week, and I remember digesting it in three days. It was, for me, simply impossible to put down.

I had read Richard Wright's *Black Boy* and *Native Son*, James Baldwin's *Another Country*, and Claude Brown's *Manchild in the Promised Land* before reading the *Autobiography*, but none of them had affected me the way Malcolm's book did. To me, Malcolm's searing words captured the essence of what it was like to be Black in America. He spoke to the deepest part of my being. I especially identified with him because I had been reared on the east side of Cleveland, Ohio, and my older brother Harold was in prison at that time for manslaughter. Thus, the narrative of Malcolm's life paralleled much of what was going on in my own life and that of many of my Black Harvard classmates, who also came from backgrounds very similar to Malcolm's.

The *Autobiography* was transformative for me on so many levels. It led me to recast not only my views about how racism works but also about how redemption is possible, even for those infected with the virus of White supremacy.

About eighteen months later and nine hundred miles west of Cambridge, a freshman student at Earlham College named Manning Marable also read *The Autobiography of Malcolm X*. He too "eagerly devoured the edited volumes of [Malcolm's] speeches and interviews," and for him Malcolm became "the icon of the Black Power movement."[1]

PRIMARY SOURCES

In his final book, *Malcolm X: A Life of Reinvention*, Marable recalls that shortly after his initial reading of the *Autobiography,* he came to a rather obvious conclusion—namely that, "[n]early all of the scholarly work on Malcolm was based on a very narrow selection of primary sources, his transcribed speeches, and secondary sources, such as newspapers [sic] articles."[2] He offers this bloviated conclusion as if his readers are, for the most part, largely unaware of how or what others had written about Malcolm's life to date. Even in the 1960s, however, most people who read Malcolm's words or others' writings on Malcolm were well aware of the inconsistencies between some parts of his speeches and recordings and the printed texts of those same speeches in publications. Marable's "insights" on the presumed lack of primary sources is a rather minor and obvious conclusion. It is also one that is over forty years old. But Marable seems to have wanted to make his readers believe that his "aha moments" about Malcolm were major discoveries by him when, in reality, they are not. Why such dramatic language then for a truism?

Human rights activists rarely have time to write much about their activism during the early stages of their involvement, but their meditative works of self-reflection provide the most introspective primary sources on their backgrounds, thoughts, and feelings. Table 1 below compares a number of African American activists in terms of their publication of books, inclusive of autobiographies, during the first ten years of their public activism. (That Martin Luther King Jr., tops this list is perhaps reflective of his scholarly background before becoming a civil rights activist.)

Table 1: Selected Activists' Writing During Their Early Careers

ACTIVIST	NUMBER OF BOOKS (INCLUDING AUTOBIOGRAPHIES) WRITTEN IN FIRST TEN YEARS OF PUBLIC NOTORIETY
Eldridge Cleaver	2
W. E. B. DuBois	2
Marcus Garvey	1
Fannie Lou Hamer	0
Martin Luther King Jr.	4
Rosa Parks	0
Asa Phillip Randolph	0
Kwame Ture (aka Stokely Carmichael)	1
Ida B. Wells-Barnett	2
Malcolm X	1

A subject's own books, of course, are but one primary source that researchers use to write biography. Interviews, speeches, and personal correspondence are also tools to flesh out the life of the subject, and, as we shall see, constitute something notably absent in Marable's book on Malcolm X. What is curious, however, about *A Life of Reinvention* is its author's overwhelming ignorance of or failure to use the primary sources—Malcolm's own *Autobiography*, his numerous speeches, other books about him, and other writings—that were at his disposal.

SPECULATION AND INNUENDO AS "SOURCES"

The part of *A Life of Reinvention* that has garnered the most publicity is the speculative nonfiction Marable offers to describe the relationship between Malcolm and a White male benefactor named William Paul Lennon. Marable's speculation about Malcolm's alleged homosexual experiences with Lennon is astonishing on many levels. For example, after presenting an elaborate description of how Malcolm "*may have* [emphasis mine]" met Lennon through classified ads, Marable notes that in the *Autobiography* Malcolm described "sexual contacts with Lennon," but that he "falsely attributed them to a character named 'Rudy.'"[3] Marable provides no facts, no primary sources, nor even any secondary sources for this remarkable assertion, which is based purely on his own conjecture. He then quotes directly from the *Autobiography*:

> [Rudy] had aside deal going, a hustle that took me right back to the old steering days in Harlem. Once a week, Rudy went to the home of this old, rich Boston blueblood, pillar of society aristocrat. He paid Rudy to undress them both, then pick up the old man like a baby, lay him on his bed, then stand over him and sprinkle him all over with talcum powder. Rudy said the old man would actually reach his climax from that.[4]

Immediately after this, as if to deflect attribution of Malcolm as a lying homosexual to himself, Marable posits innuendo as fact: "Based on circumstantial but strong evidence, Malcolm was probably describing his own homosexual encounters with Paul Lennon."[5] This is an extraordinary statement following an extraordinary assertion based on the opinion of the author and nothing more.

Speculation about Malcolm's sexuality is not new.[6] It has received, however, renewed attention since the release of Marable's book. Yet this is my primary criticism of Marable's *Malcolm X*: There is really nothing new about Marable's speculations about Malcolm. He merely exaggerates the importance to a sensational degree.

Table 2 lists the types and frequency of references Marable cites in *A Life of Reinvention*. It should be noted that the figures in this table amount to a generous assessment of the number of citations Marable provides in his book because I made no effort to distinguish between those references that were cited more than once.

Table 2: Types and Frequency of References Cited in Malcolm X: A Life of Reinvention

SOURCE TYPE	NUMBER OF TIMES CITED
Books	178
Dissertations/Theses	30
FBI Documents	19
Freedom of Information Act Documents	10
Footnotes	1,635
Interviews	8
Journal Articles	52
Newspapers and Periodicals	92
Oral Histories	16
TOTAL	*2,040*

It also should be noted that Marable separates *oral histories* from *interviews* in his book. Apparently (and I say this because Marable himself was unclear on this point), the sixteen oral histories he cites involve individuals who had direct contact with Malcolm as opposed to the interviews cited, in which individuals simply share their opinions about Malcolm.

What is curious about both of these categories, however, is Marable's omission of interviews with Malcolm's relatives who were still alive during the twenty years Marable claims it took him to write the book. Why not interview relatives such as Malcolm's widow, Betty Shabazz, who obviously knew Malcolm better during his later life than anyone else? And what about the indomitable Ella Little Collins, Malcolm's half-sister and, according to most observers, the person who witnessed Malcolm's evolution (as opposed to the pejorative term *reinvention* Marable uses in his subtitle) from Malcolm Little to Malcolm X to El-Hajj Malik El-Shabazz? Any good biographer would see his or her subject's contemporaries, relatives, friends, and enemies as primary sources, regardless of or despite the hagiographic or hypercritical material that might emerge from such interviews and oral histories.

Marable's omission or inability to secure an interview with Betty Shabazz is especially troubling since they lived in the same city (New York) and were both in academia (Marable at Columbia University and Shabazz at Medgar Evers College). That would be similar to a person living in Atlanta while doing a biography of Martin Luther King Jr., and not interviewing Coretta Scott King living just five miles away. Ilyasah Shabazz, Malcolm's third daughter, expressed her surprise about this during an April 20, 2011, interview with National Public Radio. As she noted: "There are six of us. And there are also a lot of brothers and sisters of my father's, and I would say—you know, it took Dr. Marable 20 years to do this book—and I would say in the last 20 years, probably all of them were alive. So, we were really surprised that he didn't just interview the family."[7]

Again, most thorough biographers are eager to locate and interview relatives and, in many cases, descendants of their subjects because it "humanizes" those subjects (another word repeatedly misused used by

Marable's supporters posthumously to explain his motives in writing the book). Why Marable failed to interview members of Malcolm's family who were in close proximity to him will likely remain a mystery. Yet, if evidence should be found that shows Marable attempted to conduct family interviews but failed, this would again draw into serious question the rationale of his supporters who have hailed his book as the "most comprehensive" treatment of Malcolm's life to date.

OLD BOOKS WITH NEW COVERS?

A more serious charge that can be leveled against Marable's *Malcolm X* is whether or not anything its author presents is really "new." In my opinion, the book's biggest contribution is the new details it provides about the complicity of the FBI and the New York City Police Department in Malcolm's assassination. Even this must be qualified, however, because Zak Kondo,[8] Karl Evanzz,[9] and James Douglass[10] all have written much earlier histories of the assassination that included thorough coverage of the role of local, state, and federal law-enforcement bureaus in Malcolm's death.

Evanzz is especially scathing in his review of Marable's book. He begins his critique thusly: "*Malcolm X: A Life of Reinvention* is an abomination. It is a cavalcade of innuendo and logical fallacy, and is largely 'reinvented' from previous works on the subject."[11] Concerning the assassination, Evanzz adds a small but critical piece of information that is indicative of what he dubs Marable's sloppiness in the book:

> Marable claims that the same teenager who was romantically involved with Malcolm the night of February 20 showed up at the Audubon Ballroom the next day. She sat in the front row next to a man whose name would later appear in FBI documents related to the assassination. The teenager, Marable writes, and the Newark mosque official now "live together in the same New Jersey residence, and [name deleted] has maintained absolute silence about her relationship with both Malcolm X and [name deleted]." The source

given for this allegation is Abdur-Rahman Muhammad. When I [Evanzz] asked Muhammad for his sources, he declined comment.[12]

In just this one example, Evanzz captures a major problem with Marable's book: Marable's penchant for putting two and two together and either getting five or realizing *ex post facto* that the formula he used was wrong in the first place.

A Life of Reinvention contains simply too many examples to cite here of its author's proclivity for trying to convince his readers that he has been thorough and rigorous in his research. But Marable was unable to hide the gaping holes in his research. The 1,635 footnotes in the book are a telling example of this. The number of "hostile" sources—works whose authors made similarly speculative assertions about Malcolm's life—that Marable uses in his book is shocking and amounts to a "double whammy" of speculative nonfiction.

For example, in Chapter 4 of the book, entitled "They Don't Come Like the Minister," nearly twenty-five percent, or 31 of the 128 footnotes, are from FBI sources. Marable's use of such sources represents a double-edged sword because the FBI had no love for Malcolm and could easily have placed "disinformation" in its files on Malcolm. On the one hand, those files may serve as valuable sources of information on the events surrounding Malcolm's assassination; on the other hand, they may be full of deliberate distortions, innuendo, and outright lies about Malcolm. Marable, of course, seems oblivious to this paradox and makes no mention of the FBI's notorious reputation of defaming and providing disinformation about those whom it wishes to slander. Even the star of the popular daytime television show, Judge Joe Brown, has made mention of this with regard to the assassination of Martin Luther King Jr.: "We were all transgressed upon when the FBI clouded the events in which they had a strong hand. There is nothing less than governmental complicity in what happened to Dr. King."[13] If a "TV judge," albeit one who was directly involved in the events surrounding the investigation of Dr. King's assassination, can see government complicity in the events leading up to that event, why can't Manning

Marable come to the same conclusion about Malcolm's killing? Why legitimize the FBI as a source of information on its illegal activities such as spying on Malcolm but fail to discuss its history of wreaking havoc in the lives of African American leaders such as Callie House, Marcus Garvey, A. Philip Randolph, Martin Luther King Jr., and so many others?

The arrogance of Manning Marable oozes out in so many places throughout the book. It is glaringly obvious in his use of pejorative language to describe those who had studied Malcolm X prior to the publication of *A Life of Reinvention.* Marable further notes that, in his reading of "nearly all of the literature about Malcolm produced in the 1990s," he was most struck by "its shallow character and lack of original sources."[14] Really? "Shallow character"? "Lack of original sources"? Marable saying this is like hip-hop artists criticizing the recording artists they sample in their raps. It is the lack of original sources in Marable's book that is appalling, and his criticism of the 1990s literature on Malcolm is not only arrogant but also misleading. I would venture to say that some of the best literature about Malcolm, much of which, again, is cited repeatedly by Marable in his book, came out of the 1990s. And if it was as bad as Marable claims, why does he cite so much of it in his book?

Marable's use of the terms *Malcolmology* and *Malcolmites* does not immediately endear him to those readers who have tried or are trying to expand their knowledge of Malcolm X either. Even the subtitle of his book, *A Life of Reinvention,* calls into question his motives for writing the book in the first place, implying as it does that his subject engaged in some sort of clever plotting to morph his public image into a character that best suited his own ambitions.

MANNING MARABLE: SCHOLAR OR JOURNALIST?

Quick: name two books written by W. E. B. Du Bois. Answer: *The Souls of Black Folk* and *Dusk of Dawn.* Quick: name two books written by Martin Luther King Jr.? Answer: *Stride Toward Freedom* and *Where*

Do We Go From Here? Even though you may not have read these books, you can easily attribute them to their authors and probably have heard of them. Now, name two books written by Manning Marable? Hard to do, isn't it? Perhaps it is because Marable has contributed little to Black social thought. And that is not just my opinion but one shared by others as well. Caroline B. D. Smith, for example, who wrote the entry on Marable for the book, *Contemporary Black Biography*, had this to say about her subject:

> Despite his reputation as a respected author and educator, Marable has maintained a relatively low profile [among] the country's intellectual elite. His controversial views and openly Marxist stance have alienated many in the academic world, and some have argued that his writings are too vague, too superficial, to offer tangible solutions to the urgent sociological problems facing black Americans.[15]

Smith is not the only one who has noted Marable's lack of impact on efforts to alleviate the challenges faced by Africans in the Diaspora. In an extensive interview, Abdul Alkalimat, one of the leading Marxist academics in the United States, questions Marable's contributions to scholarship and theory in the African world:

> And beyond the Malcolm X book, we have to take a look at all of Manning Marable's work to try and locate him. In other words, being in DSA (Democratic Socialists of America), sort of the left wing of the Democratic Party. That's a real political position he had held. So we have to try to understand that there are philosophical issues and deeper questions here than just the sloppy scholarship of the Malcolm X book…
>
> I think the critical question is what concepts or theoretical propositions have [sic] Marable contributed. I'm not saying in any way that none exist. I'd just like to see someone argue what they are. Clearly, he was a very prolific writer and maybe will go down as an important journalist of this period. But in terms of theory, you take—you take, for example, Walter Rodney's book [*How Europe Underdeveloped Africa*]. Rodney actually made

> fundamental contributions to theory about the historical development of Africa . . . I'm not sure that the same holds true for Marable's book.[16]

Journalism, not scholarship, is perhaps what best describes Manning Marable's body of work. More specifically, Marable was more of an opinion journalist—that is, one whose opinion bleeds through in all of his works and perhaps especially so in his last and most controversial book. Marable's opinion mattered to him, just as the opinions of broadcast media journalists on Fox News and MSNBC matter to those individuals. Their listeners crave their opinions and speculations concerning contemporary political issues, and these commentators get paid, and paid well, to provide just that. Sadly, in the case of Manning Marable and his last work of speculative nonfiction on one of the great persons in the African world, opinion took precedence over originality, and speculation superseded scholarship and a reliance on reliable sources and primary research.

ENDNOTES

1 Manning Marable, *Malcolm X: A Life of Reinvention* (New York: Viking Press, 2011), 489.

2 Ibid., 489.

3 Ibid., 66.

4 Ibid.

5 Ibid.

6 See, for example, Peter Tatchell, "Malcolm X: Gay Black Hero?" Accessed August 15, 2011, http://www.guardian.co.uk/world/2005/may/19/gayrights.usa.

7 National Public Radio, "Malcolm X's Daughter Disputes Claims in New Bio on Father," interview with Ilyasah Shabazz, April 20, 2011. Accessed August 20, 2011, http://www.npr.org/2011/04/20/135570322/malcolm-xs-daughter-addresses-controversial-claims-in-new-bio-on-father.

8 Zak Kondo, *Conspiracys (Conspiracies): Unraveling the Assassination of Malcolm X*. Washington, DC: Nubia Press, 1993.

9 Karl Evanzz, *The Judas Factor: The Plot to Kill Malcolm X*. New York: Thunder's Mouth Press, 1993.

10 J. W. Douglass, "The Murder and Martyrdom of Malcolm X," in James DiEugenio and Lisa Pease, eds., *The Assassinations: Probe Magazine on JFK, MLK, RFK, and Malcolm X*. Los Angeles: Feral House, 2002.

11 Karl Evanzz, " 'Paper Tiger': Karl Evanzz's Blistering Review of Manning Marable's *Malcolm X*." Accessed August 26, 2011, http://www.voxunion.com/?p=3646.*

12 Ibid.

13 Joseph B. Brown, "Introduction," in James DiEugenio and Lisa Pease, eds., *The Assassinations,* x.

14 Marable, *Malcolm X*, 490.

15 Caroline B. D. Smith, "Manning Marable." Accessed August 27, 2011, http://www.answers.com/topic/manning-marable.

16 Interview with Abdul Alkalimat. Accessed August 27, 2011, http://tinyurl.com/4xhjwyq.

* This essay also appears in this volume.

ROSEMARI MEALY

An Incomprehensible Omission: Women and El-Hajj Malik El-Shabazz's Ideological Development in *Malcolm X: A Life of Reinvention*—A Brief Criticism

This essay is drawn from a presentation by the author during a symposium on Manning Marable's Malcolm X: A Life of Reinvention *held at the New York Public Library, Schomburg Center for Research in Black Culture, May 19, 2011.*

It is a generally accepted principle that one of the standard goals of scholarly research is to produce new knowledge while advancing new theories of understanding. Researchers must have well-designed research plans that incorporate the most appropriate methodology for generating this new knowledge and theories of understanding. Manning Marable set out to present the definitive work on one of the most important figures of the Black liberation movement. In the resulting book, *Malcolm X: A Life of Reinvention*, Marable wrote that "in reading nearly all of the literature about Malcolm produced in the 1990s, I was struck by its shallow character and lack of original sources."[1] Ironically, some of the most acclaimed scholars of the life and times of Malcolm X, notably William (Bill) Sales, Amiri Baraka, and William Strickland, who each have critiqued or reviewed Marable's book, have made the same observations of *A Life of Reinvention*, which Marable's publisher purported to be the "definitive work . . . surpassing previous treatments in its depth and intensity, and capturing with revelatory clarity a man who constantly strove, in the great American tradition, to remake himself anew."[2]

I am very concerned about what is not included in this so-called "definitive work." Marable's publisher appears to presuppose that the author's chosen research methodology and conclusions are so irrefutable that they do not warrant even a scintilla of criticism. Such a claim also asserts that one person can produce a decisive work on an individual as complex as Malcolm X, even after twenty years of research. I define myself as a Black womanist-activist-scholar who looks at the world through a critical-race-theorist lens. Hence, in my opinion, biographers who use timelines for constructing scholarly inquiry have a responsibility to search for new facts and insights, and to reach beyond what is already known because the ultimate search is for relevance and truth, which can only be discovered through basing one's analysis in historical-sociocultural theory.

When examining *A Life of Reinvention* through this theoretical lens, I found limited scholarship and a glaring, incomprehensible omission regarding one of the most important aspects of Malcolm's political life: his thinking on questions of gender and on how his political relationships with political Black women affected his overall perspectives on the question of patriarchy. One would think that Organization of Afro-American Unity (OAAU) member Brother Herman Ferguson, who stated in an interview with Marable that Malcolm's "new commitment to gender equality confused and even outraged many members,"[3] would have propelled Marable to engage in the necessary research to ascertain whether Malcolm X really recognized the centrality of Black women's participation in the OAAU and in the overall struggle that resulted in his death. If the intent of Marable's writings was to be "definitive," then one must conclude that this seemingly incomprehensible omission actually supports the womanist argument that an omission of this nature exemplifies how gender biases are inextricably linked to the ways in which Black and progressive women, though locked out of the male discourse, are featured ever so prominently in the titillating biographical descriptions of the sexual exploits of men. Many Black and other progressive women played key roles in Malcolm X's political transformations. In *A Life of Reinvention*, however, the few such references that are made to these women are relegated to footnotes, cited from their own texts and/or other sources, or paraphrased as tangentially related to Malcolm's political development.

Recognizing that Marable was very ill during the last years of his life does not dismiss the fact that, over the course of twenty years, he did not deem it necessary to utilize the appropriate scholarly methodology of interviewing primary subjects to create new knowledge and new theories of understanding on this topic. Some of these primary subjects included Yuri Kochiyama and Maya Angelou, women whose encounters with Malcolm, as presented in *A Life of Reinvention*, Marable merely culls from previously published works or Malcolm's papers rather than presenting information from new interviews that could have helped buttress his claims to have authored the "definitive work." The omission of the voices of other women further underscores Marable's missed opportunity and/or lax scholarship. These omitted voices include the philosopher and Marxist activist-theoretician Grace Lee Boggs, actress-activist Ruby Dee, civil rights activist-scholar Dr. Gwen Patton, and journalist Selma Sparks, the latter of whom played a leading role in the development of the OAAU's newsletter, *The Blacklash*. Sparks's interviews with Malcolm X were not even mentioned in Marable's book.

Another essential Black feminist, activist, and intellectual missing from Marable's narrative is Vicky Garvin. Garvin was known within radical circles for her ability to bring diverse political groups together to coalescence around common causes. She was the key organizer and coordinator for Malcolm's Ghanaian trip. According to one source:

> Garvin played an important role in facilitating Malcolm's introductions to these politics as well as a range of international revolutionaries. She arranged meetings for Malcolm X with officials at the Algerian and Cuban embassies and with the Chinese ambassador, Huang Hua. She also served as

> the interpreter during Malcolm's meeting with Algerian officials. For both Garvin and Malcolm X, such connections proved crucial in shaping their future transnational travels and alliances.[4]

In *A Life of Reinvention*, readers are left to imagine and even to dismiss what Malcolm X's perceived opinions were of women's realities, especially as those opinions pertain to Black women in the United States. The only means readers are given to understand Malcolm's ideological development is through Marable's select, males-only, primary-source informants. This omission of women's voices amplifies the concerns of African American womanist scholars that Marable's book widens the gap in the existing literature about Malcolm X written by men because it fails to acknowledge the extraordinary contributions that African American women historically have made to constructing the leadership styles of progressive and revolutionary African American male leaders.

Ironically, the Asian American activist Yuri Kochiyama, who was a confidante of Malcolm's, has provided and shared many firsthand conversations describing Malcolm's views on women through her public discussions. For example, in a 1964 letter written to Yuri during his first visit to the newly independent progressive African nations, Malcolm wrote: "African women have asserted their right to be educated, and we need to free women here [in the United States] so that they get the same kind of education that men get."[5] Malcolm's letter revealed his positively evolving understanding of the centrality of women's equality within the liberation struggle and society.

Jill Humphries was a young scholar at Columbia University who, under Marable's tutelage, has benefited from an education equal to that received by men. She was encouraged by her mentor as a junior scholar to "engage the work."[6] It is a surmountable challenge for young scholar-activists to critically study and trace the evolution of Malcolm X / El Hajj Malik Shabazz and his political relationships with women. So I pass the baton to Jill and other young women (and men) to fashion a significant, scholarly representation of Black and progressive womanists' contributions to the ever-evolving struggle for Black liberation.

ENDNOTES

1 Manning Marable, *Malcolm X: A Life of Reinvention* (New York: Viking Press, 2011), 490.

2 Ibid., dust jacket.

3 Ibid., 374.

4 Dayo F. Gore, Jeanne Theoharis, and Komozi Woodard, *Want to Start a Revolution? Radical Women in the Black Freedom Struggle* (New York: New York University Press, 2009), 84.

5 S. E. Anderson, Interview with Yuri Kochiyama, n.d. Quoted with permission.

6 Rosemari Mealy, Interview with Jill Humphries, May 12, 2011.

GREG THOMAS

Counterrevolution...in the Flesh: The Sexual Politics of Manning Marable in Viking Press's *Malcolm X: A Life of Reinvention*

To Greg Thomas, Marable's biography of Malcolm X is a case of an established scholar using his name and elite institution to make a quick buck by exploiting the sensational at the expense of the relevant and scholarly. "Under these mantles[Marable and Columbia]," Thomas writes, "Malcolm X is absolutely questionable, in every way, while the brand of Manning Marable (i.e., his writings, motives, methods, dogmata, etc.) is absolutely unquestionable." To address this, Thomas turns the tables and "analyzes the analyzer" by asking—and answering—how Marable can exploit sex as an issue in A Life of Reinvention *while extending his speculations about Malcolm's sexuality "to a matter of accusation."*

> Harlem was their sin-den, their fleshpot. They stole off among taboo Black people, and took off whatever antiseptic, important, dignified masks they wore in their white world....I used to wonder, later on, when I was prison, what a psychiatrist would make of it all.[1]
>
> —Malcolm X

What kind of sex did old Manning like, if he actually had sex at all? Was he into oral, vaginal, anal, or all of it? Did he do it in couples? Groups? Did he use condoms or "like it raw" like Old Dirty Bastard? Before he died, had he ever turned a trick or have sex for profit, whether he liked it or not? Honestly, how many penises, apart from his alleged own (assuming he had one, of course) did this sex of Marable's involve over time from his pubescent adolescence to his waning years? And what was up with his move from one wife or marriage to another as he moved from one college or university to another in the upward mobility of his academic career? Did he take advantage of New York City's virtually endless sexual landscape, whether in the dark or in the light of day, or just a few students in the classically Greco-Roman crosshairs of Western pedagogy and pederasty? How kinky did the sex get for Marable? Did he like toys, role-play, domination, or submission? How about fisting? Did he put it on video, or like to watch, even if others would not care to see it—or even if no one cared to hear any of the answers to any of these questions at all?

Such a line of inquiry would be cast as inappropriate, or even as obscene if it were directed at Manning Marable, the institutionalized scholar. Yet this questioning is not necessarily so when that same scholar directs his focus elsewhere—at, say, certain Black subjects or at popular Black revolutionary icons—or, in the case of Professor Marable, Malcolm X/El-Hajj Malik El-Shabazz/Omowale. Indeed, the structural hypocrisy of the license Marable takes with his subject's life in his last book, *Malcolm X: A Life of Reinvention*, is huge. Strangely enough, however, such license can always come back to serve him a dose of poetic justice, and all the more so posthumously.

A colossal irony should be noted from the outset: Malcolm X was far more forthcoming and public about the details of what some might refer to as his private or personal life than any institutionalized scholar of note, perhaps more so than any political or historical figure on record. His openness, however, was no exhibition for voyeurism's sake. Where in the world are the academic scholars who can be said to emulate him in this one little respect? Be they intellectually conformist or subversive, "pacifist" or guerrilla in their position on violence or Black self-defense, revolutionary or accommodationist or reactionary.

I'm the man you think you are.[2]

—Malcolm X

The noncritical discourse published *under the name* of Manning Marable amounts to simple PR for Marable's name brand, his specific academic signature, and thus for Viking Books and its parent company, Penguin Group—not to mention his institution of employment, Columbia University. Under these mantles, Malcolm X is absolutely questionable, in *every* way, while the brand of Manning Marable (i.e., his writings, motives, methods, dogmata, etc.) is absolutely unquestionable.

How curious this is, when one man's reputation predetermines others' readings or interpretations of his writings, and when that man's individual intellectualism or intellectual individualism is embraced and elevated over the collectively minded individual, the grassroots politico, and revolutionary intellectual who is "Malcolm X." The social capital of that one author, in academia and US corporate culture at large, has come to matter more, for some, than the supposed subject of his last book: the man internationally known as "Malcolm X." Ironically, the very legendary historical figure Marable selected as the object of his study has advanced his status and standing as a professional-class academician almost half a century after that figure's assassination.

No analysis of any aspect of this Columbia University/Penguin Group/Viking Press product is complete without a critical recognition of this turning of ideological tides. Thus viewed, the noncritical discourse on *A Life of Reinvention* is but mere publicity for the intellectual-institutional status quo it upholds and the signal of a regressive sea change from a wave of Black and radical political resistance to a national as well as international culture of counterrevolution and backlash.

But what is there not to critically excoriate? Soon after his public, poetic defection from "Obamamania," Amiri Baraka wrote with precision: "[I]t is not just Marable's inclusion of tidbits of presumed sexual scandal that should interest readers that I question, but more fundamentally, what was the consciousness that created this work?"[3] The politics of sexual presumption and scandal is not irrelevant, as some all too anxiously and routinely decry. If it had no relevance, it could effect no power, no controversy, no confusion. Rather, the body politic of sex and sexuality, consciously or unconsciously, has not been duly questioned by any means as an integral part of politics in general or of Marable's purported biography of Malcolm X in particular.

> One thing that I became aware of in my traveling recently through Africa and the Middle East, in every country you go to, usually the degree of progress can never be separated from the woman. If you're in a country that's progressive, the woman is progressive....And I frankly am proud of the contribution that our women have made in the struggle for freedom, and I'm one person who's for giving them all the leeway possible because they've made a greater contribution than many of us men.[4]
>
> —Malcolm X

Predictably, much would be made of Marable's practice of sexual accusation in *A Life of Reinvention*. To be sure, sex is a source of accusation in this book whenever it is mentioned or implied. Otherwise, there is no protocol for it to become a valid subject of discussion, analysis, or political engagement. How, then, is it validated strictly to invalidate? This topic goes neglected both by uncritical apologists for Marable as well as too many of those who defend Malcolm's historical reputation as a historical reputation under assault, yet it is clearly a sexual-political assault. And it takes place in a tradition that would debase Malcolm and sex or human sexuality alike.

What questions on this topic are highly unlikely to double as free promotion for anti-"Malcolmite" publishing and academic functionaries? How about the following: How did Marable view sexuality before, during, or after he wrote about Malcolm and sexuality? Where is his historian's relationship to what has been dubbed the "history of sexuality" as a professed intellectual and a professed Black intellectual, to boot?

How does he come to exploit sex as an issue and reduce sexuality to a matter of accusation in his literary exploitation of Malcolm in the interest of counterrevolutionary reformism, not to mention academic careerism? What is Marable's sexual-political ideology as expressed in *A Life of Reinvention*, or did he ever think about sex or sexuality and its politics with any degree of self-reflexivity (or self-consciousness), even as he put some very problematic variety of these aspects to work in support of a precise political-ideological agenda or standpoint? Although contemporary academic and bourgeois audiences in North America typically assume that only Malcolm's politics of sex, gender, and sexuality can or should be interrogated as a matter of fact, it is more than important to interrogate Marable's politics of sex, gender, and sexuality as he mobilizes a certain sexual discourse to "reinvent" Malcolm X.

There is widespread sex-negative accusation without Marable's feeble attempt at substantiation in a number of sexually charged areas of *A Life of Reinvention*. For instance: (1) Marable's unrestrained and hostile representation of Malcolm's Garveyite family relations reveals a "benevolent patriarchal" representation that is racist and sexist in its anti-Garveyite evocation of Daniel Patrick Moynihan's representation of every Black family as a "tangle of pathology" in *The Negro Family: The Case for National Action*[5]; (2) there is Marable's strange, postmortem moral argument with Malcolm as a young hustler and, in this context, his sensationalist speculation concerning Malcolm and "homosexuality," which is fundamentally Western and heterosexist and infinitely less politically sophisticated than Malcolm's own treatment of race and sexuality in the *Autobiography*; (3) Marable evokes a comparable narrative of conjugal sexual dysfunction in his discussion of Malcolm's marriage to Betty; (4) Marable makes sensationalist speculation concerning Malcolm and "adultery," which is Marable's moralist term of choice for "non-monogamy" in this vast web of speculation which climaxes around the time of Malcolm's murder or assassination at an Organization of Afro-American Unity (OAAU) rally at Harlem's Audubon Ballroom on February 21, 1965; and (5) Marable's unrestrained and hostile demonization of Black radical women who are affiliated with Malcolm's brand of revolutionary politics becomes clearly evident. These women Marable brands with a malicious patriarchal demonization that helps reveal the racist and sexist character of his more "benevolent patriarchal" uses of sex, gender and sexuality to "reinvent" Malcolm X for counterrevolutionary consumption. These accusations, of course, are not exhaustive; other areas of anti-erotic accusation are certain to be targeted by others.

> You don't have to be a man to fight for freedom.[6]
>
> —Malcolm X

This book on Malcolm X by The Penguin Group's Manning Marable begins as a narrative of hostility, despite the typical objectivist pose of academic scholarship, and it sustains itself as such for its over five hundred pages. One can only conclude then, based on the political myth of objectivity, that this hostility is theoretically logical and appropriate for any intellectual consideration of Malcolm X. Marable makes no apparent effort to control or restrain it, no matter how partisan it reveals his barely objectivist academic pose to be. The very first chapter's opening lines present Earl Little, Sr., Malcolm's father: "In 1909, [Earl] married a local African-American woman, Daisy Mason, and in quick succession had three children: Ella, Mary, and Earl, Jr."[7] This sentence sets the stage for a casual charge of bigamy: "By 1917, tired of both fighting his in-laws and of white threats of violence, Earl abandoned his young wife and children as part of the great migration of Southern Blacks that began with World War I….He did not bother to get a legal divorce."[8]

Karl Evanzz was quick to note this critical point in his review, stating that Marable "offers nothing to show that he conducted a court search for the divorce record" and that he "neglects to inform us of the exact date that the couple married in 1909 and whether the marriage was done legally or by common law."[9] Abdul Alkalimat makes additional note of Marable's curious mode of citation, specifying that of Marable's sixty-three pages of footnotes, only twenty percent come from primary sources. The rest come from what Marable dubs "[previously] published work based on other people's research"–or, in the case of the instance cited, Bruce Perry, with "his police agent's attack filled with lies and innuendo."[10] In his 2011 article, "To Rethink Malcolm Means First Learning How to Think," Alkalimat further points out fifteen major examples of major claims or statements made by Marable with no evidence or footnoting whatsoever.[11] Regarding Marable's claims about Malcolm's father, Evanzz continues: "If they were not legally married, Earl had no legal obligation to file for divorce. As such, Marable's condescending tone...shows his contempt not only for Malcolm but for Malcolm's father as well. The real sin here is that Marable fails to show that he bothered to check for a marriage license or a divorce filing."[12]

Thus, "reinvented" Malcolm X, along these lines, becomes not just "the seventh son [or child] of a seventh son" (Earl Little, Sr.) and therefore destined, in the cosmology of his people, for great leadership. Instead, Marable's Malcolm becomes more or less illegitimate, the son of a bigamist and the offspring of a violent, abusive, and battering man who abandons his family. He becomes the son of a patriarch who is not benevolent enough (i.e., ideologically White and/or bourgeois) to sire a suitable "American" middle-class family—that is, not according to Marable's very obvious sexual-political norms or ideals—so instead, Marable depicts Malcolm's birth family as a "den" of Garveyites.

The number of children Earl and Daisy had "in quick succession" is no less a problem for Marable when it comes to his handling of Malcolm's mother, Louise Little (née Louise Langdon Norton). Marable is mystified by Louise and Earl's mutual attraction and their "militant Garveyite" union or romance. "Perhaps it was the attraction of opposites," he writes, focusing on Louise's "fair complexion and dark, flowing hair" as well as her "excellent Anglican elementary-level education" in fundamentally colonial-imperialist terms.[13] These terms, however, are the very racial and racist terms that Louise and her husband rejected as radical activists of the Universal Negro Improvement Association (UNIA), a movement Marable describes as merely "one of" the "largest mass movements in Black history."[14] His description reveals his own crippling preference for the views of the "pre-Ghana" W.E.B. DuBois. Marable writes that they 'paraded beneath gaudy banners of black, red, and green'.[15] Like Du Bois' writing in 1899 in *The Philadelphia Negro*, Marable's language presumes low morals and a lack of rational planning in his mention of the "quick succession" of children that resulted from Earl's first "marriage." No other explanation of material hardship prevails in his description of Earl's second marriage to Louise: "The young couple's life was hard; they had few resources, and Louise had given birth to two more children..."[16] Later, he notes, she is "pregnant again," regrettably, with "Earl's seventh child" (Malcolm) and then "yet another son," Reginald—both to Marable's subsequent sociological disapproval.[17]

Nothing separates Marable from that "Black middle class" that "looked askance at Garveyites"[18] or those who allegedly would characterize Earl Little's family as "Garveyite oddballs."[19] It is only Marable's virulent anti-Garveyism that separates his view from that of the so-called Moynihan Report. For Marable, Moynihan's mythical tangle of pathology may not be rooted in matriarchy *per se*, but in the absence of patriarchal benevolence and in the presence of the "Africa-for-the-Africans" Black radicalism historically associated with Marcus Mosiah Garvey, it is. Thus, as a rule, Malcolm's siblings were less consulted than cross-examined by Marable in the writing of his book.

Another chapter in *A Life of Reinvention*, entitled "The Legend of Detroit Red," finds Marable conducting a queer and cantankerous argument with a teenage Malcolm over morals and masculinity. The result is a postmortem monologue about class culture and class politics in which Malcolm is cast as the young son who refuses to take orders or listen while Marable promotes law and order, patriotic Americanism, and bourgeois values such as reform and civil protest in lieu of any other mode of Black resistance or revolution. Railing against crime and criminality without any critical analysis of criminalization or of the political-economic construction of crime, Marable resents the young Malcolm's "obsession with jazz, Lindy Hopping, zoot suits, and illegal hustling" in "the cultural war waged between oppressed urban Black youth and the Black bourgeoisie."[20] He similarly resents the mature, adult Malcolm's "antibourgeois attitudes"[21] in the general political war being waged between the Black pseudo-bourgeois elite and those of the Black grassroots of all age groups.

A dramatic case in point centers around Marable's treatment of Malcolm's World War II draft resistance, in which Marable contrasts his subject with "the majority of African Americans" who "had patriotically pledged their services since the first days of the war."[22] Such a comparison, however, is neither numerically possible nor feasible, much less politically desirable. The masses of "African Americans" thus are praised as "patriots" while Malcolm is singularly berated as a "buffoon."[23] Then, quite as Marable exploits Malcolm in *A Life of Reinvention* for thoroughly anti-Malcolmite ends, he briefly finds value in Earl Little, but only in order to exploit Little's much-maligned Garveyism to condemn the young, anti-elite Malcolm. Much to his middle-class horror, Marable quotes Malcolm's views on his draft resistance: "I want to get sent down South. Organize them nigger soldiers, you dig? Steal us some guns, and kill us crackers."[24] Accordingly, this Malcolm is a "bad" son, apart from an illegitimate one, as if his father or Garveyites supported U.S. warfare for imperialism in the first place. In effect, this bold, Black-Liberation-Army-style vision of Malcolm as Detroit Red is depicted as both apolitical and politically irresponsible.

Additionally, Marable gives automatic credence to an FBI report of Malcolm's draft board resistance experience over Malcolm's official autobiographical account and, once more, pathologically deploys Malcolm's sexuality in an attempt to silence or quell him. The FBI claims: "The subject was found mentally disqualified for military service for the following reasons: psychopathic personality inadequate, sexual perversion, psychiatric rejection."[25] Accordingly, Marable reinvents Malcolm as a perversion of the so-called "model of Black masculinity"[26] offered by Adam Clayton Powell, Jr., and Earl Little, Sr.—however perverse or immoral this masculinity was supposed to be for him at the outset. And this is even before he moves to smear Malcolm—and homosexuality itself—with his use of homosexuality as a scandal charge.

But when did Manning Marable become a political theorist of gender and sexuality or of how they criss-cross as analytic categories with race, class, and slavery's empire? Now *that's* a rhetorical question! In his moralism, legalism, and patriotism, Marable uncritically assumes White or Western middle-class sexual norms and ideals with an Afro-Saxonist, neo-Victorian flair. In so doing, he continues to recycle something old as something new for his imagined audience of uncritical consumers, and he emerges as the Negro reincarnation of Bruce Perry yet again, so much so that Evanzz writes: "The footnotes [of *A Life of Reinvention*] reflect heavy reliance upon people who were known enemies of Malcolm X. An earlier biographer used anonymous sources for some of his controversial claims, which was bad. Marable gives no source for some of the tabloid-type allegations, which is a million times worse."[27]

Earlier, Evanzz himself had recycled a rumor of Malcolm's alleged teenage sexual hustling in his 1992 book, *The Judas Factor: The Plot to Kill Malcolm X*. He recounted that tale, without footnoting, based on an interview he conducted with Rodnell Collins, a nephew of Malcolm's. He later claimed to have regretted spreading Collins' story and recently renounced it during a public radio interview in Washington, DC.[28] Evanzz, however, did not code Malcolm's activities as a violation of Black masculinity explicitly. Nor did he, as no enemy of Malcolm X's politics of fearless Black radicalism or grassroots revolutionism, pitch it as a voyeuristically heterosexist accusation of homosexuality.

Yet somehow, "Based on circumstantial but strong evidence," Marable writes that "Malcolm was probably describing his own homosexual encounters with Paul Lennon"[29] when he spoke to Alex Haley of "Rudy," whom Malcolm describes in some detail as a "short, light fellow, a pretty boy type" who was "half-Black and half-Italian."[30] A bunch of key terms take on bizarre new meanings in that passage. Rather than the reverse, Marable's use of the term *circumstantial* somehow comes to mean reliable and trustworthy or strong, even though no footnoted sources are used to substantiate this presumed evidence or strength, legally or extra-legally. As more than one critic has noted, without the term *probably*, there might not even be a *Malcolm X: A Life of Reinvention* to critique or condemn. Further, it is hardly clear that Marable even knows what the term *homosexuality* means beyond a method of sensationalist sexual accusation.

The level of sexual literacy evidenced in *A Life of Reinvention* is abominable. Marable notes that Malcolm once stated the following: "Once a week, Rudy went to the home of this old, rich Boston blueblood, pillar-of-society aristocrat. He paid Rudy to undress them both then pick up the old man like a baby, lay him on his bed, then stand over him and sprinkle him all over with talcum powder. Rudy said the old man would actually reach his climax from that."[31] One of the most remarkable things about the "Detroit Red," "Hustler," and "Caught" chapters of *The Autobiography of Malcolm X as Told to Alex Haley* is the antiracist history of sexuality that Malcolm audaciously crafts and meticulously analyzes within it. Moreover, he did this over a decade before Michel Foucault wrote in French his totally race-blind *La Volonté de Savoir* or *History of Sexuality*, with its culturally as well as historically specific system of sex and sexuality in the West.[32] Intellectually, Marable naturalizes and universalizes the dichotomized terms of *heterosexuality* and *homosexuality*—and for a conservative heterosexual audience, no less. His conjecture or prejudicial relationship to homosexuality is clinical and exploitive as he solidifies its stereotypical relationship to moral depravity, duplicity, and dishonesty. Marable's every gesture remains homophobic. He also immediately and stereotypically turns to Malcolm's prison record to look for more active homosexuality, if to no avail.[33] In essence, Marable's scandal-oriented treatment of the issue never departs from the standard anti-homosexual crusades of the early to mid-twentieth century to the present day.

How far this is from Audre Lorde's (*Zami*) or Joseph Beam's (*In the Life*) perspectives,[34] for they and others could easily denaturalize Marable's adopted sexual categories and values with their opposition to the bourgeois history that first created them in the nineteenth century as European bourgeois categories of identity or subjectivity. Like Chester Himes,[35] who idolized Malcolm's autobiographical representations of Harlem, Malcolm could unearth sexual-political terrain that had never been theorized before and not sufficiently theorized since. Marable, however, pastes over this political landscape of human sexuality with terms like *homosexuality* and *paid homosexual encounters*[36] while his ideologically motivated and heterosexist circumstantial "probably-tizing" lacks even the standard pretense of professional historical research.

After all, how could a Manning Marable "out" Malcolm X in any way when he himself was obviously so afraid of Malcolm and aversive to everything Malcolm had to say at every age and stage of his historic Black revolutionary life? There was always in Malcolm X what is traditionally called a spirit of *eros* or the *life force*, which is bound to meet with vicious, violent repression by this current social order when anyone like him is fully committed to, as he said, "living as fully as humanly possible." That is why he fully expected—both as a younger, anti-bourgeois street hustler and as a mature, grassroots militant who epitomized Black revolutionary love and its continued evolution—to "die at any time."[37] In short, Marable's "magnum opus" signifies a virtual regime of sexual negation that mobilizes unsupported or unsupportable accusation after accusation, including sexually charged accusations ranging from bigamy or pseudo-family pathology to homosexuality (read: homosexual depravity) and on to marital-sexual dysfunction and adultery.

Furthermore, the production of so-called evidence from Malcolm's enemies in the Nation of Islam and other highly questionable sources in *A Life of Reinvention* proceeds without shame. Marable flat-out suggests that Betty experienced sexual misery in her marriage to Malcolm, but is her alleged misery due to sexual avarice on her part, sexual impotency on Malcolm's part, or the dysfunctional sexual incompatibility of them both as a couple? Marable asserts that there were extramarital sexual affairs on both sides, repeating some imagined scenarios that ultimately do not make sense, even for him. His narrative culminates in this now-infamous sentence, "Sharon 6X may have joined [Malcolm] in his hotel room"—on the night before his assassination. [38] She was a teenager then—so he "may" be a pedophile, too, in Marable's sexual imagination. Notably, when one consults *Souls*, Marable's early-Du Boisian journal based at Columbia University, one discovers additional efforts to link Malcolm's alleged adultery to an extramarital pregnancy and an unknown child fathered by Malcolm with an unknown woman.[39]

Does not all of this qualify as some sort of sexual obsession or preoccupation with Malcolm X's sex life under the intellectual guise of biography or history—that is, if tabloid-age, North American biographical history can be considered history at all? And overall, Marable manages to negate sex or sexuality altogether, at least for himself, in ways that could easily mandate a sexual if not socio-psychoanalysis of his writing in *A Life of Reinvention* or of his ghostwritten self. When all is said and done, does Malcolm not expose and indict Marable's life against *eros*, "the life force," from the grave, all Afro-Saxonist, neo-Victorian intentions aside?

In one piece from the many schools of literature suppressed by Manning Marable's Penguin/Viking book on Malcolm X, bell hooks writes: "Contemporary thinkers do Malcolm a great disservice when they attempt to reinscribe him ironically within the very patriarchal context he so courageously challenged."[40] Angela Y. Davis also wrote an essay on this subject, but her vision of antisexist politics in the vein of Malcolm was limited to liberal legal reforms conceded by the state or the U.S. Supreme Court.[41] Conversely, hooks restricted her analysis of politics to the realm of the personal or romantic. Both, however, restrict their sexual-political field of vision to North America alone and constrict their heterosexist reflection on Malcolm and women to an emphasis on women as wives, girlfriends, or sexual partners specifically, if not exclusively.

The May 19, 2011, symposium on Malcolm X, held on the anniversary of his birthday at the Schomburg Center for Research in Black Culture in New York City featured a presentation by Rosemari Mealy, who delivered a striking message in favor of Malcolm, womanism, and Critical Race Theory. Mealy asserted that Malcolm, as a custom, would have expanded and supplemented the political language of nationalism. He would have as well championed an alternative ideological framework for his militant anti-capitalism, one that went beyond the Cold War and orthodox Western political language of communism or socialism versus capitalism. The established political languages and frameworks of race, as well as of gender and sexuality, should therefore not be reified without question. This is what self-determination means. At any rate, as an ex-Black Panther, Mealy powerfully and perceptively discussed the routine dependence of biographers on male informants and their use of women as objects of sexual discourse. She described the erasure of a long line of Black women activists who were in radical or revolutionary league with Malcolm X as she shaped and reshaped his ideological and organizational politics for collective Black liberation and Pan-African independence at home and abroad. She is radically confirmed by William H. Sales, author of *From Civil Rights to Black Liberation: Malcolm X and the Organization of Afro-American Unity.*[42] This work is much neglected by many—including Marable, who cannot afford to engage it or any of this literature at all.

From start to finish, *A Life of Reinvention* runs with the idea that Malcolm only thought "all women were, by nature, weak and unreliable,"[43] when in his own adulthood or old age, Marable runs away from Malcolm's and any sexual revolution. Indeed, if any figure is more maligned by this text than Malcolm himself, it may be those Black radical women who love the likes of Malcolm and their militant Black radical traditions. (This is apart from those who are erased or ignored.)

Both Louise Little and Betty Shabazz get mere moments of narrative sympathy only when and to the extent that they are portrayed as pitiable victims of their pathologically Black and pathologically radical soulmates—namely, Malcolm and his father. Scandalous to the extreme, Marable reaches way back in time to accuse Amy Jacques Garvey, of murder. Further, Marcus Garvey gets off the hook of accusation in *A Life of Reinvention* only when Marable indicts Amy for the death of the Reverend James Walker Hood Eason, to wit: "There is no evidence directly linking [Marcus] Garvey to the murder; several key loyalists, including Amy Jacques Garvey, his articulate and ambitious second wife, were far more ruthless than their leader and may [sic] have been involved in Eason's assassination."[44]

Still, no one gets a misogynist style of wrath in this depiction of ruthless Black radical *femme fatale* than Ella Little Collins, Malcolm's elder sister, mentor, and oftentimes savior—hence, the reason for the extremist demonization. It is Ella, whom Malcolm idolized absolutely from childhood through adulthood and for the whole of his memorable life, that Marable despises without a modicum of restraint. Malcolm's own representation of his sister in the *Autobiography* is something extraordinarily special in all of Black literature with particular regard to Western politics of gender and sexuality. He describes her after their first meeting, during her first visit to Lansing, as "the first really proud Black woman I had ever seen in my life," adding that he "had never been so impressed with anyone in [his] life."[45]

It is Ella who initiated Malcolm into the habit of writing letters when he was set to return to Boston. He describes the two of them as close, "basic types," "dominant people."[46] Ella is described as his unabashed "favorite" among his relations after he arrived in New England from Michigan.[47] When he strayed as a youth or young man, she is described as always there for him, even when exasperated with him, and entirely unjust sexual politics came explicitly to his mind in her regard: "I always had the feeling that Ella somehow admired my rebellion against the world because she, who had so much more drive and guts than most men, often felt stymied by having been born female."[48] She is described as the major force behind his prison studies and his decisive transfer to Norfolk Prison Colony, a reputedly enlightened experiment in so-called rehabilitation with a relative abundance of resources for a U.S. prison, where he launched his career in debate and fiery political oratory. And amazingly, if Malcolm had thought only Allah could convert Ella to Islam,[49] she is described as making possible his life-changing trip to Mecca and his momentous trip to Africa in the era of anti-colonial Pan-African revolution: "I was turning once again to Ella....I've said before, this is a strong, big, Black, Georgia-born woman....I had brought Ella into Islam and now she was financing me to Mecca."[50]

In reality, Malcolm never thought that all women were "by nature, weak and unreliable." This fundamentally contradicts Marable, whose representation or demonization of Ella as a Black radical woman helps shield Malcolm's subsequent Black world sexual revolution from uncritical readers or consumers of *A Life of Reinvention*. Indeed, Marable casts Ella as criminal and clinically insane, perhaps the true "villain-behind-the-villain" in his fiction of a biography. As he recites: "Over a twenty-year period, Ella was arrested an astonishing twenty-one times, and yet convicted only once."[51] Apparently, he regrets that she was not convicted more. He does not question the politics of repression and transgression on this rare occasion in which he does not idealize the state and its counterinsurgent, anti-activist operations without question—it failed, for once, insofar as it did not convict Ella twenty additional times. Was W. E. B. Du Bois equally guilty, immoral, and insane simply by virtue of his U.S. house arrest, his later Stalinism, and his political exile in Ghana? The problem for Marable once more is the Garveyite radicalism of Malcolm's family as a whole. Karl Evanzz does not miss this point:

> [Marable] uses similar tactics to malign Ella Little [Collins]—the woman who fired one of his key sources—describing her as "belligerent," "paranoid," and "reckless." While he tries to countenance his charge by citing a psychiatric evaluation, Marable knows full well that psychiatrists routinely employed such terms to describe supporters of Marcus Garvey. Their reasoning was simple: any Black person who rejects America has to be crazy.[52]

Marable uses the same state rhetoric and state position on Ella that he uses to portray the young Malcolm as a pervert and psychopath when he resists and rejects the draft. En route to another speculative accusation that puts her in the analogous place of Amy J. Garvey, Marable quotes none other than Louis Farrakhan's reference to Ella as a "genius woman" in describing the following arson attempt on Farrakhan's home: "As tensions mounted, a fire broke out in Louis's home; no one was injured, but most NOI members believed that [Ella] was responsible."[53] Is there any evil like this radical Black woman's evil in Marable's *A Life of Reinvention*? Again, Daniel Moynihan mixes quite well with Bruce Perry.

Marable cites Ella's son Rodnell Collins as an informant of sorts in his book and at times draws upon Collins' 1998 work, *Seventh Child: A Family Memoir of Malcolm X*, jointly authored with A. Peter Bailey, a former OAAU member. Marable cannot, however, overtly recognize the book, which should be absolutely central to studies of Malcolm X because it was begun by Ella herself—hence the subtitle, a "family memoir." As Rodnell notes in the preface: "Ma began tentatively working on the project in the late 1960s. For the next fifteen years or so, she compiled data, spoke on tape, and kept notes for the proposed book."[54]Moreover, the text contains passages originally written by Ella for inclusion. The chapter entitled "Ella" commences with the following: "Most of the journalists, scholars, and other who have written books or articles on Malcolm X during the past thirty years interpret or emphasize his life from various, often warring, perspectives. There is one thing they share, however: a tendency to either completely ignore or debase the pivotal, caring relationship between Malcolm and his sister, Ella Little Collins."[55]

Nonetheless, Marable debases Ella with a vengeance in *A Life of Reinvention*, writing: "Her criminal behavior and knack for evading responsibility presented him [young Malcolm] with a vivid message. Unchecked by any moral counterforce, he was set on an unsteady path that would define the next stage of his youth. Years later he would describe this time as a 'destructive detour' in an otherwise purpose-driven life."[56] He casts her by this bourgeois moralism as the criminally radical Black woman, irresponsibly responsible for what Malcolm Little would become; for his international outlaw model of masculinity," so-called;

and for his Black revolutionary detour around or away from Marable's patriotic-"American," middle-class ideal of benevolent patriarchy and heterosexism of Western empire.

> I live for change and action, only happy when it's the best there is. I am suspicious of any non-white leader who is propped up by American dollarism. The Black intelligentsia of the Western Hemisphere could aid the progress and growth of Mother Africa instead of contributing to the upkeep of the U.S.A.…The Blacks who imitate and succumb to this white propaganda I give the most degrading term possible: "Toms."…Such "Toms" really need psychoanalysis.[57]
>
> —Malcolm X

In "1965," the chapter of the *Autobiography* in which the Republican Party integrationist Alex Haley substitutes his words for those of Malcolm X the most, Malcolm can be heard plain despite of any attempt to tame, distort, and defame him. Malcolm prophesies a great deal. He predicts his assassination: "I know, too, that I could suddenly die at the hands of some white racists. Or I could die at the hands of some Negro hired by the white man. Or it could be some brainwashed Negro acting on his own idea that by eliminating me he would be helping out the white man, because I talk about the white man the way I do."[58] In the closing paragraphs of that now-classic book—which Marable's book no doubt construes as its biggest rival in the capitalist-intellectual marketplace—Malcolm also predicts his character assassination in the course and under the guise of history: "He will make use of me dead, as he has made use of me alive, as a convenient symbol of 'hatred'—and that will help him to escape facing the truth that all I have been doing is holding up a mirror….You watch. I will be labeled an 'irresponsible' Black man."[59]

The Penguin Group and Viking Press's "Manning Marable" fit this forecast of descriptions to a tee. Their commodity, and their propaganda, would present no surprises to Malcolm X himself with its much-touted "new" material and its tried-and-tired tactics of political destabilization. This is not a biography. If it must be classified as a book, instead of an operation or a maneuver, it would be more of a memoir symptomatic of somebody's *problem* with Malcolm X. It is more of an anti-Garveyite Moynihan Report mixed with Bruce Perry in the Africa-bombing age of "Obamamania" finally in undeniable decline.

Malcolm's recorded and transcribed speeches do not get nearly enough attention as the Haley's *Autobiography*, the Spike Lie (Lee) "joint" which depended on that book, or the competitive text currently under discussion. When will the more or less complete audio collections of Malcolm's oratory become widely available to the masses? Where is the unmediated Malcolm, as represented in his own words, direct and undistilled? Who will critique the often problematic editing and transcription of those of Malcolm's more famous speeches that are, relatively speaking, still easily accessible? Why has Pathfinder Press (or any other press) yet to publish more of Malcolm's speeches in the spirit of *February 1965: The Final Speeches?*[60]

And then there is the question, raised loudly or quietly by some critics, of the "Marable" book's authorship. His illness and ultimate death before its publication has raised concerns about how the book was completed. Precisely, among other things, too few have actually addressed this matter in print. It is a sort of elephant in the room of the critical discourse, which is incomplete without some critical discussion of it. For one, Todd S. Burroughs could once instantly question the book as one "written by committee."[61] In any case, it is important to note that this would not be strictly or necessarily a matter of time, sickness, or death as much as his death could have situated Marable in the position exploited by Haley, ironically, after Malcolm's murder gave him carte blanche to revise against Malcolm's will or to re-fabricate the "autobiography" for his own political bosses and for his own political ends. However, in the present era of corporate publishing, trade book "cash cows" researched and written by committee are an ever-increasing establishment-intellectual norm, regardless of the health condition of their official individual authors. In other words, "writing by committee" is hardly automatic evidence of a publishing house's posthumous betrayal; it is quite normally now evidence of more corporate collaboration between status-quo press and academic scholar from the very start or conception of their calculated consumer product projects. To date, there are no public reports of Marable's issuing deathbed protests in sudden opposition to Penguin/Viking- or Columbia University-sponsored dollarism. So when other critics speak more boldly out of print in public forums, as if the chronology of *A Life of Reinvention*'s publication could offer Marable some total or automatic absolution from their criticisms, they may seek easy escape from certain contemporary racial-capitalist realities.

Both critics and uncritical readers and reviewers have been reluctant to criticize Marable (even if his role was that of a mere collaborator in this affair) because of their personal estimation of him or his reputation as a Black or progressive colleague, friend, or presumably Marxist scholar in the White capitalist academy. Marable's name often is read instead of his text. That is, his status is upheld over Malcolm's praxis. And in these instances, Marable's careerism is disregarded along with his radical investment in reform over revolution in the form of "neo-integrationist" liberal reformism concealed by one mainstream North American interpretation of the language of "Leftism."

Marable's orientation toward Malcolm X, as opposed to Du Bois, for instance, makes sense in light of what Amiri Baraka aptly terms his "line," whether it is simply designated as social-democratic liberalism or not.[62] The noncritical discourse advertising *Malcolm X: A Life of Reinvention* can absurdly call that line objectivity ad infinitum, questioning nothing, but it would and does have a colossal, colonial problem with Malcolm X's Pan-African Black revolutionism. In the five-centuries-long tradition, its phobia of Black people and revolution has produced a pseudo-biography of counterrevolution, super-exploiting Malcolm's and our own collective flesh with the atrocious politics of sex, gender, and sexuality in tow.

ENDNOTES

1 Malcolm X, *The Autobiography of Malcolm X as Told to Alex Haley* (New York: Random House, 1965), 137-38.

2 Malcolm X, *Malcolm X Speaks: Selected Speeches and Statements* (New York: Pathfinder Press, 1993), 197.

3 Amiri Baraka, "Manning Marable's Malcolm X Book," May 4, 2011, http://theBlacklistpub.ning.com/profiles/blogs/amiri-baraka-reviews-manning.*

4 Malcolm X, "The Role of Women" (speech delivered in 1964), in *Malcolm X, By Any Means Necessary* (New York: Pathfinder Press, 1992), 179.

5 See Daniel P. Moynihan, *The Negro Family: The Case for National Action*. Washington, DC: US Department of Labor, Office of Policy Planning and Research, 1965. (Also known as the Moynihan Report.)

6 Malcolm X, *Malcolm X Speaks*, 135.

7 Manning Marable, *Malcolm X: A Life of Reinvention* (New York: Viking Press, 2011), 15.

8 Ibid., 16.

9 Karl Evanzz, "Paper Tiger: Manning Marable's Poison Pen," a book review of *Malcolm X: A Life of Reinvention*, on the blog, *Truth Continuum*, April 13, 2011, http://mxmission.blogspot.com/2011/04/paper-tiger-manning-marables-poison-pen.html.*

10 Abdul Alkalimat, "Rethinking Malcolm Means First Learning How to Think: What Was Marable Thinking? And How?" June 2011, http://echicago.illinois.edu/alkalimat-reviews-marable-june-2011.pdf.

11 Ibid.

12 Evanzz, n.p.

13 Marable, 16.

14 Ibid., 20.

15 Ibid., 19.

16 Ibid., 22.

17 Ibid., 22-24.

18 Ibid., 28.

19 Ibid., 30.

20 Ibid., 45.

21 Ibid., 50.

22 Ibid., 59.

23 Ibid., 60.

24 Malcolm via Haley, quoted in Marable, *Malcolm X: A Life of Reinvention*, 59.

25 Marable, 60.

26 Ibid.

27 Evanzz, n.p.

28 Jared A. Ball, "Malcolm X: His Ideas and His Killers w Zak Kondo and Karl Evanzz," *Vox Union*, April 15, 2011, http://www.voxunion.com/?p=3652.

29 Marable, 66.

30 Malcolm X, *The Autobiography of Malcolm X*, 161.

31 Malcolm via Haley quoted in Marable, *Malcolm X: A Life of Reinvention*, 162.

32 Michel Foucault, *La Volonté de Savoir*. Luxembourg: Messageries du Livre, 1976.

33 Marable, 66.

34 Audre Lorde, *Zami: A New Spelling of My Name—A Biomythography* (Freedom, CA: The Crossing Press, 1982); Joseph Beam, *In the Life: A Black Gay Anthology* (Boston: Alyson Press, 1986).

35 Michael Fabre, Robert Skinner (eds.), *Conversations with Chester Himes* (Jackson, MS: University Press of Mississippi, 1995).

36 Marable, 66.

37 Malcolm X, *The Autobiography of Malcolm X*, 159-60.

38 Marable, 423.

39 Garrett A. Felber, "James 67X Shabazz Oral History" (Transcript of August 1, 2007, Interview by Manning Marable). Souls 12:2 (2010) pp. 143-49.

40 bell hooks, *Outlaw Culture* (New York: Routledge, 1994) 192.

41 Angela Y. Davis, "Meditations on the Legacy of Malcolm X," in Joe Wood, ed., *Malcolm X: In Our Own Image* (New York: St. Martin's Press,1992), 46.

42 William H. Sales, Jr., *From Civil Rights to Black Liberation: Malcolm X and the Organization of Afro-American Unity* (Boston: South End Press, 1994).

43 Marable, 36.

44 Ibid., 22.

45 Malcolm X, *The Autobiography of Malcolm X*, 39-40.

46 Ibid., 41.

47 Ibid., 134.

48 Ibid., 160.

49 Ibid., 246.

50 Ibid., 365-67.

51 Marable, 42.

52 Evanzz, n.p.

53 Marable, 174-75.

54 Rodnell P. Collins with A. Peter Bailey, *Seventh Child: A Family Memoir of Malcolm X* (Secaucus, NJ: Birch Lane Press, 1998), xi.

55 Ibid., 49.

56 Marable, *Malcolm X: A Life of Reinvention*, 42.

57 Malcolm X, "I Live for Change and Action," *February 1965: The Final Speeches*. (New York: Pathfinder Press, 1992), 44.

58 Malcolm X, T*he Autobiography of Malcolm X*, 439.

59 Ibid.

60 Malcolm X, *Malcolm X: The Final Speeches*. (New York: Pathfinder Press, 1992).

61 Todd S. Burroughs, "The Fault Lies Not in Our Stars, But in Our Biographers," Drums in the Global Village, April 19, 2011, http://whosemedia.com/drums/2011/04/19/book-review-marables-malcolm-x/.

62 Baraka, n.p.

* This essay also appears in this volume.

A. PETER BAILEY

Dealing With a Few Reinventions in Manning Marable's Book on Brother Malcolm

Based on his close association with Malcolm X and his firsthand recollections of some of the people, events, and activities detailed in A Life of Reinvention, *the author of this essay calls into question the truthfulness of a number of statements attributed to him within that book.*

In 2003, after a call from Cheryl Greene, a colleague of mine who was also a researcher with Manning Marable's Malcolm X Project, I traveled to Columbia University from my home in Washington, DC, for lunch with Marable and his staff. I usually turn down requests from writers of books and articles on Brother Malcolm (which is how I always refer to him) because of my deep-seated distrust of how they might treat his life and legacy. However, I did accept interview requests for the PBS television documentaries "Eyes on the Prize II: America at the Racial Crossroads, 1965–1985" and "Make It Plain," in which I discussed the life-changing, knowledge-expanding experience of working with Brother Malcolm during the last ten months of his life, from May 1964 to February 21, 1965.

During the two-hour luncheon/interview with Marable and his staff, I answered their questions with what I consider honesty and clarity. One thing I emphasized was that I was not a member of Brother Malcolm's inner circle; I was a committed supporter who shared his economic, political, and cultural beliefs on how we, as Black people, could most effectively promote and protect our individual and group interests in a White supremacist society. I stressed these points because, all too often, when I have agreed to a speaking engagement, the person introducing me hypes up my relationship with Brother Malcolm—as in "one of Malcolm X's top aides" or "one of Malcolm X's best friends" or "a member of Malcolm X's inner circle"—and I always have to correct these inaccurate descriptions.

At one point during the luncheon, Marable expressed an interest in perusing my Malcolm X collection, but I had to turn him down because I plan to write my own book on Brother Malcolm sometime in the future. (It will be a memoir focusing on the period between 1962, when I first heard Brother Malcolm speak in person, and 1965.) After that 2003 meeting, I never heard from Marable or any of his staffers again.

Marable makes six direct references to me in his book on Brother Malcolm[1]—a book that, I must say, makes me even more hesitant to trust other scholars and more determined to write my own. Beginning on page 322, Marable accurately describes my initial meetings and conversations with Lynne Shifflett, which led to my becoming a founding member of the Organization of Afro-American Unity (OAAU), the secular organization introduced to the public by Brother Malcolm in June 1964. The same cannot be said for the mention of me and the quote attributed to me that appear on page 323, where Marable writes: "Knowing the danger posed by the Nation, Malcolm made sure his people had no illusions about what they were getting into. Bailey explained, 'Malcolm is telling us you know if you get involved with me that you might get harassed by the police and the FBI.' . . . Everyone knew this already and it didn't bother us."

First of all, I always say "Brother Malcolm" when referring to him. Then, please note that I said nothing to suggest that Brother Malcolm warned us about any danger posed by the Nation of Islam (NOI). I am certain that he spoke about those dangers with members of Muslim Mosque Inc. (MMI), and maybe even to an individual OAAU member, but I do not recall him ever warning us about anyone other than the police and the FBI. The quote cited by Marable and attributed to me does not even back up the sentence preceding it. Now, some may call this a minor point, but the deliberate misuse of a quote is misleading to readers. It is also very irritating, and very revealing, to the person being misquoted.

Continuing, on page 337, Marable writes that Brother Malcolm "also recognized that while Muslim Mosque Inc., needed to be expanded to other cities to consolidate his followers among Muslims, his priority had to be the secular political organization that *Lynne Shifflett and Peter Bailey had been quietly working to build for him* [emphasis mine]." This is a classic example of an attempt to "hype up" reality. Lynne and I were *helping* with the establishment of the OAAU. It is misleading to say otherwise. Numerous OAAU members besides Lynne and me—most notably Earl Grant, one of his top aides; Herman Ferguson and Lez Edmond of the Education Committee, and Muriel Feelings (then Gray) of the Culture Committee; Hannibal Ahmed of the Youth Committee; and Sara Mitchell, one of the organization's secretaries—were all committed to helping build up the OAAU.

Then, on page 375, Marable notes that "Peter Bailey started the OAAU's newsletter, *Blacklash*," and although this is basically true, equal credit must go to Leonard Sneed, who handled the newsletter's layout and design. Leonard was talented, creative, and committed, as can be evidenced by the nine newsletters that were published using an old mimeograph machine. We worked as a team.

On page 416, Marable writes that "there was also speculation that either BOSS [the Bureau of Special Services] or the FBI [Federal Bureau of Investigation] or perhaps their informants committed the firebombing, which was a view helped by OAAU stalwarts like Herman Ferguson and Peter Bailey. . . . The most persuasive evidence pointed to the Nation of Islam." After reading this, readers of Marable's book may erroneously conclude that Herman and I were absolving the NOI of any connection to the assassination of Brother Malcolm. That is simply not so. My belief, based both on common sense and on information provided by Professor Zak Kondo in his information-filled book, *Conspiracys (Conspiracies): Unraveling the Assassination of Malcolm X*,[2] and by scholar Paul Lee,[3] is that there is no doubt about deep NOI involvement. By the time of the assassination, however, the NOI had been so heavily infiltrated by government agencies especially hostile to Brother Malcolm that they could not plan to walk from one room in their headquarters to another without the full knowledge of BOSS and the FBI, both of which encouraged and allowed the NOI to move against him. The NOI became a willing ally of the defenders of the system of White supremacy, and that is the way it will be remembered in history.

The next mention of me appears on page 421. It refers to a meeting called by the OAAU and MMI security forces, at which those present were informed that a decision had been made to search everyone who came to any activity henceforth sponsored by either organization. Marable quotes me as saying the following: "We said that from that day forward every person that came to one of our rallies was going to be searched, and this [is] where we made a crucial error—[Malcolm] overruled this because he wanted to break away from this image of searching people before they came to rallies." The truth was that "we" did not make any decision. Rather, the security forces told those of us who were not part of that detail what they had decided, and the rest of us strongly supported their decision.

As for the "crucial error" part of that quote, my complete statement, which I made in hindsight, was that the organization should have told Brother Malcolm that, just as the president of the United States has no say-so in matters of security, he could not change a security decision made by the OAAU's security forces. Had the OAAU begun a policy of searching rally attendees, the assassins' attack plan would at least have been much more difficult to pull off. I will always regret that the organization did not carry out that policy.

On page 434, Marable presents another quote that bears no resemblance to what I actually said during the interview. He writes on that page that, on Sunday, February 21, 1965, "When Malcolm entered the

Grand Ballroom on the second floor, he was immediately encountered by Peter Bailey holding a bunch of copies of *Blacklash*. There was something in the OAAU's publication that wasn't quite right and Malcolm had ordered him not to distribute copies of the issue." First of all, I did not "encounter" Brother Malcolm that fateful day. When he came into the Audubon Ballroom, I was already there in the small lobby area near the entrance. Upon seeing me, he said "Brother Peter, when you get a chance, come backstage. I want to talk to you."

Second, I was not holding any copies of *Blacklash* when I saw Brother Malcolm. In fact, I had nothing in my hands. What Brother Malcolm asked me not to distribute was a one-page press release–type statement I had written reaffirming continued support for him after he was banned from France and his house was firebombed. When I showed the document to him in the OAAU office in the Hotel Theresa on the Saturday before the rally (not that Sunday, as Marable contends), he read it and then asked me not to distribute it at the next day's rally. I then put the release away without question, having once before been schooled by Brother Malcolm about something I had written in our first newsletter about the killing of fifteen-year-old James Powell by police officer Thomas Gilligan. In a phone conversation with Brother Malcolm about that incident, I referred to Gilligan's action as a murder. Brother Malcolm, well versed on the US legal system, told me that murder is a legal term that can only be used if a person is convicted. He said to describe the event in the newsletter article as a killing because it was that, no matter what the circumstances. (Gilligan later sued both the Southern Christian Leadership Conference and the Congress of Racial Equality for distributing flyers calling him a murderer.)

When I went backstage that day, I discovered that Brother Malcolm, despite all the intense pressure he was under, was concerned that he had hurt my feelings by asking me not to distribute the statement. "I know you put a lot of work in that statement," he told me, "I hope you understand why I asked you to not distribute it." It still amazes me that he felt the need to say that. When I speak about Brother Malcolm to students today, I use this example to show how courteous and considerate he was to those with whom he worked.

What bothers me as much as the factual errors in *A Life of Reinvention* is the tone of Marable's writing about this episode. By using words such as "immediately encountered" and "ordered," he casts the whole scene in a confrontational tone. Clarifying this is very important to me because it reads as though one of the last conversations I had with Brother Malcolm on the day he was killed had an unpleasant aspect to it. And that is *way* off course.

On page 454, Marable writes:

> . . . nearly all Malcolmites were convinced that law enforcement and the U.S. government were extensively involved in the murder. Peter Bailey, for example, charged in 1968 interviews that the NYPD and the FBI "knew that Brother Malcolm's destiny was assigned for assassination." Bailey believed that both Thomas Johnson and Norman Butler were innocent although he himself did not witness the shooting—he was waiting downstairs for Reverend Galamison—he developed a strong theory on how the assassination had occurred. "I think that Brother Malcolm was killed by trained killers," he said, not "amateurs." Bailey doubted that "the Muslims were capable of doing it." Consequently, most OAAU and MMI members decided not to be cooperative with the police . . .

First of all, I do not remember any interview in which I said that I "knew that Brother Malcolm's destiny was assigned for assassination." That's simply not my way of speaking. Additionally, when I was interviewed by Marable and his staff, I believed that Thomas 15X Johnson and Norman 3X Butler—two of the men charged with Malcolm's murder—were innocent of the assassination for which they had been convicted. I just did not believe, as the prosecutors in their case maintained, that no one would have recognized them if they had been in the Audubon Ballroom that Sunday.

As to my "doubting" that the Muslims were capable of pulling off the job on their own, I believed then and believe now that members of the NOI were willing collaborators with forces in the New York Police Department and the FBI that wanted Brother Malcolm dead. What I doubted was that the NOI could have done what they did without nods and winks from government forces. (By the way, I was not "waiting downstairs" for Reverend Galamison's arrival; I was in the small lobby area that one went through to get into the ballroom. There were no stairs there.)

Marable's statement that I called the assassins "trained killers" may be stretching the point a little bit. What I was trying to make clear in my interview was my belief that Brother Malcolm's assassination was not planned by religious zealots driven by their devotion to Elijah Muhammad (even though the ones who actually pulled the triggers may have been such) but by key members of the NOI's leadership who were driven by greed, envy, and corruption—and by those in the government who regarded Brother Malcolm as a serious threat to the US propaganda agenda, especially in Africa and the Middle East.

Finally, in note 22 on page 499, Marable discusses the book, *Seventh Child: A Family Memoir of Malcolm X*,[4] which I cowrote with Brother Malcolm's nephew Rodnell Collins, stating that it "contains much valuable information about the relationship between Ella [Brother Malcolm's older sister] and Malcolm." He then writes, "*However, Collins and his ghost writer, Peter Bailey, embellished the narrative with their own speculations* [emphasis mine]." I chuckled when I read that note. First of all, given that my name is on the book, I was not a ghostwriter. When I pointed this out to a friend of mine, who is a professor at Howard University (and who also read Marable's book from cover to cover within three weeks of its publication), he told me not to lose sleep over it. "Whatever else Marable's book is," he said, "it is not a book of profound scholarship. There are just too many maybes, perhapses, and probablies in it."

I agree. Marable's criticism of Rodnell and me for embellishing narratives with speculations is beyond chutzpah.

A LIE OF REINVENTION

ENDNOTES

1 Manning Marable, *Malcolm X: A Life of Reinvention*. New York: Viking Press, 2011.

2 Zak Kondo, *Conspiracys (Conspiracies): Unraveling the Assassination of Malcolm X*. Washington, DC: Nubia Press, 1993.

3 Paul Lee is regarded as one of the most knowledgeable authorities on the life of Brother Malcolm. He was a consultant in the making of Spike Lee's film, Malcolm X. He was also closely acquainted with George Breitman, editor of Malcolm X Speaks, the first published collection of speeches after Brother Malcolm's death.

4 Rodnell P. Collins, with A. Peter Bailey, *Seventh Child: A Family Memoir of Malcolm X*. New York: Kensington, 2002.

SUNDIATA KEITA CHA-JUA

A Life of Revolutionary Transformation: A Critique of Manning Marable's *Malcolm X: A Life of Reinvention*

Though Cha-Jua asserts that much of Manning Marable's work on Malcolm X is exemplary, he nonetheless contends that, "On analytical grounds, the verdict on A Life of Reinvention *is mixed." In this essay, he attempts to explain the difference between knowledge and information in Marable's biography, faulting that author for his lack of an interpretative framework, an omission that is not helped by the preponderance of factual errors noted in the text. Cha-Jua further examines Marable's almost complete dismissal of prior works on Malcolm, failure to include international sources, and reliance on a storytelling approach at the expense of an analytical one—factors that, in his view, make the work problematic at best.*

> I believe that there will ultimately be a clash between the oppressed and those that do the oppressing. I believe there will be a clash between those who want freedom, justice, and equality for everyone, and those who want to continue the system of exploitation. I believe there will be that kind of clash, but I don't think that it will be based on the color of the skin.[1]
>
> (Malcolm X, 1965)

INTRODUCTION

As an academically located Black scholar-activist, Manning Marable had few peers. Over the last quarter of the twentieth century and the first decade of the twenty-first, few rivaled his productivity and impact or were as involved in Black social movement organizations and institutions. His *How Capitalism Underdeveloped Black America* stands as a contemporary classic; and from a Black radical perspective, his *Race, Reform, and Rebellion* remains the most worthwhile text on the Black liberation struggle during "the long sixties" (1955–1977), the high tide of the Civil Rights and Black Power movements.[2] Through his newspaper column and radio commentary, *Along the Color Line*, syndicated in scores of Black newspapers, and on urban radio, in journal articles, and in frequent book publications, Marable informed and educated a generation of African American scholar-activists. On April 1, 2011, at the age of sixty, Manning Marable transitioned. Two days after his tragic death, what some have called his magnum opus, *Malcolm X: A Life of Reinvention*, was published posthumously. A little more than a year after publication, on April 12, 2012, Marable received the prestigious Pulitzer Prize in history for *A Life of Reinvention.*

The book has sparked a level of controversy unseen in Black Studies and the African American liberation movement in nearly two decades, not since the 1992 Clarence Thomas and Anita Hill dispute. The dispute is probably more similar to the 1968 debate over William Styron's *Nat Turner*, which sparked the John Henrik Clarke book, *William Styron's Nat Turner: Ten Black Writers Respond.*[3] In many ways, Marable's controversial book is regenerating the critical dialogue characteristic of the Black Studies transdiscipline at its best. By early July 2011, Abdul Alkalimat had linked over 150 reviews and commentaries of *A Life of Reinvention* on his website "Malcolm X: A Research Site" at www.brothermalcolm.net.[4] By summer's end that year, dozens of Black Studies departments and movement organizations had sponsored forums and symposiums on the book. Additionally, *The Black Scholar* and the *Journal of Pan-African Studies*, two premier Black Studies journals have printed forums or a special issue; and two African American–owned presses, Third World Press and Black Classic Press, have published critical anthologies responding to Marable's Malcolm X book. An interesting division exists among reviewers of *A Life of Reinvention.* Reviewers in the mainstream press and White liberal and progressive outlets have commended it; however, reviewers in Black Studies journals and Black liberation movement venues have overwhelmingly condemned it.

A Life of Reinvention is meticulously researched. Marable uncovered virtually every available source—in the United States, that is. For the most part, the book is an exemplary model of historical recovery. Unlike his predecessors, Marable had access to Malcolm's newly archived travel notebooks, of which he made superb use. Additionally, he accomplished the task of convincing Nation of Islam (NOI) leader Minister Louis Farrakhan, who himself is implicated in Malcolm's assassination, to sit for an interview and, even more improbably, to encourage other veteran NOI members to participate. Farrakhan also granted Marable access to fifty-year-old tapes of Malcolm's in-mosque sermons and lectures.

Heretofore, Marable had been an outstanding analyst of contemporary African American history and politics; in *A Life of Reinvention* he demonstrated a talent for storytelling, the province of narrative historians. Yet, in many other ways, the book is disappointing. Given Malcolm's Pan-Africanist emphasis during the last two years of his life, it is troubling that Marable barely scratched the surface of the available international sources. For instance, none of the oral histories or interviews conducted for the book was with a non-American source. This is surprising because Malcolm's life demonstrated the correctness of Gerald Horne's injunction that "a transnational research agenda for African American history in this new century is obligatory."[5] In contrast to Marable's neglect of the international dimension, Marika Sherwood, who also worked with Malcolm's travel notebooks, unearthed a plethora of international sources, including numerous people that met Malcolm during his travels. In her book, *Malcolm X Visits Abroad: April 1964 – February 1965*, Sherwood discovered, recovered, and made superb use of international sources unexplored by Marable.[6] Her investigation led her to examine US State Department records and documents in the Lyndon B. Johnson Presidential Library and Museum, sources ignored by Marable. The data gathered from her exploration of international sources led her to conclusions that differed from some of Marable's. The major problem with *A Life of Reinvention*, however, is not its inadequate exploration of international sources, but its interpretative framework.

A Life of Reinvention is a historical narrative, and because narrative histories are descriptive rather than analytical, they explain how and what but not why. Moreover, at too many points in Marable's book, telling the story took precedence over thoroughly analyzing Malcolm's intellectual and political development. As historian Lawrence Stone noted decades ago, a narrative approach can "focus attention upon the sensational," especially "stories of violence and sex."[7] And indeed, too much of *A Life of Reinvention* engages in meaningless speculation about personal sexual practices—allegations that Malcolm participated in homosexual sex and that both he and his wife Betty had extramarital affairs—and accusations that Malcolm exaggerated his criminal exploits. More significant, especially given that Marable treats Malcolm as a tragic figure, are Marable's insinuations that Malcolm's murder resulted partly from his own personal flaws. According to Marable, after Malcolm freed himself from the Nation of Islam's conservative grip, those tragic flaws led him to constantly "provoke" Elijah Muhammad and the NOI.

Significantly, the most important new information provided by *A Life of Reinvention* is political. The first is Marable's claim that Malcolm supported the racist archconservative Barry Goldwater in his quest for the US presidency. Related to this argument, Marable suggests that Malcolm shared with Goldwater a propensity for extremism and the advocacy of violence for violence's sake. Also, throughout the text, Marable occasionally implies that Malcolm was transforming himself into a mainstream civil rights activist. In the epilogue, however, Marable backs away from these latter two interpretations. Nonetheless, many of his accusations are provocative, and they contribute immensely to the book's popularity or notoriety, depending on your perspective.

A Life of Reinvention is simultaneously a sweeping narrative of El-Hajj Malik El-Shabazz / Malcolm X's life and a mundane recapitulation of what scholars uncovered decades ago. It is what Thomas Kuhn, in his book, *The Structure of Scientific Revolutions*, terms "normal science."[8]

That is, it does not represent a groundbreaking paradigm shift but rather provides more detailed information within the conventional interpretative framework. For instance, Malcolm's parents' Garveyite activities are revealed in his autobiography, and Victor Eugene Wolfenstein and Bruce Perry explored them in their biographical works on Malcolm.[9] Marable, however, presents far richer information about their lives and Black nationalist activism, but his argument is not essentially different from Perry's. Moreover, the scholarship on Malcolm has long sought to plumb his interior life, to explain his sociopsychological transformations, reconstruct his intellectual development, interrogate his shift to orthodox Islam, chart the trajectory of his politics at the time of his death, and investigate his assassination in an effort to determine who or, more precisely, what social forces murdered him. In this regard, Marable presents more about Malcolm, especially his last year, than any previous scholar; yet much of it appears to be information and not necessarily knowledge.

In many ways, *A Life of Reinvention* is as big as its subject: the world historical figure, Malcolm X. Yet, factual errors, questionable interpretations, and, from the standpoint of Black intellectual traditions, missed opportunities are embedded within Marable's sometimes mesmerizing account of Malcolm's life story. For this, the book richly deserves both commendation and condemnation.

In the following sections, I approach Manning Marable's Malcolm X book from the standpoint of the Black scholar-activist paradigm—that is, I am both concerned with it as a work of scholarship and as an intervention in the politics of the Black liberation movement. My review of the book is guided by the core intellectual principles of Black Studies—namely, that scholarship on African Americans and/or people of African descent must center the experiences, thought, and culture of Blacks; present African-descendant people as active agents; privilege Black intellectual traditions in its analytical framework; be oriented toward critiquing racial oppression in both its material and ideological manifestations; and contribute toward the empowerment and liberation of the African people under study. In this review, I outline the book's thesis, interrogate its goals, investigate several of its assertions, explore its theoretical premises, and discuss the stakes it raises for the transdiscipline of Black Studies and the African American liberation movement.

REINVENTION: AN ORDINARY THESIS

A Life of Reinvention's central argument is that Malcolm X's life was "a brilliant series of reinventions."[10] This thesis is prosaic, both in the sense that reinvention, or the process psychologists call *actualization,* is a normal, healthy human developmental experience, and it is at least a secondary thesis of the major biographical studies of the man popularly known as Malcolm X.[11] Humanistic psychologists as different as Carl Rogers and Afrocentric scholar Linda James Myers contend that human consciousness is engaged in a process of "becoming"—that is, striving toward actualization.[12] Most major studies of Malcolm explore his humanistic quest, noting his transformations in consciousness, values, and behavior from Malcolm Little to Detroit Red / Satan to Malcolm X to El-Hajj Malik El-Shabazz. Moreover, Eugene Victor Wolfenstein's sophisticated Marxist psychoanalysis focuses on excavating and explicating Malcolm's developing consciousness.[13] As Wolfenstein argues:

> Finally, when viewed from the perspective of the problematic of racist oppression and the related problem of false consciousness, Malcolm's life history falls into two distinct phases: The first, extending from his birth to his imprisonment . . . was a period of intensifying alienation and falsification of consciousness, of regression or descent into the depths of a racially oppressive society. As such it constitutes a negation of Malcolm's potential for racially self-conscious activity. The second phase, the negation of the negation, is the period during which Malcolm progressively overcame the alienation and falsification of his self-conscious activity, beginning with his conversion to Islam while he was still in prison.[14]

What is important here, are the processes by which Malcolm transformed himself, not that he did so. Wolfenstein interprets Malcolm's identity transformations as a self-liberatory process through which his participation in collective action engendered his shredding of successive veils of false consciousness as he struggled toward self-consciousness.

Wolfenstein further maintains that Malcolm was transforming himself into a revolutionary. Marable has a different interpretation. For example, he presents Malcolm's reinventions as the conscious creation of "multiple masks" to shield his "inner self from the outside world"; he also views Malcolm as a "trickster."[15] Surprisingly, this is closer to Bruce Perry's than Wolfenstein's interpretation. Perry contended that Malcolm was a "chameleon" whose "public image was carefully contrived," and that racial identity was among the inner conflicts plaguing him.[16]

Marable, on the other hand, does not engage questions about Malcolm's racial identity development. This is unfortunate because pursuing this line of analysis might have spurred him to incorporate African American psychologist William E. Cross Jr.'s theory of psychological Nigrescence in his paradigmatic work on Black identity theory.[17] Application of Cross's Nigrescence theory would have given Marable a framework through which to analyze Malcolm's reinventions. It also would have demonstrated the power of Black Studies as a transdiscipline by using knowledge from one of its subfields to illuminate Malcolm's sociopsychological, intellectual, and political development. Moreover, it would have added theoretical depth to the reinvention concept by providing an explanatory model to account for Malcolm's periodic transformations.

Theorizing about Malcolm's alleged reinventions or chameleonlike character is not the only similarity between Marable and Perry. Additionally, they share the theoretical objective of "humanizing" Malcolm.[18] Transcending the myths and legends enshrouding Malcolm is an admirable goal; no one should want a hagiographic account of Malcolm's or anyone else's life. Unfortunately, however, Marable's humanization project manifests itself largely by stressing the salacious—specifically, accusations of homosexual encounters and infidelity. The issue in that regard is not one of quantity, nor is it focused on how much space these accusations comprise in the book. Rather, it is one of impact. Every reviewer of Marable's book has commented on—the homosexuality and infidelity bared in its pages.[19] Marable's treatment of these issues has contributed much to the public's interest in *A Life of Reinvention.*

FACTUAL ERRORS AND QUESTIONABLE INTERPRETATIONS

Allegations of homosexuality with reference to Malcolm X are not new. Interestingly, they first surfaced in Perry's 1992 work, but on this question, Marable's sources are even more problematic than Perry's. Marable, for example, reinterprets a passage in the *Autobiography* in which Malcolm claims an acquaintance named Rudy had a gig in which he would undress himself and an elderly White man and then sprinkle talcum powder on the old guy, who "got off" from the experience. First, Marable alleges, based on what he describes as "circumstantial but strong evidence," that Malcolm "falsely attributed" his own "homosexual encounters" with William Paul Lennon to a "character named Rudy."[20] Second and third, Marable converts one scene from the *Autobiography*, in which no sexual intimacy occurs, into a series of "paid homosexual encounters."[21] Yet, shockingly, the only citation to corroborate his interpretation refers to Malcolm's description of that same event on page 143 of the *Autobiography*.[22] Moreover, though Marable frames this alleged act of prostitution as a speculation on one page of *A Life of Reinvention*, he later asserts that "homosexual lover" was one of Malcolm's many identities![23] Intriguingly, Marable claims he uncovered no other references to alleged incidents of homosexual behavior in Malcolm's life—not in Malcolm's youth, during his six-year incarceration, or during the rest of his life. Marable's findings thus contradict Perry's allegations.

If Marable does not believe Malcolm was gay or bisexual, why publicize unsubstantiated rumors? If Malcolm, in his Detroit Red persona, engaged in homosexual sex for money or pleasure, why does it matter? What difference does it make? With better supporting evidence than unsubstantiated rumor and third-hand reportage, readers of *A Life of Reinvention* could view this information differently, especially if Marable used it as a teachable moment. If, for instance, he took this opportunity to enlighten the public on the fluidity of sexual identities via Black queer theory by referencing the work of Cathy Cohen, Roderick Ferguson, Dwight McBride, or E. Patrick Johnson and Mae C. Henderson (to name a few) and used it to instigate a discussion of homosexuality in the African American community, one could see the inclusion of this information as useful.[24] As it is, he does not connect his "revelations" to his thesis.

Marable clearly describes his goals and research methodology in his Malcolm book. One of these goals was "to recount what actually occurred in Malcolm's life."[25] This, of course, is impossible. More importantly, it offers no insight into his process of fact selection. How did he determine factual significance—that is, which facts to include or exclude? What made questions about Malcolm's sexuality and about his and Betty's fidelity important "facts"? Why and in what ways are they relevant to Marable's goals, theoretical framework, or explanatory model? Marable never makes the case for their significance. Thus, these accusations just hang out there, disconnected from an analysis of Malcolm's identity or political development or Marable's overall thesis. Therefore, if they are true, they are historical facts of little significance; but if they are untrue, then their inclusion represents irresponsible rumormongering.

Indeed, the allegations made in *A Life of Reinvention* about Malcolm's and Betty's infidelity are based on rumor and speculation either devoid of a source or presented by only one source. For instance, Marable notes that Fifi, a Swiss national who, in an earlier conversation, claimed to love Malcolm, was at his door when he returned from dinner. He further alleges that she was the only woman permitted to enter his private space during his international travels. Yet, despite Malcolm's noting in his travel diary that after Fifi left, he took a walk in the rain "alone and feeling lonely . . . thinking of Betty," Marable speculates that

Malcolm and FiFi slept together.[26] Why? Because allegedly, he claims Malcolm uncharacteristically failed to record what transpired in his diary. Marable also uses what he claims were "Malcolm's hesitant diary entries about the *night spent with Fifi* [emphasis mine[27]]" to suggest that Betty's accusation about him sleeping with Organization of Afro-American Unity (OAAU) organizing secretary Lynne Shifflett might have been true.[28]

Interestingly, Marika Sherwood interprets the Fifi incident quite differently. In her account, Sherwood does not suggest an affair but simply quotes the notebook entry as stating the two "talked until 11 and she left" and then Malcolm, feeling lonely, went for a walk in the rain by himself. She treats the incident on its own merits and makes nothing of it. Whatever happened, it is very clear that they did not spend the night together; Fifi's leaving at such a reasonable hour suggests that they probably did not sleep together, either.

Though not definitive, two stories recounted by Sherwood are suggestive in that they shed some light on Malcolm's interaction with women during his travels. The first was told to her by Eric Anthony Abrahams, then president of the Oxford (Student) Union, which sponsored a debate on Barry Goldwater's famous 1964 quotation: "Extremism in defense of liberty is no vice. Moderation in the pursuit of justice is no virtue." According to Abrahams, "a very beautiful woman student" who had offered to walk Malcolm back to his hotel one evening "came back rather speedily." He then speculates that the woman was "sort of surprised that there was this rare Black man who turned down a beautiful woman." Though his interpretation may or may not be accurate, his facts are not in doubt: the woman returned quite quickly.

Sherwood also reports the experience of Judith Oakley, then a student at Oxford and presently a professor of anthropology at the University of Hull. Oakley claims Abrahams delivered a message that Malcolm wanted her to meet him at his hotel but that she had to bring another person along. She brought a woman named Chloe Stallibrass with her, and they met Malcolm in his room. Oakley stated that Malcolm did not talk about himself but wanted to hear about the women's "daily lives." In a revealing comment, she claims that when room service arrived with refreshments, he asked them to hide in the bathroom, observing, "Obviously, he had a reputation to protect and that is why he insisted I not come alone."[29]

Sherwood's rendition of Malcolm's time with Fifi, and Abrahams and Oakley's reports sharply contrast with Marable's speculations. The main point here is that Marable's failure to pursue international sources meant that he missed the opportunity to interview Abrahams and Oakley as well as numerous other individuals that could have shed some light on Malcolm's activities, political and otherwise.

The final alleged affair discussed in *A Life of Reinvention*, that alleging Malcolm's involvement with the eighteen-year-old Muslim woman, Sharon X Poole, is equally based on gossip and conjecture. Marable's first mention of this alleged relationship occurs on page 394; however, he provides no source. In fact, the only note for that page is a citation to a speech Malcolm gave critiquing racist ideology. Later, on page 423, Marable suggests that the night before Malcolm's murder, Poole "may have joined him in his hotel room." For this, he cites an oral history of James 67X Warren and an interview with Abdur-Rahman Muhammad. Strangely, the bibliography does not list either an interview with or an oral history of Muhammad.

Marable's allegation that Betty had an extramarital affair is likewise based on gossip, suspicion, and speculation. Betty was pregnant when Malcolm left for Africa and the Middle East on April 13, 1964. He returned on May 21, left again in July, and returned on November 24, remaining in the United States until his assassination the following year. If you place Betty's alleged affair in sociohistorical context, its logic is that a pregnant Betty began an affair that continued though the birth of her fourth child, Gamillah, born December 4, 1964, and possibly through Malcolm's assassination. Again, even if true, other than irresponsible tattling, what purpose does this so-called revelation serve?[30]

A LIE OF REINVENTION

Perhaps the most questionable interpretation of Marable's rationale is his endorsement of an apparently racist psychological profile of Malcolm's sister Ella Little Collins. Even more disturbing is that the profile in question was written in 1960, but Marable uses it to explain her behavior during the 1940s! On June 9, 1960, Dr. Elvin Semrad of the Massachusetts Mental Health Center diagnosed Collins as a "paranoid character" who "because of the militant nature of her character . . . could be considered a dangerous character." [31] Except for the term *paranoid*, the language of Semrad's report does not identify a mental disorder listed in the *Diagnostic and Statistical Manual of Mental Disorders I* (commonly referred to as *DSM I*).[32] Written in 1952, the *DSM I* was the psychiatrist's bible until the *DSM II* supplanted it in 1968. Semrad seems to have evaluated Collins as having "militant episode disorder," or "intermittent explosive disorder," a form of impulse control disorder that did not exist in 1960. Given that mental health diagnoses are social constructions, it is important to locate Semrad's assessment in its sociohistorical and discursive contexts.

Sparked by Black student-led sit-ins, the militant phase of the Civil Rights movement had exploded across the country by the time Semrad issued his assessment of Collins. Within two months of their February 1, 1960, beginnings in Greensboro, North Carolina, sit-in demonstrations involving 50,000 activists "swept through thirteen states and hundreds of communities."[33] Between 1953 and 1955, the NOI reportedly quadrupled in membership from 1,200 to about 6,000 and by 1961 increased tenfold—possibly reaching as high as 75,000 members. Additionally, by 1960, not only was Malcolm sponsoring massive rallies in Harlem, he also had become a media celebrity extolling NOI theology and his evolving political perspective in print, on radio and television, and at college campuses across the United States. Nevertheless, despite the dramatic effect of the strengthening Civil Rights movement and Malcolm's rhetoric, social activists were still seen through psychological deficit frameworks.[34] In the early 1960s, classical collective behavior theory viewed collective action as a product of individual psychology, as a manifestation of anxiety and "tension-releasing devices for pent-up frustrations," rather than societal inequities.[35] Furthermore, these theorists and mainstream US society viewed movement activists as "dangerous, threatening, extreme, or irrational."[36] Though no longer attending the mosque by June 1960, Collins still believed in NOI theology, as typified by the myth of Yacub, that all Whites were inherent devils performing wickedness against the Asiatic Black man, and that God-Allah would soon destroy them and exalt Muhammad's followers. Her beliefs would seem a textbook example of what some dubbed the social movement activists' "irrationality."[37]

It is not surprising, given Collins's beliefs and the sociohistorical and discursive context out of which came Semrad, a fifty-one-year-old White psychiatrist from Able, Nebraska, that he diagnosed Collins as "paranoid," "militant," and "dangerous." Semrad issued his diagnosis despite his observation that Collins had been "a model patient, entirely reasonable, showing wit, intelligence, and charm." Given the sociohistorical moment, the discursive context, Semrad's background, and Collins's worldview, Semrad's unfavorable diagnosis should be expected and challenged.[38]

Additionally, *A Life of Reinvention* is replete with factual errors. One example concerns the date of Malcolm's wedding. At the beginning of the last paragraph on page 145, Marable states that Malcolm and Betty drove to northern Indiana to get married on January 14, 1958; but toward the end of that same paragraph, he claims the ceremony occurred on January 4. This type of minor factual error occurs in every work and should not be a cause for alarm; however, Marable's biography of Malcolm is full of similar factual errors, plus questionable interpretations and missed opportunities.

Another example, one of a more serious nature, is Marable's attribution of the theory of Black self-activity—specifically the notion that the Black liberation movement could spark the socialist revolution—to Leon Trotsky rather than to C. L. R. James.[39] This error is compounded by the fact that the footnote reference refers to text on page 52 of Marable's *Black American Politics: From the Washington Marches to Jesse*

Jackson.[40] Moreover, the citations for notes 52 and 53, appearing on page 308 of that book, do not cite Trotsky but instead refer to Angela Davis's *Women, Race, and Class*; Gerda Lerner's edited volume *Black Women in America: Crusade for Justice*; Alfreda Duster's edited autobiography of Ida B. Wells; and Walter Rodney's *How Europe Undeveloped Africa.*[41]

The two most inflammatory political reinterpretations advanced in *A Life of Reinvention* are Malcolm's alleged support of Republican Barry Goldwater during the 1964 US presidential election and the suggestion that Malcolm's experiences during his *hajj* (pilgrimage to Mecca) led Malcolm to try and reinvent himself as a mainstream civil rights activist. In his initial mention of Goldwater,[42] Marable observes that Malcolm, after his break with the NOI, routinely condemned both Lyndon Johnson and Goldwater, usually describing Johnson as a fox and Goldwater as a wolf. Marable later draws out the similarities between Malcolm and Goldwater's alleged rhetoric of "extremism."[43] Then, referencing a letter Alex Haley wrote to his agent, Paul Reynolds, Marable claims that Malcolm backed Goldwater.[44]

According to Haley, Malcolm had written an essay entitled "Why I Am for Goldwater." Based on Marable's discussion, presumably this article was not one of the three chapters deleted from the *Autobiography*. Marable argues that though "nearly alone" among major African American leaders, Malcolm continued to support Goldwater during the fall of 1964.[45] Marable later reports that Malcolm learned of Goldwater's thrashing while in Ghana, and his last reference to Goldwater describes Malcolm's participation in a "formal debate" at Oxford University defending Goldwater's statement, "extremism in the defense of liberty is no vice . . . moderation in the pursuit of justice is no virtue."[46] In sum, Haley's mention of the essay in his letter to Reynolds is the only evidence supporting Marable's claim. Since Marable does not quote from the essay, he obviously could not access it, and since he presents no statement of support for Goldwater from Malcolm's notebooks, we can surmise that Malcolm was silent on this matter. It is entirely possible that Malcolm drafted such an argument in 1963, before he left the NOI. However, the existence of that essay would only prove that Malcolm crafted an argument in support of Goldwater at the time of its writing, not that he supported Goldwater at a later moment. According to Marika Sherwood, William Attwood, US Ambassador to Kenya, reported to the FBI that, when asked why he was in Kenya, Malcolm replied, "in order to avoid taking sides" in elections.[47] Given this statement, the silence of the notebooks, Malcolm's failure to articulate support for Goldwater in his public speeches, and the lack of corroboration by a member of the OAAU, Marable's proposition seems extremely doubtful.

Marable is correct when he notes that both Malcolm and Goldwater adopted militant, by-any-means-necessary rhetoric, but two issues should be explored before one unites the archconservative and the "becoming" Black revolutionary. First, Malcolm's argument is part of a long tradition of militant rhetoric in the Black liberation struggle. It echoes Frederick Douglass, Ida B. Wells, Robert Williams, and numerous Black activists before him. In 1857, speaking on "the philosophy of reform," Douglass declared that, "If we [Black people] ever get free from the oppressions . . . We must do this by labor, by suffering, by sacrifice, and if needs be, by our lives and the lives of others."[48] In the midst of a lynching scourge, arguing for what she called "armed self-help," Ida B. Wells avowed the following in 1892: "The lesson this teaches and which every Afro-American should ponder well, is that a Winchester rifle should have a place of honor in every Black home, and it should be used for that protection which the law refuses to give."[49] And during Malcolm's own lifetime, in response to a southern jury's inhuman verdict releasing a White man who attempted to rape a pregnant Black woman, Robert Williams asserted: "We will meet violence with violence."[50] The tradition of militant Black rhetoric and action suggests the second issue.

What is most important is the sociohistorical context in which Malcolm and Goldwater addressed their oratory. Their views only appear similar when compared in the abstract. When judged against the concrete existing circumstances they addressed, their commonality quickly fades.

Viewed from the context of the African American condition, most of Malcolm's rhetoric was not extreme but rather what Wolfenstein called "situationally rational."[51] That is, Malcolm's call for armed self-defense represented a cogent understanding of the system of anti-Black racial oppression and the gross violence used to maintain it. In that sociohistorical context, Malcolm's rhetoric was not extremism.

As Marable observes, Malcolm was a "committed student of Black folk culture" who incorporated "animal stories, rural metaphors, and trickster tales" into his speeches. He had a particular fondness for animal stories, which Perry traces back to Malcolm's love of *Aesop's Fables*. Within the tradition of working-class African American male rhetoric, Malcolm often created graphic images, what Amiri Baraka has called "word pictures," many of which exposed the violence undergirding the system of anti-Black racial oppression. Though lions often appeared in Malcolm's tales, his most popular animal stories featured the wolf and fox metaphors because they best conveyed his nightmarish interpretation of the African American condition.[52]

According to Hank Flick and Larry Powell, "Malcolm's use of animal imagery can be seen as a response to the situation and condition Blacks faced" and was "an attempt to invert the images that Blacks had of White Americans."[53] The tone and tenure of Malcolm's use of the fox and wolf metaphors and his sharp movement leftward after his departure from the NOI tends also to mitigate further against an argument that aligns him with Goldwater. Initially, Malcolm deployed the metaphors situationally depending on audience, but over time, as his political perspective moved leftward, one can detect a more radical use of the metaphor. Over time, the wolf was transformed from an allegory for White southerners to one for White conservatives, and the fox moved from a metaphor for White northerners to one for White liberals. For instance, in his speech, "God's Judgment of White America," the one after which he made his pivotal "chickens coming home to roost" comment, Malcolm argued:

> The white conservatives aren't friends of the Negro either, but they at least don't try to hide it. They are like wolves; they show their teeth in a snarl that keeps the Negro always aware of where he stands with them. But the white liberals are foxes, who also show their teeth to the Negro but pretend that they are smiling. The white liberals are more dangerous than the conservatives; they lure the Negro, and as the Negro runs from the growling wolf, he flees into the open jaws of the smiling fox.
>
> The job of the Negro civil rights leader is to make the Negro forget that the wolf and the fox both belong to the (same) family. Both are canines; and no matter which one of them the Negro places his trust in, he never ends up in the White House, but always in the dog house.[54]

Nearly a year later, in October 1964 while in Kenya, Malcolm posited the following, speaking of the Democrats and Republicans: "One is the wolf, the other is a fox. No matter what, they'll both eat you."[55] After this initial salvo, he pushed the allegory decidedly leftward, declaring: "The shrewd capitalists, the shrewd imperialists knew that the only way people would run towards the fox [Lyndon Johnson] would be if you showed them the wolf [Goldwater]. So they created a ghastly alternative."[56] If Malcolm genuinely saw Goldwater as an appalling, terrible, frightful option, to support his bid for the presidency would have been a tremendous act of cynicism.

ASSERTIONS, THEORETICAL FRAMEWORK, AND METHODOLOGY

The major assertion Marable makes in *A Life of Reinvention* is to boldly dismiss the previous literature on Malcolm. He correctly contends that, "nearly all of the scholarly work on Malcolm was based on a rather narrow selection of primary sources," declaring the following: "I was struck by its shallow character and lack of original sources."[57] Presumably, Marable's observation also applies to works published prior to the 1990s, like Goldman's *The Death and Life of Malcolm X* and Wolfenstein's *Victims of Democracy*.[58] Admittedly, the works produced during the Malcolm X resurrection of the 1990s were uneven. Some were as awful as Marable claimed, but some made important contributions, and a few were quite good. For instance, William W. Sales Jr.'s *From Civil Rights to Black Power: Malcolm X and the Organization of Afro-American Unity* is an astute analysis of the OAAU and its impact on the Black liberation movement.[59] Incidentally, Sales drew on much more than what Marable contends were merely "transcribed speeches, and secondary sources, such as newspaper articles"[60]; he used the FBI files and conducted thirteen interviews. Though Perry's work pathologizes Malcolm and his family, and Karl Evanzz's *The Judas Factor: The Plot to Kill Malcolm X* is not a full-fledged biography, neither work is shallow. And, like Sales, both made extensive use of the then-available primary sources. Like Sales, Perry and Evanzz made extensive use of the FBI files, though not necessarily the same ones Marable used. Perry and Evanzz both made greater use of oral histories and interviews than did Marable; in fact, Perry's book contains probably five times more interviews than does Marable's, both in terms of oral histories and interviews. And although Perry's focus on Malcolm's childhood acquaintances is questionable, both he and Evanzz interviewed more people than Marable.[61] Subsequently, *A Life of Reinvention* is marred by Marable's failure to engage the previous literature, not enhanced by it.

Several points in Marable's book could have benefited from engaging the earlier scholarship. For instance, Marable's allegations of Malcolm's infidelity could have been placed in conversation with two incidents described in Perry's book. From interviews with Ethel Minor, the future Communications Secretary for the Student Nonviolent Coordinating Committee (SNCC), and Sara Mitchell, both of whom were, as young women, activists in the OAAU, Perry discovered that Malcolm had opportunities to "hit on" each of them but did not. The case of Mitchell, winner of a Harlem beauty contest, is particularly suggestive because, as Perry relates, Malcolm reputedly arrived at her home one night exhausted, claiming, "I just want to sleep." According to her story, despite what Perry claims was a "double entendre," Malcolm simply "curled up and went to sleep." Summing up these incidents, Perry concluded that Malcolm "had enormous self-control."[62]

Do these incidents "prove" that Malcolm did not have affairs with Fifi, Shifflett, or Poole? Of course not. But when combined with the stories told by Sherwood and given the highly speculative nature of the allegations, these corresponding incidents, which occurred during the same historical moment, should raise doubts.

MISSED OPPORTUNITIES AND BLACK STUDIES

Marable does an outstanding job of describing the sociohistorical context in which Malcolm lived, but he does a less sterling job of situating him in the intellectual and cultural context of his times, especially the 1960s. Hence, *A Life of Reinvention* is silent on a number of questions of import to Black Studies scholars. Perhaps, the most serious missed opportunity concerns Marable's failure to explore the intellectual roots of Malcolm's evolving thought.

For instance, he reports that Malcolm "devoured" the works of "W. E. B. Du Bois, Carter G. Woodson, and J. A. Rogers" and that he "studied the history of the transatlantic slave trade, the impact of the 'peculiar institution' of chattel slavery in the United States, and African American revolts."[63] Yet, what specific works did he read? Concerning Du Bois, it would matter greatly, for instance, whether Malcolm read *The Philadelphia Negro* or *Black Reconstruction*. Despite his prison reading, or maybe because of it, Marable relates that Malcolm developed an "interpretation of enslavement" that "cast Black culture as utterly decimated by the institution of slavery" and "racial oppression."[64] As Malcolm's famous metaphor of the house slave and the field slave attests, he was capable of distilling physical resistance from his studies. Consistent with the dominant intellectual climate, however, he saw African American culture as distorted and pathological.

Also consistent with the times, Malcolm appeared ignorant of African cultural retentions or of the ways enslaved African Americans deployed cultural resistance. Was his thinking on these issues shaped by E. Franklin Frazier's *The Negro Family in the United States*, Abram Kardiner and Lionel Ovesey's *Mark of Oppression*, or Stanley Elkin's *Slavery: A Problem in American Life and Culture*?[65] Malcolm seems to have maintained his ignorance and negative interpretation of African American culture throughout his NOI days. This is not surprising, since as Richard King observed, "It was only by the end of the 1960s that a consensus emerged, particularly among African American intellectuals, that African American culture was a culture of 'creativity and resistance.'"[66] Somehow, during the mid-1960s, Malcolm broke with the pathological view and became an advocate of cultural revolution, of excavating the African elements in African American culture.

What role then did scholarship play in Malcolm's break from the pathological view of African American culture? Did he subscribe to or regularly read the *Journal of Negro History*, *Phylon*, *Journal of Negro Education*, or *Freedomways*? Did Lerone Bennett's *Before the Mayflower*, published in 1962, influence him? How did his intellectual explorations contribute to what Marable contends was his ability to reinvent himself? Unfortunately, Marable does not explore the intellectual roots of Malcolm's developing radical political and cultural perspectives after his release from prison.

A Life of Reinvention also misses opportunities to connect individuals with whom Malcolm worked to political developments, especially Black Power–era, Black nationalist organizations inspired by his praxis. Herman Ferguson and Milton Henry represent two such examples. Ferguson sat for four oral histories relating to Marable's Malcolm X project and is one of the most quoted figures in the book. He appears on sixteen pages and is quoted no fewer than fourteen times, yet his later activities as a founding member and minister of education of the Republic of New Africa is never revealed. Even more curiously, Marable presents Milton Henry simply as "Malcolm's good friend," "an attorney," and "leader of Michigan's Freedom Now Party" (FNP),[67] when Henry's role in Malcolm's life and in the Black liberation movement as a whole was much greater. He was the co-owner of the Afro-American Broadcasting Company, the firm that issued Malcolm's most famous speeches: "Message to the Grassroots" and "The Ballot or the Bullet." In addition to his role in the FNP, Henry was involved in the Group on Advanced Leadership (GOAL). Given the detailed nature of Marable's coverage of Malcolm's international travel, it is surprising that he does not mention Henry's presence in Egypt, where he joined Malcolm to cover his lobbying at the Organization of African Unity's (OAU) second summit in 1964. Henry broadcasted an interview with Malcolm from Egypt back to Detroit. Additionally, when Malcolm left the ship where the members of the African liberation movements were housed at the summit, he relocated to the Nile Hilton, where he shared a room with Henry. It was during his stay with Henry at the Hilton that Malcolm was rushed to the hospital suffering from the ingestion of a toxic substance.[68]

Sherwood maintains that Henry was not a peripheral figure during Malcolm's stay in Egypt for the OAU summit but notes that after Malcolm's assassination, he co-led the Malcolm X Society with his brother, Richard. It was this group that sponsored the Black Government Conference that led to the formation of the Republic of New Africa, in which he and Betty Shabazz served as vice presidents. Was Marable aware of these facts or did he deem them not historically significant?[69]

CONCLUSION: THE STAKES FOR BLACK STUDIES AND THE BLACK LIBERATION MOVEMENT

The primary task of a scholar using historical methodologies is to uncover data—facts, if you will—to sift through them, make selections, and then to analyze and organize the data into a coherent story or narrative. Manning Marable should be commended for the enormous amount of new information he and his score of student researchers uncovered. Among the most important new sources the Marable team exhumed are Malcolm's notebooks, tapes of his early NOI sermons and lectures, and interviews with Louis Farrakhan and NOI members that knew Malcolm. This new data allowed Marable to construct a more detailed account of Malcolm's life than any previous scholar.

The last two hundred pages of *A Life of Reinvention* are particularly engrossing—more so for their forensic nature than for their literary style, but engrossing nonetheless. Marable achieves his goal of exposing the extent of illegal government surveillance, identifying the traitors in Malcolm's organizations, and naming the killers, albeit much of this information was already known. Nevertheless, despite the book's shortcomings on the international front, on empirical grounds it is a tremendous accomplishment.

Much of the uproar over Marable's book on Malcolm, however, concerns the validity of several of the "facts" Marable presents. Two issues are important in this regard. First, given the speculative character and sparse corroboration for most of Marable's "facts" about Malcolm's homosexual encounters and his and Betty's extramarital affairs, one wonders why he included information that is circumstantial at best. Second, assuming these "facts" are true, what role do they serve in the larger narrative? Why are they historically significant? For the most part, Marable's allegations seem to hang out there, disconnected from a larger analysis. The lone exception is Marable's discussion of Malcolm's initial sexual difficulties with Betty. The "fact" of this deeply personal issue has historical significance because John and Ethel Sharieff used knowledge of it to ridicule Malcolm, thereby widening the split between him and the NOI. The other sex-related "facts" do not rise to the level of historical significance, and only in a very casual sense does Marable connect them to his reinvention thesis.

On analytical grounds, the verdict on *A Life of Reinvention* is mixed. For the most part, its readers learn nothing new of significance; Marable merely provides greater detail about things already known. The political speculations about Malcolm—that he supported Goldwater, embraced violence, or was mainstreaming his views and becoming a civil rights leader—simply do not hold up to scrutiny. Fortunately, the book's epilogue, titled "Reflections on a Revolutionary Vision," largely makes up for the analytical failings in the body of the work. In that chapter, Marable brings coherence to a series of arguments dispersed throughout the text. For example, he corrects textual implications that Malcolm was evolving into a liberal integrationist or that he advocated violence for its own sake. Marable's conclusion that Malcolm was shifting his vision of Black self-determination away from the separate-state idea to a more pragmatic proto-nationalism, based on proportional representation tied to a broader Pan-Africanist vision and linked to Third World revolution, is a plausible interpretation of Malcolm's political trajectory. It is eerily similar, however, to Marable's own Social Democratic politics.

Perhaps it is too early to judge, but like the specter of Malcolm's assassination, haunting questions remain unanswered. What is the historical significance of *A Life of Reinvention*? What is its impact on Black Studies? In the short-term, the book has sent a bolt of energy throughout the discipline. I doubt any previous work in Black Studies has elicited such an extensive and passionate response. It is likely that it will inspire Black Studies departments to offer several new courses on Malcolm. Marable's empirical accomplishments and failures should also spur Black Studies scholar-activists on the humanities side of the discipline to adopt a similar large-scale, research-team approach. To accomplish the tasks of the discipline in the future, these scholar-activists will need to move beyond the lone-researcher model and even beyond Marable's own senior researcher–research assistant model to create genuine research teams composed of several highly engaged and competent scholar-activists.

Marable's greatest contribution has been to resurrect Malcolm X. In doing so, he has ignited a firestorm throughout the discipline and the movement. Struggling over the meaning of our most important icon puts the core mission and the National Council for Black Studies slogan—academic excellence, cultural grounding, and social responsibility—back in the forefront of the discipline. Debates over Malcolm, especially our "last" Malcolm, serve only to revive the radical critical tendency of research and analysis in both the discipline and the movement.

ENDNOTES

1 Malcolm X, *The Autobiography of Malcolm X as Told to Alex Haley*, New York: Random House, 1965.

2 Manning Marable, *How Capitalism Underdeveloped Black America: Problems in Race, Political Economy, and Society*, Cambridge, MA: South End Press, 1983; Marable, *Race, Reform, and Rebellion: The Second Reconstruction and Beyond in Black America, 1945–2006* (3rd ed.), Oxford, MS: University Press of Mississippi, 2007.

3 William Styron, *The Confessions of Nat Turner*, New York: Random House, 1967; John Henrik Clarke, *William Styron's Nat Turner: Ten Black Writers Respond,* Westport, CT: Greenwood Press, 1987. ***

4 Abdul Alkalimat, ed., "Malcolm X: A Research Site," (launched May 19, 1999: University of Toledo and Twenty-First Century Books), http://www.brothermalcolm.net/index.html.

5 Gerald Horne, "Toward a Transnational Research Agenda for African American History in the 21st Century," *Journal of African American History, 3* (2006), 288–303.

6 Marika Sherwood, *Malcolm X Visits Abroad: April 1964 – February 1965.* Hollywood, CA: Tsehai Publishers, 2011.

7 Lawrence Stone, "Revival of Narrative: Reflections on New Old History," *Past and Present, 85*, (November 1979), 23.

8 Thomas S. Kuhn, *The Structure of Scientific Revolutions* (3rd ed.) (Chicago: University of Chicago Press, 1970/1962), 10.

9 Malcolm X, *The Autobiography*; Eugene Victor Wolfenstein, *Victims of Democracy: Malcolm X and the Black Revolution,* Berkeley: University of California Press, 1981; Bruce Perry, *Malcolm: The Life of a Man that Changed Black America*, Barrytown, NY: Station Hill, 1991.

10 Marable, *Malcolm X: A Life of Reinvention*, 10.

11 I consider Peter Goldman, *The Death and Life of Malcolm X* (New York: Harper & Row, 1973); Wolfenstein, *Victims of Democracy*; Perry,

Malcolm: The Life of a Man that Changed Black America; Karl Evanzz, *The Judas Factor: The Plot to Kill Malcolm X* (Thunders Mouth Press, 1992); and Marable, *Malcolm X: A Life of Reinvention* to constitute the major biographies. These studies do not exhaust the important work on Malcolm X.

12 Carl Rogers, *On Becoming a Person: A Therapist's View of Psychotherapy*, London: Constable, 1961; Linda James Myers, "Theoretical and Conceptual Approaches to African and African American Psychology," in Helen A. Neville, Brendesha M. Tynes, and Shawn O. Utsey (eds.), *Handbook of African American Psychology* (Los Angeles: Sage, 2009), 44.

13 Wolfenstein, *Victims of Democracy.*

14 Ibid., 39.

15 Marable, *Malcolm X: A Life of Reinvention*, 10, 11.

16 Perry, *Malcolm: The Life of a Man*, ix–x, 36–45. Perry confuses what linguists and sociologists call "code switching" with insecurity and the lack of a grounded identity.

17 See William E. Cross Jr., "The Negro-to-Black Conversion Experience," *Black World, 9* (July 1971), 13–27; William E. Cross Jr., *Shades of Black: Diversity in African American Identity*, Philadelphia: Temple University Press, 1995; Beverly J. Vandiver, Peony E. Fhagen-Smith, Kevin O. Cokley, William E. Cross Jr., and Frank C. Worrell, "Cross's Nigrescence Model: From Theory to Scale to Theory," *Journal of Multicultural Counseling and Development, 3* (July 1, 2001), 174–200; Beverly J. Vandiver, William E. Cross Jr., Frank C. Worrell, and Peony E. Fhagen-Smith, "Validating the Cross Racial Identity Scale," *Journal of Counseling Psychology, 1* (2002), 71–85.

18 Marable, *Malcolm X: A Life of Reinvention*, 12; Perry, *Malcolm: The Life of a Man*, 75–77, 82–83.

19 See, for example, Bill Fletcher Jr., "Manning Marable and the Malcolm X Biography Controversy: A Response to Critics," *Black Commentator*, July 7, 2011, http://www.Blackcommentator.com/434/434_aw_marable_malcolm_controversy_share.html#.

20 Marable, *Malcolm X: A Life of Reinvention*, 65.

21 Ibid., 506.

22 Marable identifies the sources for his interpretation as Perry citations of Malcolm "Shorty" Jarvis and Rodnell Collins, Malcolm's sister Ella Little Collins's son. Jarvis and Collins both alleged that Malcolm and Jarvis had a deal to rub powder over the body of a wealthy White millionaire, presumably Paul Lennon. See Perry, *Malcolm X: The Life of a Man*, 75–77, 82–83; see also Rodnell P. Collins and Peter A. Bailey, *Seventh Son: A Family Memoir of Malcolm X* (New York: Kensington, 2002), 76.

23 Marable, *Malcolm X: A Life of Reinvention*, 66, 73.

24 For works on Black queer identity, see Cathy Cohen, *The Boundaries of Blackness: AIDS and the Breakdown of Black Politics* (Chicago: University of Chicago Press, 1999); Roderick Ferguson, "Race-ing Homonormativity: Citizenship, Sociology and Gay Identity," in E. Patrick Johnson and Mae G. Henderson (eds.), *Black Queer Studies: A Critical Anthology* (Durham, NC: Duke University Press, 2005), 52–67; Dwight McBride, "Straight Black Studies: On African American Studies, James Baldwin, and Black Queer Studies," in Johnson and Henderson, *Black Queer Studies*, 68–89; or E. Patrick Johnson, "'Quare' Studies, or (Almost) Everything I Know about Queer Studies I Learned from My Grandmother," in Johnson and Henderson, *Black Queer Studies*, 124–57.

25 Marable, *Malcolm X: A Life of Reinvention*, 12.

26 Ibid., 385–86.

27 I italicize this phrase to emphasize its inappropriateness since, by Marable's own acknowledgment, they did not spend the night together.

28 Marable, *Malcolm X: A Life of Reinvention*, 379.

29 Sherwood, *Malcolm X Visits Abroad*, 154–55; Marable, *Malcolm X: A Life of Reinvention,* 383, 391; Malcolm X, "Communication and Reality," in John Henrik Clarke (ed.), *Malcolm X: The Man and His Times* (New York: Macmillan, 1969), 307–20.

30 Marable, *Malcolm X: A Life of Reinvention*, 551, 565. Marable's sources for his speculation about Poole seem to be an oral history with James 67X Warren and an interview with Abdur- Rahman Muhammad. His tentative phrasing suggests neither confirmed Poole's presence with Malcolm at the Hilton. Strangely, he does not mention the FBI, so either their surveillance did not confirm her presence or he chose not to use them as a source for this allegation. The former seems likely, given that Marable uses FBI sources throughout the book. Indeed, they are the

book's primary sources regarding Betty's alleged affair with Charles Kenyatta. Amazingly, according to one FBI report, the two planned to marry.

31 Marable, *Malcolm X: A Life of Reinvention*, 40; The Psychologist, "Explosive disorder," http://www.psychologistanywhereanytime.com/disorders_psychologist_and_psychologists/psychologist_explosive_disorder.htm.

32 American Psychiatric Association, *Diagnostic and Statistical Manual of Mental Disorders*, Washington, DC: American Psychiatric Association, 1952, http://www.psychiatryonline.com/DSMPDF/dsm-i.pdf

33 Aldon Morris, "Black Southern Student Sit-In Movement: An Analysis of Internal Organization," *American Sociological Review, 46* (December 1981), 745, 764; Barbara Ransby, *Ella Baker and the Black Freedom Movement: A Radical Democratic Vision* (Chapel Hill: University of North Carolina Press, 2003), 237.

34 Marable, *Malcolm X: A Life of Reinvention*, 123.

35 Steven M. Buechler, *Social Movements in Advanced Capitalism: The Political Economy and Cultural Construction of Social Activism* (Oxford: University of Oxford Press, 2000), 20–21.

36 Ibid., 21.

37 Aldon Morris, *The Origins of the Civil Rights Movement: Black Communities Organizing for Change* (New York: The Free Press, 1984), 276–77; Steven M. Buechler, *Social Movements in Advanced Capitalism*, 20–21.

38 Stephanie Adler and Max Day, "Learning to Do Psychotherapy With Psychotic Patients: In Memory of Elvin Semrad, MD," *Psychiatric Times, 2* (February 5, 2010), 1, http://www.psychiatrictimes.com/display/article/10168/1519938.

39 Marable, *Malcolm X: A Life of Reinvention,* 302, 536–37 n.

40 Manning Marable, *Black American Politics: From the Washington Marches to Jesse Jackson* (London: Verso, 1985), 52.

41 Angela Davis, *Women, Race, and Class* (New York: Vintage; 1st Vintage Books edition, February 12, 1983); Gerda Lerner, *Black Women in White America: A Documentary History* (New York: Vintage Books Edition,

1972); Alfreda Duster (ed.), *Crusade for Justice: The Autobiography of Ida B. Wells* (Chicago: University Of Chicago Press, 1991); Walter Rodney, *How Europe Undeveloped Africa* (Washington, DC: Howard University Press; Revised edition, November 1981).

42 Ibid., 3, 11.

43 Ibid., 213.

44 Ibid., 352.

45 Ibid., 367.

46 Ibid., 383, 391.

47 Sherwood, *Malcolm X Visits Abroad*, 113.

48 Frederick Douglass, "The Significance of Emancipation in the West Indies," (Speech presented in Canandaigua, New York, August 3, 1857), in John W. Blassingame (ed.), *The Frederick Douglass Papers—Series One: Speeches, Debates, and Interviews (Volume 3: 1855–63)* (New Haven, CT: Yale University Press), 204.

49 Ida B. Wells, *Southern Horrors: Lynch Law in All Its Phases* (New York: St. Martin's Press, 1996/1892), 22–3; Robert Williams, *Negroes with Guns* (Chicago: Third World Press, 1973), 63.

50 Timothy B. Tyson, *Radio Free Dixie: Robert F. Williams and the Roots of Black Power* (Chapel Hill: University of North Carolina Press, 1999), 149.

51 Wolfenstein, *Victims of Democracy*, 78–86.

52 Malcolm also may have been attracted to *these tales* because of Aesop's former slave status and the distinct possibly that he was an African. Frank M. Snowden Jr., questions the validity of Maximus Planudes's account that Aesop was Ethiopian but later seems to give credence to this contention. See Marable, *Malcolm X: A Life of Reinvention*, 11; Perry, *Malcolm: The Life of a Man*, 109, 177, 371; J. A. Rogers, *World's Great Men of Color Vol. 1: Asia and Africa*, and *Historical Figures Before Christ, Including Aesop, Hannibal, Cleopatra, Zenobia, Askia the Great, and Many Others* (New York: Simon & Shuster, 1996/1946), 73–80; Frank M. Snowden Jr., *Blacks in Antiquity: Ethiopians in the Greco-Roman Experience* (Cambridge, MA: Belknap Press of Harvard University Press, 1970), 6, 188.

53 Hank Flick and Larry Powell, "Animal Imagery in the Rhetoric of Malcolm X," *Journal of Black Studies, 4* (June 1988), 438, 442.

54 Malcolm X, "God's Judgment of White America (The Chickens Come Home to Roost),"(Speech delivered December 4, 1963), *The Black Commentator*, http://www.Blackcommentator.com/91/91_malcolm.html.

55 "Kenya: The House of Wolves and Foxes," http://fwambancfwamba.wordpress.com/2007/01/30/kenyathe-wolf-intends-to-make-you-his-meal.

56 Ibid.

57 Marable, *Malcolm X: A Life of Reinvention*, 489, 490.

58 Marable did interview Goldman, however, and made extensive use of his work in the text.

59 William W. Sales Jr., *From Civil Rights to Black Liberation: Malcolm X and the Organization of Afro-American Unity.* Boston: South End Press, 1994.

60 Marable, *Malcolm X: A Life of Reinvention*, 490.

61 Perry, *Malcolm X: The Life of a Man*, 382–83, 521–29; Evanzz, *The Judas Factor*, 325–26, 372–74.

62 Perry, *Malcolm X: The Life of a Man*, 274–75; Clayborne Carson, *In Struggle: SNCC and the Black Awakening of the 1960s* (Cambridge, MA: Harvard University Press), 1981, 267–68.

63 Marable, *Malcolm X: A Life of Reinvention*, 91.

64 Ibid., 408.

65 E. Franklin Frazier, *The Negro Family in the United States*, Chicago: University of Chicago Press, 1939; Stanley Elkins, *Slavery: A Problem in American Institutional Life*, Chicago: University of Chicago Press, 1959; Abram Kardiner and Lionel Ovesey, *The Mark of Oppression*, Cleveland, OH: Meridian Press, 1951.

66 Richard King, *Race, Culture, and the Intellectuals, 1940–1970* (Washington, DC: Woodrow Wilson Center Press and Baltimore: John Hopkins University Press, 2004), 125.

67 Marable, *Malcolm X: A Life of Reinvention*, 418.

68 Ibid., 565, 267–68, 273, 323, 324, 328, 350, 374–76, 389, 416, 419, 429, 437, 440, 456, 418.

69 Sherwood, *Malcolm X Travels Abroad*, 85; "Background on the International Dimensions of the African American Struggle: Part 2, The Global Struggle's Links to Detroit's 1967 Rebellion," *Workers World*, August 13, 2007, http://www.workers.org/2007/us/detroit1967-0816/index.html.

*** This book is also available from Black Classic Press, *www.blackclassicbooks.com*

EUGENE PURYEAR

It's Not That Complicated—Malcolm X Was a Revolutionary: Confused Terminology, Concepts Mar Marable Biography

Though this author offers that Marable's book adds much-needed texture and depth to several periods of Malcolm X's life, he concedes that it ultimately fails to frame Malcolm and the overall Black struggle for freedom adequately or to situate him appropriately within the broader Black cultural experience of his time. The result is little that is revelatory and much that is dubious regarding Malcolm's evolving revolutionary stances and political direction.

In the years since his death, El-Hajj Malik El-Shabazz (Malcolm X) has become recognized as more than simply a Black leader but as a world-historic figure. For millions, he is a symbol of dignity, strength, militancy, and self-determination. The incisive prose of his autobiography, in particular, is imprinted on millions of minds across the world as an incredible story of personal and political transformation. What Malcolm was transforming into has remained, however, the subject of enormous debate. Political forces from the socialist left all the way to the leader of the Republican National Committee now claim his legacy.

The late Manning Marable's new biography of Malcolm X, *Malcolm X: A Life of Reinvention,*[1] promised to unveil new details and dimensions of Malcolm's life, helping us understand more fully where he was coming from, and ultimately where he was going. The product of twenty years of research, completed with hundreds of thousands of dollars in support from both Viking Press and Columbia University, Marable's book adds texture and depth to several periods of Malcolm's life and will undoubtedly serve as a key resource for those who want to go beyond *The Autobiography of Malcolm X as Told to Alex Haley*, published in 1965.[2]

Marable repeatedly points out that Malcolm's *Autobiography* is part fact and part fictive, constructed by the political and personal agendas of Alex Haley, a Republican, and Malcolm, who emphasized different aspects of his life as his political world changed. Marable's biography of the man focuses attention on Malcolm's frequent and growing connections to both global Islam and the anticolonial movements of Africa in particular, but as an analytical work, it fails to deal adequately with Malcolm's political influences, his ideological development, and his evolving strategy for Black liberation. Those who consider these the most critical questions and who have been attracted to Malcolm as a symbol of revolution are likely to be disappointed with the book. Several reviews have highlighted Marable's uneven research and accused him of irresponsibly resorting to conjecture when making provocative and sometimes scandalous claims about Malcolm's personal life. Although certainly far more remains to be said about both, this review will address Marable's failure to frame Malcolm and the overall Black freedom struggle adequately.

As such, while Marable constantly hints at various themes, he often develops ideas and concepts haphazardly. One of his themes, for instance, is that Malcolm exaggerated certain details of his youth while obscuring others for rhetorical purposes. He argues that Malcolm "presented himself as the embodiment of the two central figures of African-American folk culture, simultaneously the hustler/trickster and the preacher/minister."[3] His discussion never reaches its potential, however, as Marable uses the trickster theme in conflicting ways. The decidedly negative undertone to that discussion ignores the complexity of folkloric tricksters like Br'er Rabbit, whose deceptions were celebrated as strategies to outwit his oppressors. Rather than consistently situating

Malcolm X within the broader Black cultural experience, Marable substitutes an eclectic and unfocused approach.

A LIFE OF REINVENTION'S CONFUSED AND CONFUSING TERMINOLOGY

Marable's book fails to give a clear assessment of Malcolm, in large part because it fails to frame adequately the movement of which he was a part. Marable's discussions of the Black Civil Rights movement in the United States are often quite shallow and confusing. For example, his constant use of the term *integrationist* is a poor substitute for serious political analysis of the Civil Rights leadership against which Malcolm was often set in contrast. Although a biography cannot be expected to elaborate on all issues, this nomenclature is of crucial importance in a book on Malcolm X. In worthless textbooks across the country, the Civil Rights movement is often split between the so-called violent separatist likes of Malcolm X and the so-called peaceful integrationist persona of Martin Luther King Jr. These terms, however, do not allow the readers of those texts to make meaningful sense of the evolving movement and its swirling debates.

The term *integrationist* is often used to give the false impression that such activists were concerned principally about intermingling with Whites. Undoubtedly, many African Americans saw in integration the promise of a better world in which racism would be eliminated and society as a whole would grow. Yet, integration was fundamentally a strategy aimed at winning Black communities equal access to the services and opportunities offered to Whites. It was an effort to make the United States fulfill its promise of equality before the law. Desiring desegregation of the public bus lines, for example, says nothing in particular about one's attitudes toward interactions with Whites. Rather, it is a statement about rights—namely, about the equal right to choose the most convenient seat on a mode of transportation. Civil Rights marchers sang of freedom, not integration.

A century earlier, many Black abolitionists advocated for social equality, or the right to form relationships across racial lines. But was the upshot of their struggle that they wanted to consort with Whites? Hardly. The crux of their politics was that they were engaged in a righteous struggle against slavery.

It is likewise dubious to what extent Marable's integrationist label fosters any understanding of the worldview of a fiery militant like Gloria Richardson, whose Civil Rights movement activities Marable discusses in his book. Richardson also desired the desegregation of education and all public services, but in her general attitude toward the local White power structure, she had far more in common with Malcolm X than with the leaders of moderate Civil Rights groups. Marable, however, suggests that Malcolm contradicted himself by appearing on stage with Richardson.[4] Though Marable clearly favors integrationism as a political strategy, he simultaneously implies that the activists who pursued this strategy were less concerned with Black pride. This is the false framework that textbooks have used to sanitize Civil Rights workers' Black consciousness and sense of obligation to their community.

MISREPRESENTING THE HISTORIC ROLE OF THE NATION OF ISLAM

This same framework also mirrors, ironically, the analysis put forward by the Nation of Islam (NOI) in the 1950s, which equated anything short of its separatist program to be a betrayal of the Black community. Clearly, Marable is not partial to the NOI. His references to the group as a "cult" and to its leader, Elijah Muhammad, as a "young gigolo" betray his thinly disguised contempt for the organization.[5] Unfortunately, readers of Marable's work will walk away from its pages knowing all the details of the NOI's underside without gaining a clear understanding of its historical significance.

The NOI tapped into the awakening national consciousness of the African American community in the 1950s. Organized along capitalist lines, it was a self-help organization whose day-to-day activities shared much in common with other ethnic-based organizations that served migrant and immigrant communities in other periods of US history. The NOI's program of creating a self-contained economic community was no idle chatter. Under Muhammad's leadership, it set up a complex and sophisticated set of business enterprises. Its messages of Black capitalism—"buy Black" and "support your own"—appealed to a sector of small business owners and aspiring entrepreneurs in the Black ghettos of America's northern and western cities, which became the organization's main areas of strength. At the same time, the NOI's program of uplift, which focused on Blacks winning their freedom and national equality without begging or bowing, touched a raw nerve among Black workers frustrated with the country's slow pace of change.

Elijah Muhammad controlled an organization of tens of thousands and revenues that ran into the tens of millions. He had thousands of completely committed warriors ready to execute any order. So why would Marable call him a gigolo, a most inappropriate and demeaning label? Academic historians never use such terms for the powerful, habitually philandering men of Washington, DC, like John F. Kennedy. And why call the NOI a cult? What religious group would not fit this description, especially in its infancy? Marable sneers at the NOI's creation myth, but is there a different creation myth for any religion that would qualify as being scientifically or historically accurate? (Instead of evaluating different political currents solely by their rhetoric and form, revolutionary Marxists look for the roots and substance of their demands. From this perspective, the NOI's core demand for self-determination is historically justifiable, even if the means it adopted for reaching that goal were not totally desirable.)

Although the Christianity-based Civil Rights leadership stood in contradiction to Elijah Muhammad's particular brand of separatism, the NOI was part of the same Black national awakening. Instead of grappling with and explaining the historical roots of the NOI's separatism, however, Marable falls back on a shallow pragmatic argument. He asserts that, in a 1960 debate, Civil Rights leader Bayard Rustin "closed the trap" on Malcolm by forcing him to admit to the NOI's program for a separate state. Given that Rustin could "recount the major reforms that had taken place, and the practical impossibility of a [B]lack state," Marable says, "the essential weakness of the Nation of Islam had been exposed."[6] However, political ideas cannot be assessed purely on the grounds of what is practical in the short term. The balance of political and social forces is always subject to change. Rustin's pragmatic reformism, to which Marable was partial, excluded radical and revolutionary visions of any sort and argued that activists must work to modify, not replace, the existing capitalist system. Lacking a clear exposition of both the Civil Rights struggle and Black Nationalism, Marable's book fails to make sense of the subsequent evolution of both Malcolm and the movement.

MISREADING MALCOLM'S POLITICAL EVOLUTION

In 1964 and 1965, Malcolm's last years, the Civil Rights movement accomplished the legal and political dismantling of Jim Crow segregation in what amounted to a political revolution. During those years, Black political forces across the spectrum turned toward the question of how to turn legal, formal equality into real social and economic equality. Malcolm found himself in a transitional period during which he strove to launch a full-fledged Black liberation movement. He wanted to help give direction to that expanding movement rather than stand apart from it, as Elijah Muhammad mandated. As Marable notes, Malcolm's subsequent departure from the NOI was not personal, but primarily political—a point that gets somewhat lost in the book's digressions into what I call *mosque gossip*.

In famous speeches such as "Message to the Grassroots" and "Ballot or the Bullet," Malcolm did not eschew politics. Rather, he suggested that Black people use their voting rights to develop an alternative power base. He remained deeply critical of the traditional Civil Rights leadership but advocated for a Black united front in which various political currents could contend. He also insisted on making self-defense a reality, not just a slogan, and held out the idea that a Black Nationalist army might eventually form if the Black masses were not given full rights. Yet Marable principally evaluates Malcolm on the bases of separatist versus integrationist, violence versus nonviolence, and revolutionary versus practical strategies. In each category, he suggests Malcolm moved from the former to the latter, becoming more moderate. He also asserts that Malcolm eventually implicitly acknowledged the correctness of his longtime foes in the movement.

For instance, he continually tries to suggest that Malcolm contradicted himself with his advocacy of using the political system to achieve certain reforms. He further calls it a "glaring inconsistency" for Malcolm to advocate Blacks' use of the ballot to effect change while arguing that neither major party had anything to offer the Black struggle.[7] Indeed, in Marable's world, there clearly is no room for electoral politics outside of the Democratic Party, and the only practical options for Black people in the United States are the two major political parties.

Malcolm's actual views on this were entirely different. His famous "Ballot or the Bullet" speech, which called for Blacks to consider forming a Black Nationalist party, was decidedly in step with the times. He made some of his most important speeches on this subject in Detroit, the heart of the nascent Freedom Now Party, which aimed to organize independent Black political action. Malcolm had also seen the Mississippi Freedom Democratic Party (MFDP) turned away from the larger Democratic Party's convention in Atlantic City, and it was no accident or contradiction that MFDP leader Fannie Lou Hamer showed up in Harlem in December 1964 to hear him speak. Nor was it coincidental that the year Malcolm was assassinated, the Lowndes County Freedom Organization, which attempted to utilize voting rights for the purposes of self-determination, was born in Alabama.

Even on theoretical terms, there is nothing inconsistent about condemning the two major parties while suggesting that Black people vote strategically. A revolutionary makes use of all tactics that advance the struggle at a particular moment, provided that this does not foster illusions in the current system. In his pamphlet, "Left-Wing Communism: An Infantile Disorder," Lenin laid out the importance of utilizing electoral tactics as a method to heighten class consciousness and push forward revolutionary politics.[8] Far from calling it a glaring inconsistency, he saw it as an obligation for revolutionaries participating in elections to point out how ruling-class parties cannot meet people's needs. As one who came out of a Marxist tradition, Marable undoubtedly was aware of these classic formulations of reform and revolution. He mentions the dialectical relationship between the two in *A Life of Reinvention*, but in the book's afterword, he sets them up as mutually exclusive, explaining that the "mature" Malcolm believed the ballot could be used to achieve "meaningful social change," "despite" his "revolutionary rhetoric."[9]

Marable further details how Malcolm endorsed revolutionary violence in Africa but did not yet advocate for such a military struggle inside the United States. If this were a contradiction, as he suggests it was, then he would effectively disqualify nearly every self-proclaimed revolutionary in this land who has not actively called for immediate armed action.

Marable notes that Malcolm, in his latter days, claimed that he no longer knew "how to define [his] particular ideology." Rather than portray this as a drift toward liberalism or as a period simply of confusion—as Marable does—Malcolm's political crossroads should be put instead in the context of the Black liberation movement. Malcolm searched for answers, looking for potential examples in Africa, questioning the legitimacy of the capitalist economic system, and considering new strategies to advance the Black struggle. His last year of political development and experimentation did not leave us with a unified system of thought, but it did leave a clear spirit of resistance, militancy, and defiance.

An honest appraisal suggests not that Malcolm was moving toward integrationism but that the integrationists were moving toward him. It is no accident that Malcolm's legacy was evoked constantly when the "Black Power" slogan emerged a year after his death. The notion of Black Power—Black political, economic, and cultural control over majority-Black communities—could appeal to individuals who advocated both integrationist and separatist strategies in years prior. It could take liberal variants, stressing the need for Black representatives to be in charge of existing structures. It could have its rhetorically more separatist expressions. It could also take on varied meanings for revolutionaries. Each variant shared a common frame of reference: the struggle for self-determination.

This helps explain the contest over Malcolm's political legacy, which began shortly after his death. Organizations of all types—from the Congress of Racial Equality (CORE) to the cultural nationalists in the organization US to the Black Panther Party—all saw themselves as inheritors of Malcolm's evolving outlook. Various shades of nationalists, socialists, Pan-Africanists, and anarchists all lay claim to at least certain aspects of his political legacy. Liberal Democrats cited Malcolm's influence when running for political offices that had previously been occupied only by White politicians. This again speaks to the inadequacy of setting up mutually exclusive separatist and integrationist camps, for these forces overlapped and came together in complex ways.

MISAPPROPRIATING MALCOLM'S RADICALISM

Though Marable cannot have been expected to resolve all these questions, his whole discussion of Malcolm's political trajectory is clouded by generalizations like "meaningful social change" and "transformative." In the process, he omits the substance of Malcolm's radicalism. Regardless of his organizational trajectory, Malcolm clearly asserted that without taking on capitalism it would be impossible to uproot various forms of oppression, racism in particular. Many can admire Malcolm's particular traits or isolated speeches, but without a basic acceptance of these facts, none can lay claim to his political legacy.

Malcolm may have been the inspiration for a number of Black Power groups, but it is worth considering what sort of social and economic vision he would have attached to this demand. The leadership of CORE, the direct-action organization, made the transition from what Marable calls the integrationist camp to a more Malcolm-aligned one in 1966. By the early 1970s, however, many of these same CORE leaders had become Nixon-aligned. Their particular brand of Black Power won rhetorical, moral, and material support in the halls of Congress, foundation boardrooms, and corporate suites. Black liberal figures also took on some of the symbolism and rhetoric of the Black Power movement, but they too sought an accommodation, albeit of a different type, with US monopoly capitalism.

The political significance of Malcolm X is that he was the antithesis of such accommodationist thinking. He would not have accepted merely a new face to the structures of the capitalist system. Malcolm increasingly compared the plight of Black people in the United States to the anticolonial struggles in Asia and Africa. He clearly saw that changes in leadership had been insufficient to uproot the control of the former colonizers. Malcolm's critique of capitalism was not uncommon in his period, however. Even as new avenues for reform opened, the limits of capitalism created the central tension of Black politics between 1965 and 1975. Likewise, the revolutionaries in Africa with whom Malcolm interacted focused increasingly on economics as the pivot point for the next period of struggle. They advocated a variety of programs from nonaligned economics to African socialism. Many ultimately oriented toward industrialization in conjunction with the socialist bloc as the only path to overcome the legacies of underdevelopment. These experiences, as well as the experiences of the Vietnam War, would have undoubtedly influenced Malcolm's political evolution.

A REVOLUTIONARY TO THE END?

In Marable's final chapter, "Reflections of a Revolutionary Legacy," he attempts to sum up Malcolm's legacy, writing: "What Malcolm sought was a fundamental restructuring of wealth and power in the United States—not a violent social revolution, but radical and meaningful change nevertheless."[10] It is in these last sections, however, that Marable most clearly stumbles. How can one forsake revolution while also possessing a revolutionary legacy? What definition of revolution is Marable using? I suspect none. As with his use of the terms *integrationist*, *separatist*, *race-neutral*, and *Bonapartist*, as well as a few loaded Cold War terms that he throws into his text, Marable's use of terms relating to revolution and meaningful change are not clearly defined and, as such, fail as analytical categories.

That Malcolm supposedly "reinvented" himself is no real revelation, as this is common among all sorts of people. It is especially so for leaders who must navigate complex political ruptures. The takeaway for most readers, unfortunately, will be that Malcolm was evolving toward a form of liberalism or that he potentially was never a revolutionary at all.

Putting aside Marable's claims of having produced a definitive biography, *A Life of Reinvention* has raised more questions than it answers. Some of these questions may be irresponsible and some may confuse matters that should be crystal clear, but Marable's biography of Malcolm X has at least shown the need to study and debate Malcolm's legacy and the movements from which he sprang.

ENDNOTES

1 Manning Marable, *Malcolm X: A Life of Reinvention*, New York: Viking Press, 2011.

2 Malcolm X, *The Autobiography of Malcolm X as Told to Alex Haley*, New York: Random House, 1965.

3 Marable, *Malcolm X: A Life of Reinvention*, 11.

4 Ibid., 298.

5 Ibid., 183.

6 Ibid., 176–77.

7 Ibid., 307.

8 V. I. Lenin, *Left-Wing Communism: An Infantile Disorder*. Geelong, Australia: Resistance Books, 1999 (originally published in 1920).

9 Marable, *Malcolm X: A Life of Reinvention*, 484.

10 Ibid., 483.

KARL EVANZZ

Jared Ball Radio Interview with Karl Evanzz on WPFW 89.3 FM, April 15, 2011

JB: Mr. Evanzz, you have ignited another round of discussion with your just-published review of Manning Marable's book, *Malcolm X: A Life of Reinvention* and the subsequent discussion of [your review] not being accepted as originally planned by *TheRoot.com*. And that is the subject of an article this morning in the "Lifestyle" section of the *Washington Post*. Let me just ask you: Your review starts by saying, "*Malcolm X: A Life of Reinvention* is an abomination. It is a cavalcade of innuendo and logical fallacy, and is largely reinvented from previous works on the subject." Could you quickly summarize your reasons for this statement and what you looked to outline in that review?

KE: Sure. I say it's a cavalcade, meaning a parade, of innuendo because from the first pages Marable begins an unprovoked attack upon Malcolm X's legacy and upon everybody who was related to Malcolm X. He calls Malcolm X's father a bigamist. He calls Malcolm X a homosexual. He calls Malcolm X's sister, Ella Collins, a paranoid schizophrenic and a reckless woman. It's one diatribe after another. And he has virtually no documentation to support these scurrilous accusations.

That's why I began the review with a strong denunciation of Mr. Marable. You know, the people he is talking about...I get personally offended, let me say this, when somebody makes allegations against anybody that they *know* are not true... .Marable knows a lot of the stuff he said was not true, and he knows some of it was outright prevarication and lies.

I had never met Manning Marable, but in 2005 he went on "Democracy Now!" [a radio newsmagazine] promoting his book—February 21, in fact, the anniversary of Malcolm X's assassination. And he said that Alex Haley, Malcolm X's biographer, was an FBI informant. So a Canadian reporter [named Malcolm Azania] called and asked me what I thought about it. And I said that I don't believe that for one second because I had seen parts of the declassified files on Alex Haley, and I can tell you point-blank that he resisted numerous attempts by the FBI to convert him into an informant. So I was outraged by that.

I really get outraged when these ivory tower intellectuals come on and want to pummel somebody who's dead. Attack somebody who is *alive!* Say something negative about Minister Farrakhan or some of these other clowns running around out here [saying], you know, "Malcolm did this" or "Malcolm did that, but I'm ten times better than Malcolm." Don't do that! It is rude and irresponsible for these so-called "public intellectuals" to consistently condemn Malcolm X and brother Dr. King.

JB: Obviously, there is a lot more to this book. It is more than 600 pages, and I am, again, still working through it. A lot of it does deal with [Malcolm's] background, his history, the assassination. In fact, I saw where someone showed that [there are] only seven pages that actually deal with these more salacious accounts as you describe. Could you talk a little bit about...

KE: Let me make a comment about that.

JB: Sure.

KE: See, that's the problem with the media. Like you said, it's seven or eight pages of scurrilous material, but in actuality, it's a lot more than that. Here is what happens: these idiots in the media, and no offense to you personally... but if you go to some of these gay websites, for example, or some of these racist websites, they have already extracted those comments about Malcolm X being gay and such and such. They are making all these jokes, and that's what gets picked up and repeated and becomes part of the folklore of a person's history. Not what he did but what he did, allegedly, in the bedroom. So if you don't have documentation for what somebody did in their personal life, don't bring it up.

This whole thing about this letter, for example, that Malcolm wrote to Elijah Muhammad that is quoted in the book about his problems with Betty Shabazz... I had a White man call me back in 1993 and offer me that same letter. I said, "Where did you get the letter from, Sir?" He never could tell me where he got the letter from. So the provenance of that letter is suspect to begin with. I talked to Wilfred Little, Malcolm X's brother, and said, "Can you vouch for this letter?" He said, "Let me tell you this, it sounds like Malcolm and it might have been Malcolm, but I cannot vouch for that letter." People have to understand that the FBI at the time was actually faking letters, writing letters to Elijah Muhammad, and writing letters to Malcolm X that were completely fabricated. People need to check the sourcing on things before they go quoting it and saying "Aha! I *gotcha*!"

And the other thing I want to say is that Malcolm X never said he was a saint. He never said that he was perfect. So for these little knuckleheads to go out here and pick every little piece of lint that they can find and say, "See, I told you he wasn't perfect!" is stupid. You can't find any Catholic saint who was perfect. People go off on these tangents, and what they are doing makes no sense whatsoever.

JB: Could you quickly outline your own theory of the assassination of Malcolm X? Because even as we are here to discuss it, I don't want the entire discussion to avoid this issue and the importance in general of Malcolm X, beyond just discussion of Marable's book.

KE: Well, let me clarify this too. One of the bloggers said that my attack on Marable is personal. But if you look at the review, you will see that I cite page numbers, page after page in the review, showing that it is about the book and not about Marable.

Now, my theory of Malcolm X's assassination is very cut and dry. Basically, in March of 1964, Elijah Muhammad—and this is in the FBI file, by the way…it's declassified, no big secret here—Elijah Muhammad called Louis Farrakhan in Boston, and he said it's time to "close his [meaning Malcolm's] eyes." He said, and I'm paraphrasing now [that] if we [the Nation of Islam] let Malcolm X live, he will just be running around the country putting us down, and I can't have that. A few months later, Elijah Muhammad, Jr., went to New York and had a meeting with the Fruit of Islam. And he told them to go to Malcolm's house and cut that nigger's tongue out and bring it to [him], and [he would] stamp it approved.

So a year before Malcolm is killed, you had these top Nation of Islam leaders planning to assassinate Malcolm X. At the same time, Malcolm X had been going to Africa and pushing his UN [United Nations] petition condemning the United States government for violating the human rights of the African Americans. So the CIA was using informants inside the Black community and so was the FBI, trying to get somebody—something—going in there [to] get Malcolm X killed because he [was] going to embarrass the American government before the world by taking us before the UN.

So you had two different factions that wanted Malcolm X dead, and it just so happened that their interests collided or coalesced. That's my theory: elements within the Black community let themselves become pawns of the intelligence community and they worked out a plan to kill Malcolm X.

There were numerous attempts to kill him after March 1964 until he was actually killed. Everyone knows by now that one of the [body] guards on the stage when Malcolm was killed [Gene Roberts] was an undercover New York police detective. The audience [contained] four or five undercover police detectives, and Malcolm's organization was infiltrated by the FBI. His phone was tapped. There were FBI agents following Malcolm around the clock. He knew this. He would look behind him sometimes and he would see these White guys following him with these crew cuts and these jive suits on, so he knew who they were. They were not discrete about it because they were trying to let him know that 'we've got you [and] we're going to take care of you'.

And that's why, at the end, Malcolm had pretty much given up. By the week he died, he was, like, I can't fight it. They bombed his house the week before, which was Valentine's Day. They bombed the man's house with fire bombs...and by the way, the participants [in that bombing] were Captain Joseph of the Newark mosque and Alvan Farrakhan, Louis Farrakhan's brother, who has also been implicated as one of the people who threw the fire bombs at Malcolm's house. So let those brothers who sit here and kiss Farrakhan's feet think about that one.

JB: How do you feel Marable's work handles this question of Malcolm X's assassination? Do you think Marable does a fair job in covering these aspects and properly attributing conclusions drawn to work previously done on the subject?

KE: The second half of the book I don't have any problems with, and let me tell you why. It's not plagiarism, *per se*, but the second half of the book is basically a reconstitution of my books on the Nation of Islam and of Zak Kondo's book on the assassination. So I don't have any argument with that. He is quoting *me*! However, when he goes so far as to say that Norman 3X Butler was innocent because he was hurt on the day of the assassination—that his leg was hurt and he was at the doctor's office—that's completely bogus.

Now this is one problem with the book: [Marable] criticizes my work, on page 490, as not being original source material, but he says that Norman Butler was injured that day. But if he had read the trial transcript, which *is* original source material, he would have seen that Norman Butler's own doctor said that's bull crap. [He said], "I didn't see him on February 21, I saw him on February 25, four days after the assassination." So Norman Butler's story, that he was too hurt to be at the crime, is completely bogus. In fact, there is a photograph of a man resembling Norman 3X Butler right outside the Audubon as they are taking Malcolm X's body to the hospital.

JB: To be fair, it is not just you who Marable dismisses on page 490. All of the books written in the 1990s are dismissed.

KE: Yes, he dismisses every book written in the 1990s about Malcolm X's life and his assassination. Well, that's *everything* that has been written about Malcolm X.

JB: One of our audience's questions about your criticism is that you seem to have done precisely what Marable has done regarding source material for making allegations about Malcolm's sexuality or sexual practice, and yet you remain obviously critical of him. On page 8 of your book, *The Judas Factor*, you describe Malcolm as accepting payment to allow men to perform fellatio on him. And you, like Marable, offer your source. Could you respond to that? How is this different than what you accuse Marable of?

KE: I can clarify that really easily. People should understand, and I will send you a copy of the letter. I wrote *The Judas Factor* in 1981. I submitted it to publishers, and Toni Morrison [then an editor at Random House] liked the book. She wanted to buy it, but after a couple of months she called me back and said… I can't give you a contract because these two White guys I work with don't want to buy it because, she said, they said nobody knows who Malcolm X is. This is 1981. So I stuck the book back in the drawer and worked on it periodically for the next ten years. And when Malcolm became "popular," of course, I had publishers beating my door down.

Now I got that information [about Malcolm X's sexual exploits] from the same person that Marable [got] it from, a putative relative of Malcolm X. It was in 1981 when I wrote [the book], so keep that in mind. And I am thinking this guy is a true lover of Malcolm X because he is supposedly his nephew. Well, it turns out that this person is not actually related by blood to Malcolm X. If you look at some of these other books, he is cited as a source of some of the more salacious stuff about Malcolm X. So the point I'm making is I did not get a second source on that information. I accepted it because I thought this person was a true-blue Malcolm X supporter. If I had to do it over again and, in fact, when I do the twentieth-anniversary edition of the book, I am going to take that out. That was my first mistake.

The point I was trying to make here though is that this was a common practice in the ghetto when I was a kid. I mean when I hung out in gangs in St. Louis in the early to mid-1960s, there were gay guys who would give young teenagers like myself five dollars to let them perform fellatio on us. So I figured, you know, that if what this guy says is true, this is more than likely what Malcolm was doing. So I take the blame for trusting someone I thought could be trusted with that information. However, I did not use two sources, which was my mistake. I will correct that.

JB: You also mentioned to me that there is a big difference between the resources available and the length of time involved in the research between yours and Marable's book.

KE: That is precisely right. You have to remember, I was in law school at the time I wrote that book—and I'm raising two kids. So I'm researching the book and writing...I'm not making that as an excuse, I'm only saying that this was over thirty years ago when I wrote the book. Times are a lot different now and a lot more information is available. So I'm researching the book and I'm one person—researching, writing, and editing. Marable had over *twenty* assistants! Marable had hundreds of thousands of dollars at his disposal. So what I did in 1981 and what he did in 2011 is apples and oranges. There is *no* comparison.

JB: In the last few moments we have left, I don't want this entire discussion to only be about Marable's book. What few words would you like to leave our listeners with regarding Malcolm X? What is his importance, as you see it, even in 2011?

KE: My biggest impression of Malcolm X is that he was a prophet. If people go back and read the epilogue [of *The Autobiography of Malcolm X*] he said something very profound. He said, I made a lot of mistakes out there, and now I have to go and clean this mess up. He was, of course, talking about those teachings, like [that] Fard Muhammad was God and that sort of stuff. But he also said that he hoped people would read his book [the *Autobiography*] and learn from [his] mistakes and see that if they don't correct society, if society does not start accepting minorities as part of the game, [then] in twenty to thirty years, we are going to have a subculture of gangsters, of unemployable Black men and Latino men, who have no choice but to go into a life of crime. And this is the situation we have today. We have where a Black man or a Latino commits one crime, one felony, and they are permanently locked out of the job market for life. And then people wonder why these brothers turn to a life of crime.

I've seen my own son and a lot of young men who go out here and apply for a job and they have a felony arrest, let's say for stealing a carton of cigarettes, and that White man on that job will say I can't hire you because you're a convicted felon. So what you're creating is a permanent underclass in this society, who will have no choice ultimately but to turn against this society and wreak havoc.

Malcolm was a prophet about that. He made that very clear that if you don't listen now, you'll listen later. To me, that is one of the most important things about that autobiography. I think everyone should read that book and really try to get Malcolm's message. He recognized his mistakes and he was also saying, "I love this country whether you believe it or not. But I'm telling you that if you don't make some changes, there is going to be hell to pay."

KARL EVANZZ

Paper Tiger: Manning Marable's Poison Pen

The author of this essay was among the first to publicly, and with serious detail, critique Manning Marable's Malcolm X book. The coeditors of this volume acknowledge that his initial review of Malcolm X: A Life of Reinvention *is as much responsible for launching the process of critical response that is this book as was the Marable book itself.*

Malcolm X: A Life of Reinvention is an abomination. It is a cavalcade of innuendo and logical fallacy, and is largely "reinvented" from previous works on the subject.

It may serve as grounds for at least two defamation actions. The publisher would do well to consider recalling the book and issuing an apology for two reasons: a man labeled an "alleged murderer" has never been formally accused or convicted of that crime, and a woman mentioned by name is accused of committing adultery forty-six years ago. As such, there is virtually no way to verify the allegation.

Marable, who died on April 1, 2011, takes cheap shots at Malcolm X, Malcolm's parents, Betty Shabazz, Malcolm's siblings, and almost anyone with a familial nexus to Malcolm X.

[The book's] official release on the forty-third anniversary of the assassination of Dr. Martin Luther King, Jr., is symbolic because this book amounts to an assassination of Malcolm X's character. Marable's friends dare to call this his "magnum opus." To use street vernacular, this ain't his magnum nothin'. It is merely the logical culmination of a life spent in the ivory tower writing books of scant interest beyond the tower walls. If the so-called public intellectuals praising the book were Marable's true friends, they might have at least apprised him of the hostile tone and the lack of vetting on key allegations, the central one being Malcolm X's alleged homosexual affair. The media ran with this allegation without checking its validity.

Malcolm X, Marable claims, "falsely attributed" his own sexual encounters with an older White male to a friend named Rudy. "Based on circumstantial but strong evidence, Malcolm was *probably* [emphasis mine] describing his own homosexual encounter with Paul Lennon. The revelations of his involvement with Lennon produced much speculation about Malcolm's sexual orientation." Speculation by whom? Marable, that's who.

There are four footnotes for this page, but none substantiates this scurrilous assertion, one that would be grounds for libel were either party alive. The claim is juxtaposed by dozens of pages relating to Malcolm's maturation into selling drugs, pimping (including White women), burglary, and other crimes. If you look at the mug shot—the first in a pallid sixteen-page photo section—you see the face of a thug you do not want to tangle with.

Moreover, there is nothing in Malcolm X's far superior [autobiographical] work to suggest that there was any touching of genitalia, let alone oral or anal sodomy. In fact, Malcolm X's autobiography clearly shows (in the chapter titled "Caught") how amusing he found the strange things that made White "johns" reach orgasm. (One man, he wrote, ejaculated by sitting outside a bedroom door listening to a Black couple making whoopee.)

Nor does Marable offer proof that the employer was homosexual, bisexual, or asexual. The only logical conclusion from the facts is that the man [Lennon] had unusual recreational habits. Marable offers no proof that the man didn't pay women to pour powder on him from time to time, for example, or that anyone employed by the man was homosexual. His proffer is a want ad for a male secretary. The ad ran twice over a three-day period in one newspaper on one occasion.

Another example of logical fallacy here is the one used to denigrate Malcolm X's father, Earl Little, Sr., who is accused of bigamy. "Earl abandoned his young wife and children....He did not bother to get a legal divorce," he writes. Marable cites other authors to support this claim, but none of them establishes that he checked court records to confirm this allegation. He offers nothing to show that he conducted a court search for the divorce record. On the opening page of Chapter One, Marable writes: "In 1909, he [Earl] married a local African American woman, Daisy Mason, and in quick succession had three children: Ella, Mary, and Earl, Jr." Notice the problem? Marable neglects to inform us of the exact date that the couple married in 1909 and whether the marriage was done legally or by common law. Again, his notes show no indication that he searched court records for a marriage license. Did Marable know the date of the marriage? If they were not legally married, Earl had no legal obligation to file for divorce. As such, Marable's condescending tone—"he [Earl] did not bother"—shows his contempt not only for Malcolm but for Malcolm's father as well. The real sin here is that Marable fails to show that he bothered to check for a marriage license or a divorce filing.

Marable uses similar tactics to malign Ella Little—the woman who fired one of his key sources—describing her as "belligerent," "paranoid" and "reckless." [Though] he tries to countenance his charge by citing a psychiatric evaluation, Marable knows full well that psychiatrists routinely employed such terms to describe supporters of Marcus Garvey. Their reasoning was simple: any Black person who rejects America has to be crazy.

In the preface, Marable boasts that his book will "reconstruct the full contours of his [Malcolm's] remarkable life," and proceeds to contrive the most mean-spirited biography of Malcolm X in two decades.

The footnotes reflect heavy reliance upon people who were known enemies of Malcolm X. An earlier biographer used anonymous sources for some of his controversial claims, which was bad. Marable gives no source for some of the tabloid-type allegations, which is a million times worse.

According to Marable, Malcolm was having an extramarital affair with one of his secretaries, an affair that lasted until his death. Keep in mind that Malcolm knew by early 1965 that he was under constant surveillance by the FBI as well as by members of the Nation of Islam. How do we know? Because Malcolm X said so repeatedly in speeches and his posthumous memoir. "Elijah seems to know every move I make," Haley quotes him (Epilogue) saying in the final days of his short life. On February 16, Malcolm X told Haley: "I have been marked for death in the next five days. I have the names of five Black Muslims who have been chosen to kill me. I will announce them at the meeting."

On February 21, five Black Muslims killed him while his wife and four little girls watched in horror.

FBI files show that agents worked in eight-hour shifts to keep Malcolm under around-the-clock surveillance in weeks prior to his death. Malcolm told Haley and others that he would see them watching him as they took notes while he left his house, as he went to the drugstore to get a newspaper, and as he went to his office. FBI documents confirm his suspicions.

Note further that Black Muslims were threatening to kill him to prevent him from testifying in a Los Angeles paternity case filed against Elijah Muhammad by two of his teenage secretaries.

With those kinds of stressors, an extramarital affair the night before he died seems highly unlikely, and he certainly would not have chosen a teenage girl at a time when he was scheduled to testify against Black Muslim leader Elijah Muhammad else for doing the same thing.

After claiming that Betty Shabazz had an affair with one of Malcolm's assistants guarding his family, Marable alleges that Malcolm X pursued yet another extramarital relationship.

He also claims that Malcolm met with Alex Haley on February 20 to discuss their joint book project, took Betty to a friend's house for her to spend the night, and then rented a cheap hotel room where he "may have" had the teenage secretary as a bed warmer. By that logic, he may have met with Olive Oyl, Bluto, and Popeye that night as well.

There are numerous published accounts from those close to Malcolm that he was near his breaking point by then. Black Muslims had bombed his home on Valentine's Day because Malcolm refused to move out of the house pending a judgment over its ownership.

Marable claims that the same teenager who was romantically involved with Malcolm the night of February 20 showed up at the Audubon Ballroom the next day. She sat in the front row next to a man whose name would later appear in FBI documents related to the assassination.

The teenager, Marable writes, and the Newark mosque official now "live together in the same New Jersey residence, and [name deleted] has maintained absolute silence about her relationship with both Malcolm X and [name deleted]." The source given for this allegation is Abdur-Rahman Muhammad. When I asked Muhammad for his sources, he declined comment. Despite the obvious lack of due diligence, Marable spares no opportunity to praise his own ingenuity and tenacity.

"*After years* [my emphasis] of research," he writes in [the chapter entitled] "Life Beyond the Legend," "I discovered that several chapters had been deleted [from the biography] prior to publication—chapters that envisioned the construction of a united front of Negroes led by the Black Muslims." Yeah, and Columbus "discovered" America. The word "years" has to be a typographical error. Surely he means after *minutes* of research. This is from the front page of the "Life" section of *USA Today*:

> MEMORIES FOR SALE: A manuscript of Alex Haley's first book, The Autobiography of Malcolm X, sold for $100,000 at an auction to settle claims against the late author's estate. The buyer was Detroit entertainment lawyer Gregory Reed, who also paid $21,500 for *three deleted chapters of the book* [emphasis mine]."

The date of the story? October 2, 1992.

The story ran in practically every major newspaper and Black magazine in the next two months. Any college student could have signed on to Nexis or other news databases and found that in five minutes or less. A Google search for *Malcolm X*, *autobiography*, and *missing chapters* generated more than 4,000 hits on April 4, 2011 [the official publication date of Marable book].

As a former professional researcher (I worked in the news research department of *The Washington Post* for more than a decade), I immediately recognized Marable's fraud, one of many in this pedestrian publication.

The late professor uncovers no significant new material, yet he has the *chutzpah* to dismiss with a flick of his wrist earlier books about Malcolm's life and assassination. In reading, Marable writes, "*all* [emphasis mine] of the literature about Malcolm produced in the 1990s, I was struck by its shallow character and lack of original sources."

When I began reading Chapter Seven, I felt like I was revisiting my biography of Elijah Muhammad. It deals with marital discord between Nation of Islam leader Elijah Muhammad and [his wife] Clara Muhammad. The chapter's first four pages read like a "reinvention" of chapters from *The Messenger*, published by Pantheon Books in 1999. I checked the footnotes for those four pages and noticed that seven of the first ten [footnotes on page 521] cite *The Messenger* as the source. Why didn't Marable use the original source material? He makes no mention of the FBI's national and Chicago files on Clara Muhammad.

Marable has two primary arguments: (1) the intelligence community and the New York Police Department deliberately ignored serious threats against Malcolm's X life, and (2) there is overwhelming evidence that the five assassins came from the Nation of Islam's Newark mosque. That's it.

His first argument is based upon research in my first book, *The Judas Factor: The Plot to Kill Malcolm X*, published in November 1992. His second argument—and the one that the media chose to ignore for the past two decades—is based upon the research of Zak Kondo of Baltimore City Community College. *Conspiracys: Unraveling the Assassination of Malcolm X* is without question the most authoritative examination of the mechanics of the assassination.

Marable had hundreds of thousands of dollars at his disposal for more than a decade. He had over twenty researchers at his disposal. Given far less capital and manpower, both David J. Garrow and Taylor Branch separately produced three-volume works of encyclopedic detail on Malcolm's contemporary, Dr. Martin Luther King, Jr.

Despite his acknowledgments of gratitude to other prominent researchers and benefactors, Marable's book is a single volume with questionable documentation.

Poor exposition and inexcusable typographical errors taint the book. When I communicated with Marable [in] June [2010] regarding a statement obtained from Linward X Cathcart by New York police after the assassination, his reply referred to "Linwood" Cathcart. I advised him of the misspelling and cautioned him to check his manuscript for the mistake.

One of his assistants replied under his name and told me that Marable dictated his responses for her to relay. She blamed herself for misspelling the name and assured me that the book had the proper spelling. There are two references to Cathcart's full name in the book, and both times the name is spelled "Linwood." It is also misspelled in the index.

A LIE OF REINVENTION

In the prologue, Marable describes Malcolm X's memoir as a "cautionary tale about human waste and the tragedies produced by racial segregation."

Human waste? As in feces and urine?

"No man has more accurately described and analyzed the existential, political, social, moral and spiritual plight of a victimized people than has Malcolm X in this book," an objective reviewer wrote about *The Autobiography of Malcolm X.*

A Life of Reinvention, by contrast, is immediately forgettable. It was written by a chronic pen pusher who lived a rather unremarkable middle class existence but nonetheless implies that Malcolm X was an amateur this or a mediocre that.

"I'm the man you think you are," Malcolm X said. Malcolm X was at the top of the class in school, on top of the hustling game during his hoodlum years, and a hellraiser in prison. He was national spokesman for a Black organization that barely functioned before he joined in 1952. He was, finally, a revolutionary known and respected by other prominent revolutionaries—Fidel Castro, Ben Bella, and Che Guevara, to name a few.

He was, in short, a black panther of a man. By contrast, Marable was just another paper tiger.

WILLIAM A. SALES, JR.

Jared Ball Interview with William Sales, June 3, 2011[1]

JB: Before we can get too far into it, can you just summarize what you were doing in your book, many years ago, that is still, again, just as powerful and relevant? What is it [that] you sought to capture in your book, *From Civil Rights to Black Liberation: Malcolm X and the Organization of Afro-American Unity;* then what [did] you [think] of Marable's book; and, most importantly, what you think of the relevance of Malcolm X in 2011?

WS: My book was born of a project by a group of scholars called the Malcolm X Work Group that [got] together in 1987 to address the tremendous gap in our understanding and knowledge about Malcolm X. My book was devoted to establishing Malcolm as a thinker and theoretician of Black liberation and, specifically, to focus on the last eleven months of his life, after he left the Nation of Islam, as a reflection of the most mature period in his thought and his activity.

JB: I want to remind people that at the end of the summer, Professor Sales and Professor [Rosemari] Mealy...among many others, Professor [William] Strickland, who was also at that panel at the Schomburg, will all be contributors to a book I'm coediting with Dr. Todd Steven Burroughs [featuring] writers who respond to Marable's book. That book of essays will [be published] by Black Classic Press. And we're thrilled to have professors Sales and Mealy and others involved in that.

But one of the points I was trying to make was what Marable had not done in his book—was that he had left out a lot of and [had] not built upon the great research that you and others had already laid down: giving us an idea of what Malcolm was really trying to get done at the end of his life [and] what made him the threat to national security and to the softer elements within the progressive social movements and to other reactionary forces as well. For instance, you really outlined the basic aims and objectives of the OAAU. Something as simple as that outlining was not done in Marable's book.

WS: Not at all.

JB: And you give a view of the truly radical politics of the OAAU. And you even explain the origins of the name of that organization and what it was originally meant to be called. Let's start there, with the description of those basic names and objectives and what the original name of the organization was set to be and why it was changed...

WS: The Organization of Afro-American Unity was conceived by Malcolm X as the hemispheric affiliate of the Organization of African Unity, which was the highest organizational development of Pan-Africanism in the 1960s. In 1963, the OAU had come to existence, and less than a year later Malcolm was traveling in Africa. And he received the support of the Pan-African forces there, and he begins to see that the OAAU should come to existence to link African-descended people in the Diaspora with the Pan-Africanist movements on the continent of Africa. One reason he felt that such an international configuration of Pan-Africanists was essential is because he defined the enemy of Black people everywhere as the North Atlantic Treaty Organization. And I thought that was prescient, when we consider today what's going on in Africa with the NATO bombing of Libya, that, as early as 1964, Malcolm made explicit statements that we were not just fighting against racism in the United States, but that racism was most fundamenentally reflected in an internationalist coalition, organized militarily, known as NATO. Originally, the OAAU was conceived as a national liberation movement, and there was terminology bandied around to that extent. What Malcolm was trying to set up was an African American Freedom Army, and terminology of that sense was used. But very soon it was realized that there had to be a public manifestation of this organization, and the terminology OAAU would be more appropriate to what Malcolm wanted to do.

What he was really trying to create fundamentally was a Black united front—that is, a coalition of various class and strata forces inside the Black community that would be organized around the agenda of the most dispossessed strata, which he gave voice to for the first time in the twentieth century. That was the idea: that there would be an organization that would undertake total responsibility for the process of protecting, organizing, mobilizing, and struggling for the liberation of Black people and that would be an international construct. What I was trying to identify in my text [was] the various components of what Malcolm tried to put in place, to put that thing together.

JB: We'll try to come back to the OAAU a moment, but let's get back to a specific response to Manning Marable. He interviewed Muhammad Ahmed, formerly of RAM—the Revolutionary Action Movement—in his book but doesn't bring into the description the relationship between RAM and Malcolm X that you describe in much greater detail.

WS: That's right.

JB: And, in fact, he only uses his discussion [with] Ahmed to speculate as to the psychological state of Malcolm X at the end of his life as opposed of talking about, strategically and tactically and politically and ideologically, what he [Malcolm] was trying to get to. If you could start there and summarize the broader concern of Marable's book, and then we'll come back to what you do with yours.

WS: There are so many flaws in Manning's book, one sometimes doesn't know where to begin. First of all, I think it's fundamentally compromised by the necessities of the commercial market. The salacious and the sensational, which actually occupy a few pages among hundreds, are projected as the essence of the real Malcolm, compared to some alleged "idealized" Malcolm that appears in the *Autobiography*.[2] First of all, this book is an unwarranted attack on the *Autobiography*. And I would say up front not that people should read Manning's book, but definitely the starting point for any serious study of Malcolm is the *Autobiography* and will always remain so.

The second thing is that the book completely ignores two decades of scholarship on Malcolm X. Now you'll have large parts of that in his [Manning's] bibliography. But it seems to me [that], in many ways, he wrote the book without reference to his own bibliography. For instance, I mentioned the Malcolm X Work Group, which emerged in the latter part of the 1980s. Out of that effort came two international conferences on Malcolm X and a number of books and articles and websites devoted to the serious study of Malcolm. None of that process is mentioned in Manning's book. He refuses to seriously engage other scholars and their positions in his text. He simply, in his introduction, dismisses the whole two decades of scholarship and the scholarly traditions that have emerged in African American Studies. That's a travesty that can't go without [mentioning].

Manning also distorts the meanings of Malcolm's words through selective quotations, along with his own asides and annotations, which consistently turn the meaning of Malcolm's words in a particular direction—away from revolution, away from "By Any Means Necessary," into a more narrow, confined electoral politics— [toward] what some have identified as a Social Democratic mode. One way you can get at that is through a very close analysis of the text. And, of course, when one doesn't know Malcolm's words, it's very hard to get out the text these kinds of contradictions between Malcolm and Manning, but it's essential. Fortunately, a number of us now have been looking at this text very closely and [examining] the various contradictions, line by line, between Malcolm and Manning.

I'll give you one selective manipulation. For instance, Manning said that Malcolm accepted the possibility of liberalism since he acknowledged the Declaration of Independence and the US Constitution in the OAAU's founding statement. However, Manning fails to mention, in the very next section of that OAAU founding document, where Malcolm asserts the OAAU's commitment to self-defense. In addition, Manning fails to discuss why a revolutionary might cite those two documents. Don't forget that the Declaration of Independence establishes the right of people's violent rebellion and revolution as a fundamental human right when you're oppressed. The US Constitution recognizes the right of people to keep and bear arms. Ho Chi Minh quoted the Declaration of Independence in the Vietnamese constitution, but I would not argue that that would have made Ho accepting [of] the possibility of a liberal solution in Vietnam. So you get these kinds of manipulations.

There are others I could mention. He [Marable] says, for instance, at another point, that Malcolm has finally come to the point of repudiating violence. The problem with that statement was the way he made it in the book. Manning made it as if Malcolm had, at some point, embraced not self-defense but some sort of aggressive violence against White people. And this is something that Malcolm never did and explicitly repudiated. So Manning would put words in Malcolm's mouth, and those distortions were in a particular direction. [They] repudiated the [likelihood] of considering the option of self-defense in the process of struggling for self-determination.

JB: I noticed the recent news that President Obama has refused again to join the World Conference Against Racism—convened, well, by the world itself. And given this rejection, this second refusal to participate, [he is] following right in line with President Bush's refusal to attend the first one in 2001. But it's interesting to note [that] in Marable, in the Epilogue, the World Conference Against Racism [most] likely would have been the fulfillment of Malcolm X's international vision. At the same time, he is positioning [that] Malcolm has prefigured—he said "anticipated"—the election of a Black president, saying it was the success of some kind of Black united front. Baraka has made a similar mistake. But my point being [is that] if those gatherings are the modern-day fulfillment of Malcolm's international vision, what does it mean that Obama has refused to participate in two of them while, at the same time, being fashioned by Marable and Peniel Joseph and others as the extension of the political legacy of Malcolm X and Martin Luther King?

WS: I think the most glaring contradiction between Manning's vision of Obama being the fulfillment of Malcolm is [the] bombing of Libya—that is, the first US president to launch an overt attack on an African country in the twenty-first century is Barack Obama. And there's no way you can square Malcolm's anti-war stance and his anti-NATO stance with Obama's present policy in North Africa more generally with AFRICOM [the United States Africa Command] all around the African continent. This is the most glaring example.

Of course, the deeper meaning of Obama refusing to participate in what we [call] Durban II—the follow-up of the World Conference Against Racism, Racial Discrimination, Xenophobia, and Other Forms of Racial and Ethnic Oppression—[is that] it shows that he's also not free of the Zionist lobby in the United States. That every international position he takes has to be harmonized with the interests of the state of Israel. And it shows that [that] is more important in his thinking than the needs of the African continent or African Americans, for that part. But I think if one sits down in a quiet room and systematically goes through [what] Obama says he's about, it becomes quite clear that he's not the fulfillment of Dr. King or Malcolm X.

JB: We're going to reward the patience of at least one of our callers. Good morning to you, caller.

CALLER #1: I just wanted to comment. Professor Sales, I'm not familiar with [your] work. What do you think is behind the conspiracy [that] Cornel West [raises] about Obama's ties to Zionist and Wall Street oligarchs? What is behind maligning and the ridiculing these very brave people who are speaking the truth?

WS: The mass media's been corporatized and [is] in the service of those who have no interest in the truth [or] about our oppression seeing the light of day or even the role of the present President of the United States in advancing that oppression. So it's no surprise that critics of the Obama administration are attacked and vilified. What you will not see is any of the administration's defenders engaging the criticisms being directed of the administration or Obama because their interests cannot prevail against a disinterested discussion and debate about what's going on. You get vilification and an isolation of critics of the administration.

JB: I want to remind the audience that you've been an outspoken critic of many administrations. A month or so [ago], you took part in rallies to [support] Black-led critical responses to America's foreign policy. Some observers are saying that Obama's foreign policy is worse than Bush's in this unilateral aggression overseas in Libya without consent of Congress since even Bush, no matter how we say he did it, got consent from Congress for the ultimately unjust and illegal wars that he sought to impose on the world.

WS: I think basically what we should never forget is that Barack Obama is a Harvard-trained corporate lawyer who didn't have the benefit of being raised by Black parents. So at certain crucial points in his development, he was completely outside of the main motion of African Americans. Let me be specific about that. I was very much involved with students during the anti-apartheid campaigns in the early 1980s and middle-1980s at Columbia [University], at the time Barack Obama was at Columbia. None of the activists who were involved at Columbia knew anything about the presence of Barack Obama on that campus, which tells me that, in the formative periods of his development, he was not able to benefit from that contemporary manifestation of the Black tradition of resistance. We should really never lose sight of who Obama is. And secondly, when we look at the kinds of people he surrounded himself with, his policymakers, [we see that] these are not people who are in any way indebted to the Black community or sympathetic to our tradition of resistance and struggle. When we understand who Obama is and how close he is, not to the Black community, but to the heights of the corporate elite, then we can understand why we have continuity between the Bush administration and the Obama administration. [We also see] that Obama can give a much better "cover" to imperialist escapades around the world than Bush ever could because he gives the veneer of some way being associated with the struggle against the various forces that he, in fact, represents.

JB: I just want to remind people who are not familiar with Professor Sales's work in general and specifically this book, *From Civil Rights to Black Liberation: Malcolm X and the Organization of Afro-American Unity*, [that] if you want to get an overview of the trajectories within Black liberation politics specifically with how they impacted Malcolm X and engage in a comparison-contrast between what Sales and others have done and what Marable has done, you can just simply look at the sections that I have here in front of me, where Professor Sales breaks [this] down [in his chapter], "The OAAU and the Politics of the Black United Front." There's [another] section here, "The Basic Aims and Objectives of the OAAU," [and others]: "The OAAU Structure and Activities," "The OAAU Liberation School," "The Quest for International and Pan-Africanist Legitimacy for the OAAU," "The OAAU and the Civil Rights Movement: Building the United Front," "The OAAU and Developing a Student Movement," [and] "The Black Student Movement and the OAAU." Just in these brief pages and sections, not to mention the rest of the book itself, you see not only what Marable did not do but the trajectories and tendencies within Black American struggle and politics that impacted Malcolm and were impacted by Malcolm that are left out of many discussions about Malcolm by Marable and by many others.

Caller, thank you for your patience...

CALLER #2: Thanks for the discussion. It's a great one. I have not read Professor Sales's book. I'm ashamed to say that, but I will pick it up because it [is about] a very special point of Malcolm's life we need to know about. I have read Marable's book. He seems to dismiss Dr. John Henrik

Clarke's contribution. He seems to miss many of the militant activists, the radical aspects. I wanted to know Professor Sales's opinions of this, and if he mentioned Dr. Clarke in his book.

JB: Great question. Professor Sales?

WS: Dr. Clarke was one of my mentors. I learned African American history from Dr. Clarke, and I called upon him extensively in the research of the creation of the OAAU. He was central to that process. It was Dr. Clarke who helped Malcolm crystallize his idea of a hemispheric affiliate of the Organization of African Unity. Now one of the reasons Manning couldn't deal with the role of Dr. Clarke and the other Black nationalists is that Manning is not sympathetic to, nor does he understand, Black nationalism. Therefore, the few glimpses you get of his analysis of Black nationalism in the text are distorted and really reflect stereotypes of Black nationalism that originate in the White majoritarian sectors of our society.

You can't understand Malcolm without a detailed understanding of Black Nationalism. And the development of Black Nationalism in the 1960s—its much more explicit Pan-Africanism, how the class component gets introduced into Black Nationalism, how it moves from a cultural nationalism to a revolutionary Black Nationalism—none of this is understood by Manning, and none of this is understood by Manning on how it impacts Malcolm's development.

JB: And to answer the question, Dr. Clarke is referenced on several occasions in the book as well as the other important nationalists often ignored by some of the discussions.

CALLER #3: Thank you for letting me speak....I am an uneducated man....I do see the President as a scrim or a draw curtain of imperialism....To use him [a mixed-race person, who is not oriented to struggle because of that] as a go-between is certainly an opportunity for an imperialistic White power structure of this entire world. So give me your thoughts of my uneducated response. [Laughs]

JB: [Laughs] Bob Marley said, "I have no education, only inspiration. If I had been educationed, I'd be a…fool." I left out a word there, but I think that's appropriate here. Professor Sales, I'm going to ask you for a concluding comment because we're up against the end of the program. Please go ahead.

WS: In the last twenty-five to thirty years, we've had inside the Black community the maturation of a bourgeoisie that has no allegiance to the community. While some of those people may be of mixed race, mixed race is not a defining characteristic of the group. While Barack Obama, for instance, is of mixed race, Clarence Thomas is not. What's more important is the *class* interests of the group, and Obama fits squarely inside that development.

What I can say in summarizing Malcolm and the OAAU is that the OAAU was Malcolm's organizational attempt to give Black people an international personality and to organize us as a legitimate Black Liberation Movement. And even though it wasn't conceived as an inter-class united front, it put the interests of the poorest and most dispossessed Black people at the center of that effort. That is, Malcolm took into account explicitly the whole question of class. And then, when he talked about Blackness or, more specifically, what we might call "the cultural question," he always tried to root Black peoples' notion of racial identity in the cultural characteristics of what he called "the field Negro": the class of Black people who were most dispossessed and oppressed and [who] in no way identified with their oppressor. And so, today what we learn from Malcolm is that a part of our liberation as a people must be to develop this notion of peoplehood and the fundamental human rights that are associated with peoplehood—to develop this notion of Black culture that's rooted in the most dispossessed and oppressed Black people and their need for struggle.

And Rosemari Mealy was absolutely correct. One of the most important transformations that Malcolm was ever to experience was the realization of the very powerful and essential role that women played in the struggle for liberation and his new conception of the role for Black women. No legitimate scholar of Malcolm should ignore this.

And lastly, one cannot come to grips with Malcolm without a detailed discussion of the role of violence and self-defense and how that's an issue that has to be taken up. And what's so heroic about Malcolm is that he did, in fact, seriously engage in that whole discussion. What do you do when somebody's coming to destroy you as a people? What rights do you have? You have the right to resist. You have the right of self-defense. How should that right be exercised? Do you really have a choice? If you want to be free, if you're a nation and you want to be free, history tells us that, out of necessity, that's a violent process. Malcolm did not look away from that. He did not step way from that and all of its implications. And we have to thank him for that.

ENDNOTES

1 This interview aired on Ball's radio program, "Super Funky Soul Power Hour," on June 3, 2011. Fully archived audio of the complete interview can be found online at: http://www.voxunion.com/malcolm-x-and-the-oaauafro-american-freedom-fighters/.

2 Sales is referring here to *The Autobiography of Malcolm X: As Told to Alex Haley* (New York: Grove Press, 1965).

ZAK KONDO

Jared Ball Interview with Zak Kondo, April 11, 2011[1]

JB: Please summarize your theory of the assassination of Malcolm X.

ZK: ...I began to expand my thesis and had to do a lot more research. Doing the research was very painstaking. If you read my book, there are almost 1,300 endnotes. It took me eleven years from start to finish to do that book. I read tens of thousands of government documents, primarily FBI documents. I read everything that was published on Malcolm X. I got to know Malcolm's family... Malcolm's brothers, Wilfred and Philbert and Robert; Malcolm's younger brother, who wrote the introduction to my book. And so, anyway, when I initially began researching the assassination of Malcolm X, I had a political motive. My political motive was [that] I couldn't accept the idea that the Nation of Islam killed Malcolm or was even involved in Malcolm's assassination.

So when I began this book, it was designed primarily to exonerate, to free the Nation of Islam from any dealings with Malcolm's assassination. And as I began to do my research, I began to realize that the Nation of Islam was, in fact, involved in Malcolm's assassination. But, of course, I also wanted to figure out the other forces who were involved. So, in the end, after my eleven years of study, I found that basically three forces came together to assassinate Malcolm: the Nation of Islam, from which the assassins came; the Federal Bureau of Investigation—that is, the FBI, [which] basically, in many ways, helped to set up Malcolm to be murdered through all types of counterintelligence techniques and tactics; and then the third group was the NYPD, the New York City Police Department, but specifically what they called the "Red Squad"—the secret counterintelligence unit known as BOSSI: the Bureau of Special Services and Investigations.[2] My research found that these three forces together, playing different roles, were responsible for the assassination of Malcolm X.

JB: What threat to the state did Malcolm X represent?

ZK: Let me start first with the FBI. Malcolm was a danger, both domestically and internationally, to the FBI. What you have to keep in mind is that the Federal Bureau of Investigation, during the 1950s, during the 1960s, was engaged in some of the most amoral, unethical, violent, and despicable operations that you could ever imagine against what they referred to as "domestic dissidents"—that is, those people who lived within the United States who may have been critical of the United States or may have been critical of the government. The truth of the matter is that FBI Director J. Edgar Hoover, who pretty much made the bureau a mirror of himself, had issues with people over almost anything imaginable, and that would have been grounds for him and the FBI to basically come after you. I don't say that loosely at all. The FBI—during the 40s, 50s, 60s, and even after Hoover's death—didn't need a whole lot of reasons but, for Malcolm, they had a whole *bunch* of reasons!

First off, Malcolm was affiliated with some of the most radical movements in the United States at that particular time—the Revolutionary Action Movement (RAM), for example. If you read FBI documents on Malcolm, they [agents] always had a subsection in the various documents in which they would isolate his relationship with the Revolutionary Action Movement, which was basically a group of some of our most important revolutionaries in the US [during the 60's]. These were Africans who pretty much believed that the only way for us to be empowered was through violent revolution. So [the FBI] had Malcolm affiliated with them, etc., etc., etc. during this particular time, up until 1964 and 1965.

For example, Malcolm X gave a speech on April 3, 1964, in Cleveland, Ohio, in which he basically talked about Black revolution. These were the types of things that the FBI [was] basically concerned about, and they would have agents there. They [the FBI] would have informants there [and] they would record and analyze his speeches. If you go back to the spring of 1964, Malcolm constantly talked about the importance of Africans organizing rifle clubs. Well, in his files, the FBI would have a section dealing with Malcolm and rifle clubs. So these were the types of things, on the domestic level, that made Malcolm X a threat.

But he was probably viewed more as a threat on the international level than anything else. Malcolm really became, with all due respect to Paul Robeson and, of course, [Marcus] Garvey, Malcolm was probably the most important internationalist that the African community in the United States ever produced. For example, in 1964, Malcolm spent twenty-five weeks in Africa and Asia. While in these places, he met with several heads of state. Wherever he went, people already knew who Malcolm X was. Of course, what he was trying to do was forge relationships between Africans in the Diaspora and, specifically, Africans from the United States, and, of course, Africans on the continent. He was also trying to make the OAAU, the Organization of Afro-American Unity, which is an organization he founded in June of 1964... a part of the OAU, the Organization of African Unity. And, of course, [the federal government] made note of each of these things. And so, my point is that between Malcolm's domestic radicalism and Malcolm's internationalism, Malcolm was viewed as a major threat to the United States.

And the other thing, too, that you always have to keep in mind [is that] Malcolm was probably one of the most effective critics of the United States during this time. And you have to be sensitive to the fact that this was during the Cold War, in which the United States was constantly sensitive to how it was being portrayed [globally]. And you got Malcolm going all over the world basically talking about the hypocrisy of the United States—how the United States be talking about democracy on the one hand and then Jim Crowism was still alive and well on the other. These types of things very much embarrassed the United States, and we have all types of documents—State Department documents, CIA documents, and, of course, the FBI documents—in which members of the White power structure were constantly talking about their concerns over Malcolm's constant internationalism and how it was going to impact on American foreign policy and America's international image throughout the world.

JB: So what then are your thoughts on Marable's *Malcolm X*?

ZK: The Marable book is interesting. First of all, I'm glad that the book is out because what it has done is to spark a new interest in Malcolm. What I think is very disappointing is the focus of the book, the fact that Marable, it seems, was very interested in what I refer to as "tabloid issues." On the one hand, he wanted to write the definitive study on Malcolm X; then, on the other hand, he seemed committed to go underneath Malcolm's sheets. He [was] trying to pull out things that his publisher is marketing as new information.

Like, for example, there is this new thing going around the Internet now that Marable uncovered the fact that Malcolm *may have had* what they're defining as "gay liaisons" back when he was a young hood in his late teens or early twenties. Well, if you read Bruce Perry—he published a book in 1991 called *Malcolm X: The Life of the Man Who Changed Black America*—... he basically made the same accusations. It didn't get no play [then, or since], although it did give some people in the gay community an opportunity to say, "Well, Malcolm may have been one of us." Other than that, it didn't go anywhere. Well, all Marable has done is pretty much repackaged that story line as new information, and now they are marketing it like this is something extraordinary. The truth is, as was the problem with the Perry book, the evidence that this information is based on is not credible enough to really be able to measure it one way or another.[3]

Some of the other things, which, in some ways, [are] actually kind of comical [in Marable's book are] that more information about this particular book is focused on the assassination than anything else. Now, I had some conversations with Marable. We were working on this program together to try to get Malcolm's lone assassin—who is still alive—we were trying to figure out a way to get him in prison. And it's kind of interesting that when I talked to Marable, he was basically saying to me that my book was extraordinary and that [he and other scholars "owe" me] this and that. And so, it's curious that when [his] book comes out, I noticed he didn't interview me for the book with regards to the assassination. I'm going through the book, and I was surprised to find that what he does with me is he [cites] me as a "see also" citation. He didn't even use me as a *footnote*!

But this is somewhat ironic. As you go through his book, if you read my book first and then you go through his book, what you are going to basically see is that all he's done is to regurgitate my thesis. He's regurgitating pretty much the same information that I got in my book. He may rephrase things here or there, but he's not giving attribution. That's a little disappointing.

Then, as you go through his book, you begin to realize that in order to market this book as if it's doing something new, he does that with a lot of people. I noticed [that] he does that with Perry. The only people he really gives credit to, I noticed, he gives Peter Goldman quite a bit of play. Peter Goldman published a book in 1973 called *The Death and Life of Malcolm X,* and he added an afterword in 1979. He was a senior editor of *Newsweek* magazine. And my book pretty much goes after [Goldman's] quite a bit.

So it's an interesting situation here because I'm not seeing a whole lot of new information from [Marable's] book, although they want to market it like this guy has broken this new ground. Maybe it's just me. Maybe I'm just too close to the subject matter, but I ain't seein' it! It's unfortunate that Marable died last week because we can't ask him, we can't debate him, we can't engage him, we can't dialogue with him, we can't call him out.

One of the other tragedies is that the graduate students who were his assistants, who helped him to do the research, from what I can gather with regard to them, they're not going to be much help in all this either because it seems like, even if they did some of the research, they don't seem to know much about what's going on with [it]. That's one of the tragedies: [Marable] basically left us with a mess, but [he's] not in a position to clean it up. We can't clean this mess up, and yet, if he gets his way, this book will redefine Malcolm X.

JB: While some of our differences with Marable's work are straightforward [and] easily identified, others are far more complicated or nuanced. Regardless of all the debate around the content or body of Marable's book, one area where I am absolute is in my complete disagreement with Marable's conclusions. Examples of this include my disagreement with the way Marable describes Frantz Fanon's views on race [and] the end of racial hierarchies. [Also] Marable's need, much like [that of] his protégé, Peniel Joseph, to describe Barack Obama as an extension of some Black Nationalist electoral shift in the balance of power, which I think itself extends from Marable's poor representations of Malcolm's legendary speech, "The Ballot or the Bullet"—a speech that had nothing to do with using the vote to produce [a] kind of Wall Street-funded, Africa-bombing, poor-child-defunding, [General Electric]-jobs-adviser-having, nuclear-energy-lobbyist-Chief-of-Staff-having, public-education-crippling-President—regardless of her or his color.

Could you then respond to two other areas of Marable's work ... on Malcolm X with which I have serious issues: the first being Marable's description of the 2001 World Conference Against Racism in South Africa as being "in many ways the fulfillment of Malcolm's international vision"; and [the second being] Marable also saying, "In the final months of his life Malcolm resisted identification as a Black nationalist seeking ideological shelter under the race-neutral concepts of pan-Africanism and Third World revolution." I have to note that Obama refused to participate in the follow up to the World Conference Against Racism in 2009.

ZK: The new thing in town among Africans of the so-called Left is this—and it's not really new—but [it's] this whole anti-racism thing. Malcolm, I don't think, would fit in that. Malcolm wasn't just about anti-racism. Malcolm was about destroying White supremacy. What I'm suggesting here is that Malcolm's focus wasn't in trying to save anybody from racism. As far as White people were concerned, he wasn't even interested in trying to save White people. Malcolm's philosophy [was]: What do we do to stop racism from oppressing my people?

Now, would Malcolm have attended that particular conference? I don't know, but I don't think I would bet much money on it, and I certainly wouldn't think it as being real responsible to make it seem as though a conference like that is what really defines Malcolm. [That] is what it seems to me [Marable] is saying ... [that this] was Malcolm's mission. I don't think so. Malcolm was about empowering African people, and a conference like that, to me, doesn't seem like it would do anything necessarily to empower African people.

Black Nationalism primarily deals with domestic [North] America—that is, [with] Africans in the United States developing a nation within a nation. Clearly, Malcolm was about Pan-Africanism—that's real clear. Malcolm was scheduled to be the main attraction at what was called the Afro-Asian Conference, scheduled for June, 1965, in Indonesia. You could make an argument that certainly Malcolm appreciated so-called Third Worldism in addition to Pan-Africanism. So, on that level, I would argue that [Marable did] make a reasonable argument that Malcolm did embrace Pan-Africanism and that Malcolm was opening up as far as other people of color [were concerned]. And the fact that [Malcolm] went to Asia and African throughout 1964, I think, substantiates that, in and of itself.

But one does not exclude the other. Just because there might be something to that doesn't mean necessarily that [Malcolm] was pulling away from Black Nationalism. I think, clearly, Malcolm was a Black Nationalist. Now, was he *the* Black Nationalist of the US organization? Was he *the* Black Nationalist of some of the other, more defined Black Nationalist organizations of the 1960s? I would suggest to you that Malcolm's Black Nationalism, in many ways, was broader. Malcolm embraced a more broad-based Black Nationalism. But I would suggest to you that Malcolm died as a Black Nationalist, Malcolm died as a Pan-Africanist, and Malcolm died as a so-called orthodox Sunni Muslim.

JB: And then what of the last known living assassin of Malcolm X, William Bradley?

ZK: Right now, there are two actual assassins of Malcolm X. There was a five-man murder team that killed Malcolm on February 21, 1965, at 3:10 p.m. at the Audubon Ballroom in New York City. Two of them are still alive. One [is] Talmadge Hayer, who fired the forty-five [pistol] and did time for killing Malcolm. The other is Bradley, who actually delivered the death blow. He's the one that fired a J. C. Higgins twelve-gauge, sawed-off, double-barreled shotgun from fifteen feet into Malcolm's chest and stomach. That's what *killed* Malcolm.

[Bradley] is also still alive. He never did a day in prison for Malcolm's assassination, although he has been in prison here and there for a total of maybe about eight or nine years for other crimes that he has committed. I give you a list at the end of my book of the five-man murder team, even though when I wrote my book four of them were still alive. The other two have since died.

And one of the things that [Marable's publishers] are marketing Marable's book for is that, you know, this great *revelation* that [he has] uncovered … .This is not new information, but they are kind of putting it out there like [it's] new information. My book deals with all of that.

ENDNOTES

1 The full interview with Zak Kondo, from which this excerpt is drawn, was conducted during one of Ball's classes at Morgan State University on April 5, 2011. That interview aired on Ball's radio program, "Super Funky Soul Power Hour," on April 11, 2011. Fully archived audio of the complete interview can be found online at: http://www.voxunion.com/malcolm-x-his-ideas-and-his-killers-w-karl-evanzz-and-zak-kondo/.

2 This unit is referred to alternately throughout Marable's book and by many other authors and reviewers, including those in this book, as simply "BOSS" rather than "BOSSI."

3 Both revelations are based on the same source—Malcolm Jarvis, known as "Shorty" in *The Autobiography of Malcolm X, As Told to Alex Haley* (New York: Grove Press, 1965.)

AMIRI BARAKA

Manning Marable's Malcolm X Book

On March 30 I waited for a car that Manning Marable was supposed to send to pick me up at my house so that we could meet later that day in his office at Columbia University because he wanted to interview me as part of an oral history project. I had met with him two weeks before to discuss how Columbia would handle my papers, that is when we scheduled this last project. But the car never came. I called another driver I knew, a friend of mine and we drove to Columbia, but Marable was not there. It seemed no one at the Africana Studies Department knew where he was. Finally some word got to me that Manning had gone back into the hospital. I went back home, the next day I got the news on the Internet that he had died.

The strangeness of that missed appointment was weird enough, but the fact that his last work on Malcolm X was to be released three days later made the whole ending of our living relationship a frustrating incomplete denouement.

Initially, a friend of mine gave me a copy of the book at a happy discount. Taking it on one of my frequent trips out of town, I began to read. I gave that first copy to my wife when I returned because she had also, as many other people had, been clamoring to read it. As well as asking me relentlessly had I read it. I bought another copy of the book at the Chicago airport, and I guess started to get into the book seriously.

A LIE OF REINVENTION

I have known Manning for a number of years. Actually I met him while he was still teaching in Colorado. I even worked under him, when I taught briefly at Columbia University, when he was chairman of the Africana Studies Department at Columbia. As well, I have appreciated one of his books, the DuBois (*Black Radical Democrat*) work and at least appreciated the theme of *How Capitalism Underdeveloped Black America*, as well as the entire stance of his acknowledgement of the important aspects of American (Black American) history, which had to be grasped.

But as recently as a few weeks ago, ironically I had written him a letter about his journal *Souls* about an essay that quoted a man[1] who had been accused of participating in the assassination, making some demeaning remarks about Malcolm. My letter questioned the "intelligence" of including the quote since it offered nothing significant to the piece. This was not just loose criticism; I really wanted to know just what purpose the inclusion served.

But with the publication of what some have called "his magnum opus" *Malcolm X: A Life of Reinvention* it is not just Marable's inclusion of tidbits of presumed sexual scandal that should interest readers that I question, but more fundamentally, *what was the consciousness that created this work?*

First of all, I don't think we can just bull's-eye the writer's intentions, we must include Marable's consciousness as the overall shaper of his intentions, as well as his method. Originally from Ohio, Marable was a freshman in college in 1969; he did not graduate until 1971. He has been attached to Academic institutions since 1974, Smith, Tuskegee, University of San Francisco, Cornell, Colgate, Purdue, Ohio State, University of Colorado, and Columbia. It is no denigration of his life to say that Manning was an academic, a well principled one, but an academic nevertheless.

But Marable did have a political aspect to his life, which I understood and why I think he was a very principled academic. He did understand that the "purely" academic was fabrication of the essentially unengaged. That whatever you might do, there was a conscious political stance that your political consciousness had to assume, even if you refused to take it. So his "membership" in the 1970's National Political Assembly chaired by Richard Hatcher, Mayor of Gary, Indiana, Rep. Charles Diggs, the congressman from Detroit and myself as chairman of the Congress of African Peoples, signified that he was aware and a partisan of that attempt to raise and institutionalize Black political consciousness as a way to organize Black people nationally to struggle for Black political power.

In 1974 Marable joined the Democratic Socialists of America (DSA), and for a time was even a Vice Chairman of that organization which is called "Left" but is not a Marxist and certainly not a Marxist-Leninist organization. It is one of those organizations like the group that split from Lenin's 2nd International, which he called socialists in word but chauvinists in reality. So that it is important that we recognize the specific political base upon which Manning's "observations" may be judged. He is not simply "observing." He is making judgments.

So, for instance, for Marable to consistently, throughout his book, call the Nation of Islam (NOI) a "sect" is a judgment not an observation. The NOI certainly has and had more influence on society than DSA, certainly on Black people. The meaning as a small breakaway group of a religious order only used now to connote a "jocular or illiterate" character (according to the Oxford English Dictionary) is spurious.

But then in relationship to revolutionary Marxism or Marxism–Leninism, DSA certainly fits the description. My point being that Marable must be judged by what he says not by what others say he "intended." The best thing about the book, of course, is that it raises Malcolm X to the height of our conversation again, and this is a very good thing in this Obama election period. (Post racial it ain't!)

The very profile of Malcolm's life, the outline of his life of struggle needs to be spread across the world again, if only to re-awaken the fiercest "blackness" in us to fight this newly packaged "same ol' same ol'" emergence of white supremacy and racism.

Whatever Marable is saying or pointing out, in the end, is to convince us of the superiority of social democracy which he refers to as "the Left," which is anything from DSA to the Trotskyists. The characterization of Bayard Rustin's "superior" reasoning in a debate with Malcolm or the response of James Farmer to Malcolm's bringing a "body guard" to Farmer's house, "Do you think I want to kill you?" tries to render Malcolm some paranoid case when indeed there were people plotting very actively to kill him.

Ultimately, it is Marable's own political line that renders the book weakened by his consistent attempts to "reduce" Malcolm's known qualities and status with many largely unsubstantiated injections, many described by Marable himself as "rumors." Is there, for instance, any real evidence of Malcolm's or Betty's sexual trysts. People who knew Charles Kenyatta, for example, in Harlem, will quickly recall a vainglorious fool & liar. Could much of this rumor material actually have come from Marable's "official" sources, the FBI, CIA, BOSS, NYPD[2], as well as those in the NOI who hated him? About Malcolm, a sentence like Marable's "That evening Sharon 6X may have joined him in his hotel" is inexcusable.

When I wrote the FBI asking them to release surveillance materials they had gathered on me, at first the director even denied such papers existed. It was Allen Ginsberg's lawyer who finally got an admission that such papers existed, and that I could get them for ten cents a page. But when I got the papers, it was my wife, Amina, who said how do we know that the information they haven't crossed out is stuff they want us to see and so confuse us about what was really going on.

I would submit that is exactly what those agencies would do in this case! To assume because you are given "access" to certain information, that that information is not "cooked," as people around law enforcement say, is to labor in deep naiveté as to whom you are dealing with!

Marable never made any pretensions about being a "revolutionary." His hookup with the DSA is open acknowledgment that he rejected Lenin's prescription for a revolutionary organization, or party of the advanced, or such concepts as "The Dictatorship of the Proletariat." In fact the DSA says they are not a party, aligning themselves very clearly with Lenin's opponents in the 2nd International.

Such people, social democrats, are open opponents of revolution, so that at base Marable was opposed to the political logic of Malcolm's efforts to make revolution. Marable is even more dismissive of the Nation of Islam which he brands a "cult" a "sect" dismissing the fact that even as a religious organization, the NOI had a distinct political message, and that it was this message, I think, more than the direct attraction of Islam, that drew the thousands to it.

If Marable was giving a deeper understanding of Elijah Muhammad's call for Five States in the South, he would have mentioned the relationship of this concept to Lenin's formulation of an Afro American Nation in the black belt South (called that because that was the largest single concentration of Afro Americans in the U.S.). It was not simply some Negro fantasy.

If Marable actually understood the political legitimacy of Malcolm's Black Nationalism and how Malcolm's constant exposure to the revolutionary aspects of the Civil Rights movement and the more militant Black Liberation Movement shaped his thinking and made his whole presentation more overtly political and that this was not only negative to the core of the NOI bureaucracy but certainly to the FBI, &c. They have even written Malcolm X was much safer to them in the Nation than as a loose cannon roaming the planet outside of it. They understood that what Malcolm was saying, even in "The Ballot or the Bullet" was dangerous stuff. That his admission that all white people might not be the Devil was not morphing into a Dr. King replica but an understanding, as he said at Oxford University, that when Black people made their revolution there would be some white people joining them.

The meeting with the Klan was not Malcolm's idea, certainly it was Elijah Muhammad's as it had been Marcus Garvey's idea before him. Malcolm's Black Nationalism became more deliberately a Revolutionary Nationalism, such as Mao Tse Tsung (or Cabral or Nkrumah) spoke of, necessary to rally the nation's forces together to make first a national revolution to overthrow foreign domination and followed by a revolution to destroy capitalism.

Importantly, Marable does draw a clearer picture of Malcolm's childhood and early days, especially indicating the Garvey influence his parents taught him and how that would make him open to what Elijah Muhammad taught, unlike the obscure flashbacks of Spike Lee's version of Malcolm's early days. Though Marable ascribes some wholly political "defiance" to the conked hair and zoot suits of the '40s rather than understanding that there was also a deep organic cultural expression that is always evident in Black life. It is not just a formal reaction to white society. African pants are similarly draped. Access to straightening combs or conkolene are a product of the period, and certainly if any straight hair is gonna be imitated, there was some here before the Latinos.

The "antibourgeois" attitude of the Black youth culture is organic and an expression of the gestalt of black life in the U.S. and Marable seems not to wholly understand it. For instance his take on BeBop as the music of "the hepcats (sic) who broke mostly sharply from swing, developing a black oriented sound at the margins of musical taste and commercialism." BeBop was a revolutionary music, dismissing Tin Pan Alley commercialism and raising the blues and improvisation again as principal to black music.

The essential "disconnection " in the book is Marable's failure to understand the revolutionary aspects of Black Nationalism, as a struggle for " Self Determination, Self Respect and Self Defense." A struggle for equal democratic rights expressed on the sidewalks of an oppressor nation by an oppressed Afro American nationality.

What the book does is try to remove Malcolm from the context and character of an Afro American revolutionary and "make him more human," by dismantling that portrait by redrawing him with the rumors, assumptions, speculations, questionable guesses and the intentionally twisted seeing of the state and his enemies.

Was Captain Joseph (who later changed his name to Yusuf Shah) close to Malcolm? He appeared on television calling Malcolm "Benedict Arnold" and told Spike Lee that I had come up to the Mosque and stood up to question Malcolm and Malcolm told me to "sit down until you get rid of that white woman." I met Malcolm only once, the month before he was murdered. This was in Muhammad Babu's room at the Waldorf Astoria. Babu had just finished leading the revolution in Zanzibar, and would later become Minister of Economics for Tanzania (which was Zanzibar and Tanganyika).

At that meeting Malcolm responded to my demeaning of the NAACP by saying I should be trying, instead, to join the NAACP, to make a point about Black people needing a "United Front." That idea was not an attempt at "trying to become respectable," to paraphrase Marable, Malcolm had come to realize that no sectarianism could make the revolution we needed. Interestingly, Stokely Carmichael (Kwame Ture) also called for the building of a Black United Front, and Martin Luther King, when he visited my house in Newark, a week before he was murdered, called for the same political strategy. It was such a front that was a major part of the national democratic coalition that elected Obama.

As for Yusuf Shah, when Spike Lee repeated Shah's wild allegations about me in his book *How I Made The Movie X [By Any Means Necessary]*, I asked a college friend of mine, who had become my part time lawyer, Hudson Reed, to file a suit against Shah demanding he be questioned in court for any "exculpatory" evidence relating to the murder of Malcolm X, particularly as to the involvement of himself and organized crime. A short time later, Shah, who had moved to Massachusetts, died in his sleep. Marable reports that Captain Joseph/Yusuf Shah's FBI file was "empty"!

It is Marable's misunderstanding of the revolutionary aspect of Black Nationalism that challenges the portrait not only of Malcolm but of the period and its organizations as well. He treats the split between Malcolm X and the NOI much like he assumes the police did. (Though this is patently false.) As a struggle between "two warring black gangs," a sect splitting from the main.

So that there is much more from Marable framing Malcolm's murder as directed by the NOI, rather than the state. Marable's general portrait of Malcolm is as a doomed and confused individual about whom he could say that "Malcolm extensively read history but he was not a historian." As if the academic title "HISTORIAN" conferred a more scientific understanding of history than any grassroots' scholar might have. Simple class bias.

To say of the NOI that it was not a radical organization obscures the Black Nationalist confrontation with the white racist oppressor nation. Marable thinks that the Trots of the SWP [Socialist Workers Party] or the members of the CP [Communist Party] or the Committees of Correspondence are more radical. That means he has not even understood Lenin's directive as pointed out in Stalin's *Foundations of Leninism*, in "The National Question,"

. . . The revolutionary character of a national movement under the conditions of imperialist oppression does not necessarily presuppose the existence of proletarian elements in the movement, the existence of a revolutionary or a republican programme of the movement, the existence of a democratic basis of the movement. The struggle that the Emir of Afghanistan is waging for the independence of Afghanistan is objectively a revolutionary struggle, despite the monarchist view of the Emir and his associates, for it weakens, disintegrates and undermines imperialism; whereas the struggle waged by such 'desperate' democrats and 'socialists', 'revolutionaries' and republicans . . . was a reactionary struggle. ...Lenin was right in saying that the national movement of the oppressed countries should be appraised not from the point of view of formal democracy but from the point of view of the actual results, as shown by the general balance sheet of struggle against imperialism.[3]

Marable thinks that the Trots like the SWP or the *soi disant* Marxists in CPUSA or the Committees of Correspondence (a breakaway from the CPUSA) or the DSA are more radical than the NOI or Malcolm X. Perhaps on paper. But not in the real world of the Harlem streets. Malcolm came out the NOI, Dr. King from the reformist SCLC. But both men were more objectively revolutionary on those Harlem streets or in those southern marches than any of the social democratic formations and the social democrats ought to face this.

Marable spends most of his time trying to make the NOI Malcolm's murderers. Information from FBI, BOSS, CIA, NYPD, would tend to push this view, for obvious reasons. In this vein Marable says that Malcolm's Africa trips "made his murder all the more necessary from an institutional standpoint." That Malcolm's actions "had been all too provocative" to Elijah Muhammad and the NOI. But what about the Imperialist U.S. state and its agencies of detection and murder? They would be more provoked and better able to end such provocation. If there's a well-known murderer of Malcolm X still running loose as Marable and others have pointed out, how is it he remains free and we must presume that those agencies of the state know this as well as Marable and the others!

But even as he keeps hammering away that it was the Nation of Islam, he still says contradictorily "The fatwa, or death warrant, may or may not have been signed by Elijah Muhammad, there is no way of knowing." Many of Marable's claims fall under the same category.

He even quotes Malcolm after he was refused entrance into France that he had been making a "serious mistake" by focusing attention on the NOI Chicago headquarters "thinking all my problems were coming from Chicago and they're not." Asked then from where, Malcolm said "From Washington."

Marable also tells us that even today the FBI refuses to release its reports on Malcolm's assassination. Yet he will quote one of those agencies without question. Of Betty Shabazz' death Marable says flatly, of Malcolm's daughter Qubilah . . . "her disturbed twelve-year old son set fire one night to his grandmother's apartment." How does he know this? Is an official government "information" release that impressive? There are many doubts about that murder; shouldn't some of them have been investigated?

Some of the characterizations in the book are simply incorrect and suffer from only knowing about the movement on paper. Marable saying about Stokely Carmichael, after splitting with "pacifist" Bob Moses and SNCC that he would subsequently join the Black Panthers is such an example. Carmichael didn't join the Panthers; he was "drafted" along with Rap Brown.

Marable says in effect that Malcolm misunderstood Martin Luther King's influence on Black people. He didn't misunderstand that influence: he was trying to provide an alternative to it. Though ultimately I believe both leaders later conclusion that a United Front would be the most formidable instrument to achieve equal rights and self-determination for the Afro American people, I would have liked to have seen Malcolm and Martin in the same organization, and for that matter Garvey & Du Bois. They could argue all day and all night and in the end some of us might not agree on the majority's decision, but like the Congress of the United States we'd have to say, "I don't even agree with that . . . but that's what we voted to do!"

Interestingly, on the back of the book are three academics who represent the same social democratic thought as Professor Marable. [Skip] Gates who disparages Africa, looks for racism in Cuba, not Cambridge, and says the Harvard Yard is his nation.

My friend Cornel West who in response to me calling out at the Left Forum, "Where are the socialists, where are the communists" shouts "I'm a Christian!" And Michael Eric Dyson who wrote a book on Dr. King calling it the "True Dr. King" somewhat like Marable's approach to Malcolm. But who and what else would you expect in the paper "Garden of Even" of "Post Racial America?" So it is necessary that we rid ourselves of the real leaders of our struggle, in favor of Academics who want to tell us we were following flawed leaders with flawed ideas. We don't need equal rights and self-determination, an appointment to an Ivy League school will do just fine.

ENDNOTES

1 This man, Thomas 15X, is the same one Marable quotes in *A Life of Reinvention* as claiming that the Nation of Islam burned Malcolm's house down.

2 These abbreviations stand for the Federal Bureau of Investigation, the Central Intelligence Agency, the Bureau of Special Services, and the New York Police Department, respectively.

3 Joseph P. Stalin, *Foundations of Leninism*, (New York: International Publishers, 1984), 77.

MARGO ARNOLD

Blues for Manning Marable

This essay's response to Marable's Malcolm X book raises issues that identify some of the dynamics that existed "below the waterline" for Marable. It isolates and explores the role played by Columbia University in its influence over Manning Marable—a member of its faculty and administration—and ultimately over the memory of Malcolm X. It also attempts to "read" Marable, the man, and to unveil some of the experiences he brought to A Life of Reinvention.

Marable's book has given us the blues.

—Black Radical Collective Consciousness[1]

In the United States Constitution, the rights of 450,000 enslaved Africans, with a history of 168 years of residency in America, were ignored. Blacks were recognized only as property. Thurgood Marshall, the first African American to sit on the Supreme Court, characterized this omission and discrepancy best when he described America's Constitution as "defective from the start."[2] Frantz Fanon claimed that Black people in American society were not even regarded as fully "human."[3] Derrick Bell assessed African Americans in the twenty-first century as being still "the people at the bottom of the well."[4]

Indeed, we Africans in America have never been regarded as truly part of the American sociopolitical system. Coping with the "truth" of the inferior status designated to Africans in the Americas has never been easy. Is it any wonder then that spirituals, jazz, hip-hop, and the blues sprang from our midst?

A LIE OF REINVENTION

Manning Marable's *Malcolm X: A Life of Reinvention* matters greatly because of the man he chose to reinvent: Malcolm X, the twentieth-century Black Nationalist leader who declared war on the status of the "Negro" in America. Malcolm taught that this status was over. The Negro, in his view, was no more—done! America instead would have to deal with African Americans, Black people who were proud of their heritage and ready to address their fate as full-fledged men and women, not as individuals counted as three-fifths of a person. No, Malcolm said, count us as *five-fifths* of a person!

Malcolm also believed that if America was not ready to give up White supremacy and superiority, then integration was not the answer to the so-called "race problem." According to the integrationists and their supporters, however, Malcolm was going too fast. He was asking for too much in the twentieth century, a mere five hundred years after the inception of the European system of Black inferiority.

Manning Marable was commissioned to halt the remnants of Malcolm's movement forty-six years after his assassination. Like Gunnar Myrdal's *An American Dilemma*,[5] that comprehensive and imposing study that was so sorely needed to help America shape a plan to address its "Negro problem" after World War II, Marable's book provides America and the world with a new, dynamic approach to its "Malcolm X problem" and a thorough revision of the legacy of Malcolm and Black Nationalism.

Marable set out in his book to prove something that he believed the world of ideas needed. He claimed that his purpose was to unveil the lesser-known layers of Malcolm's personality, to go beyond the legend of Malcolm X to remind readers that Malcolm had "the normal contradictions that all human beings have,"[6] and to address distortions in Malcolm's *The Autobiography of Malcolm X as Told to Alex Haley*.[7] As he wrote, "In many ways, . . . [the *Autobiography*] is more Haley's than its author's because Malcolm died" in February 1965 before the book was published.[8] Yet, Marable's own book is more about its author's interpretation of the Black Nationalism of the 1960s and 1970s than about the life story of Malcolm X.

Edward Carr, the renowned twentieth-century historiographer, warned that belief in historical facts independent of the interpretation of the historian is a preposterous fallacy that is hard to eradicate.[9] *A Life of Reinvention* is an irresponsible text on the life of Malcolm X, his movement, and the struggle for Black Nationalism, primarily because of its use of questionable evidence and its author's reliance on a huge number of assumptions and so-called "facts" to regulate Malcolm—speculations that often are prefaced with the words *might*, *probably*, and *may have* or couched as presumptions (e.g., "he [Malcolm] *calculated*," p. 338; "he *sensed*," p. 339; "he *believed*," p. 340; "he *expected*," p. 341; etc. [emphasis mine]).

Marable also repeatedly refers to his subject as a "militant"[10] when the most apt description of Malcolm X is that of a *revolutionary*. He further interprets Malcolm X as a man who experienced a metamorphosis from "an angry Black militant into a multicultural American icon."[11] He even presents Malcolm's wife, Betty Shabazz, as an icon of multicultural assimilation, noting that by the 1970s she "was invited as an honored guest to a Washington, DC, fundraising gala promotion for the reelection of Richard Nixon."[12] Why would Marable even include that mention? Was it to confirm his own view that Malcolm's own family wanted to obscure any attempts to remember the "angry black militant"?

Many have defended Marable's right to deliver his own perspectives on Malcolm and Malcolm's significance to the Black Nationalism movement (and to the Black Power and Black Arts movements of the same period). Critics of the book, noting that Malcolm also had a profound impact on global African revolutionary history, have considered it a turncoat text. According to Marika Sherwood, author of *Malcolm X: Visiting Abroad April 1964 – February 1965*: "The book is grossly disappointing and appears . . . to indicate that Marable did not value Malcolm X and his contributions to the still ongoing struggles."[13] Amiri

Baraka contends that Marable's work is reflective of "institutional dishonesty," a process of "knowing" where there is "no way of knowing, as evidenced in the many times Marable writes that Malcolm "misunderstood" this or that and makes claims such as "Malcolm read history but was not a historian."[14] Marable, however, claimed that *A Life of Reinvention* is an attempt to substantiate and give fresh perspectives on some important aspects of Black Nationalism in America.

To be certain, Marable's book has triggered some invigorating intellectual debates, especially in Black Studies circles. But what its author has attempted to prove in *A Life of Reinvention* has given some Black Studies scholars a special case of the blues. It gives them the blues as they struggle to understand how one such scholar can so grossly misrepresent Malcolm X's life. It also gives them the blues when that same scholar refers to the term *Black Power* as mainly a "slogan."[15]

The important question for Black Studies scholars is this: Can the academy evaluate Malcolm X, or will the community of thinkers outside academia have to take the leadership in evaluating revolutionaries? Social and cultural theorist Sylvia Wynter, in discussing Marable's book recently in an interview with Greg Thomas (one of the contributors to this volume), recalled Amiri Baraka's (then LeRoi Jones) 1963 suggestion that "we need to look at the West from a landscape outside the West"[16] to understand Marable's mission.

In that vein, revolutionary studies need to focus on the revolutionary contributions of its icons. Does the discipline of Black Studies provide the tools for understanding the character of White supremacy, the African American struggle, and the liberation fighters of the twentieth and twenty-first centuries? Does it provide the tools for understanding the contributions of Malcolm X, Robert F. Williams, Angela Davis, Amiri Baraka, Assata Shakur, Steve Biko, Elaine Brown, Stokely Carmichael, Fred Hampton, and Medgar Evers? Williams, for example, a leader of the Republic of New Africa Movement, called for retaliatory violence in the 1960s, a revolutionary stance that caused him to have to flee to Cuba and later China. Is not his revolutionary stance far more important to the liberation of African Americans than understanding any alleged idiosyncrasies of his personality or background, such as Marable attempts to do in his biography of Malcolm X?

Magnus Bassey, in his recent text, *Malcolm X and African American Self-Consciousness*, focuses on Malcolm X's contributions to global struggles against oppression and to his potential to influence today's intellectuals and activists.[17] Unlike Bassey's study, however, Marable cannot make room for a revitalization of self-determination or Black Nationalism. His avid effort to unveil Malcolm's alleged flaws includes an attempt to discredit and dismantle the remnants of Black Nationalism in the twenty-first century.

The significance of Black Nationalism will continue to be debated, but Marable's biography does not provide the depth needed to understand it. Nor does Marable achieve his stated goal of "humanizing" Malcolm X. He merely simplifies the human being who was the forerunner of the Black Nationalism, Black Power, and Black Arts movements, and whose legacy is embodied in the lyrics of Sly and the Family Stone's 1969 hit, "Stand":

Stand,
For the things you know are right,
It's the truth that the truth makes them so uptight . . .

Stand,
You've been sitting much too long.
There's a permanent crease in your right and wrong . . .

Stand,
There's a midget standing tall
And the giant beside him about to fall . . .

Stand,
Don't you know that you are free,
Well, at least in your mind if you want to be . . . [18]

Black Nationalism evolved when African Americans "stood" and addressed the ills of colonialism, neocolonialism, discrimination, White superiority, wide-scale poverty, and, simply put, the pathology of functioning as "less thans" in America. To discredit Malcolm X, who was a major catalyst of these movements, is to discredit a people's attempts at freedom and revolution and give them, collectively, the blues.

HOW DID MARABLE'S BOOK GET SO BLACK AND BLUE?

To answer this question, more light needs to be shed on Manning Marable, the man. Understanding Marable is essential to any effort to understand *his understanding* of Malcolm X's life story and his need to reinvent it.

Manning Marable was hailed as a Negro in Dayton, Ohio, when he was born in 1950. He grew into a smart kid who learned, aspired, and achieved. By 1976, when he received his PhD in American History from the University of Maryland, Marable was what Carter G. Woodson referred to as "the finished product."[19] Credentialed, proud, and recognized as a man of prestige, Marable began his work teaching, advocating, organizing, writing, and publishing important works including his syndicated newspaper column *Along the Color Line*; his books—*The Great Wells of Democracy: The Meaning of Race in American Life*; *Race, Reform and Rebellion*; and *The Autobiography of Medgar Evers*—and his preeminent reader, *Beyond Boundaries*.[20] He was a professor with currency in the field of Black Studies, who culminated his career with *Malcolm X: A Life of Reinvention.* The latter text, he asserted, would help readers become more "objective" in studying and evaluating the history of Malcolm X.[21]

Yet, Marable's final book compels reflection on who Marable became in his journey to academic recognition as well as who he *could* have become had he not internalized simple, knee-jerk reductions of Black Nationalism. To understand why he needed to "reinvent" Malcolm X, and for whom, we must first consider Marable's need to "humanize" Malcolm and make him less of a radical Black revolutionary.[22] Before doing that, however, we must recognize the many reasons why we still need to remember Malcolm X as a Black radical visionary.

Malcolm X taught a generation of African Americans the power of calling themselves by a new name—*Black*—as not only a unifying concept but as part of a new worldview. He unveiled the reality that the so-called Negroes of his day were utilizing much of their energy trying to gain acceptance by and status from Whites. His message even influenced a number of integrationists, including Robert Gore, community relations director of the Congress for Racial Equality (CORE), who stated: "I must confess that it did my heart a world of good to sit back and listen to Mr. X list the sins of the white man toward the Black man in America."[23]

Malcolm X taught that freedom from Negro status was within reach. He reinvented the Negro as Black, African American, with his brazen and profound Black Nationalist confrontation of the devastating effects of racism and oppression. He emboldened an entire generation of people to love the beauty of their own brilliance, their smiles, their styles, their rhythms, and their resistance. Other proud and strident voices came forth from his message, proclaiming that they, too, were Black and beautiful like Stokely, like Baraka, like Sonia, like Angela, like Fundi—*like Malcolm!*[24]

Malcolm used nationalism, which Maulana Karenga subsequently described as "a profound commitment to community, to peoplehood, and the right and responsibility of a people to exist,"[25] to advocate in defense of Black people and their self-interests globally. But he explained it in ways that everyday Black folk could understand, stating, for example:

"You don't stick a knife in a man's back nine inches and then pull it out six inches and say you're making progress."[26]

Malcolm's mission was to restore African Americans back to a consciousness of health and self-determination. Marable, however, seems not to value the seriousness of Malcolm's mission. Indeed, his book reflects an unswerving passion for dismissing the accomplishments of Malcolm X and the Black Nationalism movement as a whole. It further reveals Marable's investment in the premise that Malcolm's message and leadership, his call for a mental return to Africa's cultural values as a first step to liberation, was far less important than some other (and far more salacious and trivial) aspects of Malcolm's life experiences.

As Paulo Freire maintained, "reading the word" is "reading the world."[27] Malcolm knew that the mental status of African people in America is often unveiled in the ways they relate (or choose not to relate) to their own culture and race. It is evidenced in how we talk, what we value, who we value, how we dress, even how we walk. Remembering Malcolm's exhortations about the power of names and the power of who reads whom, we must resist Marable's decision to read Malcolm X through a liberal and anti–Black Nationalist, anti-revolutionary worldview.

James Baldwin once wrote that "Aunt Jemima and Uncle Tom are dead, their places taken by a group of amazingly well-adjusted young men and women . . . ferociously literate, well dressed and scrubbed, who are never laughed at . . . "[28] Those "well-adjusted" Blacks are often those well trained not to resist, either radically or ferociously. For his part, Malcolm X was ferocious in his stance against racism and oppression. *A Life of Reinvention*, on the other hand, reflects Manning Marable's performance of what W. E. B. Du Bois referred to as the Negro's "double-consciousness" or intellectual two-ness: "this sense of always looking at one's self through the eyes of others, of measuring one's soul by the tape of a world that looks on in amused contempt and pity."[29]

Marable's double-consciousness, Du Bois (and perhaps Malcolm) would contend, was rooted in the process of "seasoning" or training that took place in Barbados and other islands of the Caribbean to which enslaved Africans were brought and prepared to be "slaves," or inferiors, in the Americas. This process generated harmful psychological constructs in the minds of the enslaved, constructs that African American intellectuals must work against actively to achieve and reflect psychological health and avoid the blues.

Thus, the notion of a blues for Manning Marable is a fitting one. Marable was a scholar who worked for decades trying to make a difference, but his contributions ended up imploding on him with the publication of his final work, a book that prevents many from seeing him as any kind of visionary. To those critics, he was simply a well-trained academic and, unlike Malcolm X, neither radical, ferocious, nor revolutionary.

THE ACADEMIC APPROPRIATION OF MALCOLM X

An earlier text by Marable, *Living Black History*,[30] reveals the extent to which forces within the American power structure literally supported his work as a Columbia University professor and, more specifically, his work on this most recent biography of Malcolm X. Marable noted in that text, for example, that Columbia University owned the Audubon Ballroom where Malcolm was assassinated (it always goes back to who owns the land!), and that it, for decades, had expressed no interest in supporting the establishment of the Malcolm X Center for Self-Determination on that site. Indeed, the university opposed this move and sought to tear down the building and construct another in its place.

For more than a decade, Harlem community activists protested against the Audubon's destruction and, in 1990, an organization of community groups was formed to fight for landmark status to honor the building. They called themselves the "Save the Audubon Coalition" (STAC) and counted among their supporters attorney William Kunstler and the Center for Constitutional Rights. Their slogan was "FIGHT AGAINST COLUMBIA UNIVERSITY."

I propose that to achieve its goal of destroying the site where Malcolm X died, Columbia needed a "Negro" with enough currency in the Harlem community to advocate in its interest. Marable was given the job, and he did a fine one.

With the help of then-Mayor David Dinkins, who also later became a professor of Public Affairs at Columbia, Marable achieved a compromise that halted the Harlem protests. The compromise was that Columbia would save forty-five percent of the original Audubon building, including the site of Malcolm's death, and erect a memorial within the new building it planned to construct on the remaining land. The university also agreed to establish a Malcolm X scholarship for "minorities" seeking to attend its medical school, and (another crumb!) to give Malcolm's daughters some money. In 1995, the new building on the Audubon site opened. Only a small space and an exhibit commemorated the spot where Malcolm fell.

The first twelve pages of *A Life of Reinvention* proudly discuss this coup against the Black community of Harlem. Those pages clearly reveal that Marable was not a revolutionary (and it would probably take one to truly understand the mind and life of Malcolm X). They also show that he was no community activist or supporter of community activism, either. This was evidenced again when, ten years later, on Malcolm X's eightieth birthday (May 19, 2005), with the assistance and under the guidance of Marable, officials of Columbia University and New York City, along with the children of Malcolm and Betty (by then also deceased) and other members of their family, marked the opening of the The Malcolm X and Dr. Betty Shabazz Memorial and Education Center. The center, erected "to promote a global understanding of the universal battle against all forms of discrimination," was located in a small section of the new Audubon building.

In *Living Black History*, Marable recalls the words of Lee Bollinger, Columbia's president, who spoke at the opening ceremonies for the Betty Shabazz center and asked: "Why has it taken four decades for the memorabilia of one of black America's most illustrious giants to be archived and placed on public display?"[31] Could Marable not see the duplicity in this statement? The answer to Bollinger's question? The fear of Black Power.

Malcolm X was, to White America, "the Coming of the Lord"—that is, one sent to deliver final judgment. To African Americans, he was a giant and, as eulogized by actor Ossie Davis, "our Black Shining Prince."[32] Marable's response to that question, however, led him to criticize Betty's and Malcolm's family. He responded with not even a hint of discontent toward Columbia University or its president.

Instead, Marable facilitated the ten-year process of helping Columbia University to control the performance of memory tied to Malcolm X's assassination site. He also worked diligently for five years to get the Malcolm X Archives transferred to Columbia, meeting with the university's attorneys and those of Malcolm's widow and family, with various city officials, and with the New York Economic Development Corporation to broker an agreement.[33]

Marable may have gotten Columbia University interested in the value of Malcolm's archives, but he failed to help Columbia address the desires of its surrounding community—namely, to honor appropriately one of its (claimed) own, Malcolm X, with a landmark building. For his failure to stand up with and for the Harlem community in its quest to preserve and honor Malcolm X, Marable gave Harlemites—and, once again, Black Radical Collective Consciousness—the blues.

But making archives available to a university can be a good thing. So too can helping a university to understand the significance and importance of yielding to the voices of the community. However, the institutionalization of Black radicals and Black radicalism is dangerous. Marable's assignment culminated in the establishment, under his direction, of the Malcolm X Project at Columbia University. As the project's website notes, Columbia University made two additional major contributions to Malcolm X's legacy: (1) the contribution of a "robust, web-based, multimedia version of *The Autobiography of Malcolm X as Told to Alex Haley*"; and (2) "the research and development of a biography of Malcolm X written by Dr. Manning Marable."[34]

Marable facilitated the process of bringing Malcolm and Betty's progeny to the table to close the deal for Columbia. He then set out to do his work, in what would be his dying feat, of "reinventing" Malcolm X as a tragic, confused figure rather than as an icon of Black Nationalism and Black Power revolutionism.

ADD IT UP

Basil Davidson, African history scholar and author of *The Black Man's Burden*, reminds us of the notorious brilliance of the Europeans' master plan. That brilliance is revealed, Davidson contends, in the continuous remodeling of Eurocentric infrastructures to perpetuate racism for economic reasons. It is evidenced in the European colonialists' ability to continue to succeed in plundering African countries, even after so-called decolonization, while barely putting a dent in the wealth gained from their former colonies.[35]

A Life of Reinvention reveals that the "master's plan" is ongoing. Feeling blue for Manning Marable is an appropriate response to his Malcolm X book. Marable's fraudulent, demeaning text has backfired on him. It has reopened the floodgates for the Black Radical Collective Consciousness to give greater focus to Malcolm X and the revolutionary Black Nationalist movement.

Marable also greatly underestimated the consciousness of African Americans—those from the hip-hop generation and winding back—many of whom choose willfully to ignore his suggestion that we, as Amiri Baraka put it, "rid ourselves of the real leaders of our struggle in favor of Academics who want to tell us we were following flawed leaders with flawed ideas."[36] Were that the case, Baraka continues, "We don't need equal rights and self-determination, an appointment to an Ivy League school will do just fine."[37]

Like Baraka, the Black Radical Collective Consciousness refuses to let go of the image of Malcolm X as one of our most important revolutionary leaders. It refuses to let go, either of the iconic image, the actual person, or the ongoing revolutionary struggle that we still call "X." It further contends that Manning Marable, in *A Life of Reinvention*, reinvented himself and himself alone.

ENDNOTES

1 Black Radical Collective Consciousness can be understood as both a cultural memory and a political sensibility. The radicalness of this collective consciousness is its full emphasis on the liberation of Black people.

2 In 1987, Marshall gave a controversial speech on the occasion of the bicentennial celebrations of the US Constitution. Marshall stated, "the government [the founding fathers] devised was defective from the start, requiring several amendments, a civil war, and major social transformations to attain the system of constitutional government and its respect for the freedoms and individual rights, we hold as fundamental today." Cited in Tinsley E. Yarbrough, *The Rehnquist Court and the Constitution* (New York: Oxford University Press USA, 2001), 64–65.

3 Frantz Fanon, *The Wretched of the Earth*, New York: Grove Press, 1965; Lewis R. Gordon, "Through the Zone of Nonbeing: A Reading of *Black Skin, White Masks* in Celebration of Fanon's Eightieth Birthday," 2011, http://www.jhfc.duke.edu/wko/dossiers/1.3/lgordon.pdf.

4 Derrick Bell, *Faces at the Bottom of the Well: The Permanence of Racism*. New York: Basic Books, 1992.

5 Gunnar Myrdal, *An American Dilemma: The Negro Problem and Modern Democracy*. New York: Harper & Brothers, 1944.

6 Manning Marable, *Malcolm X: A Life of Reinvention* (New York: Viking Press, 2011), 24.

A LIE OF REINVENTION

7 Malcolm X, *The Autobiography of Malcolm X as Told to Alex Haley*. New York: Ballantine Books, 1987.

8 Marable, *Malcolm X: A Life of Reinvention*, 21.

9 Edwin Carr, *What is History?* (New York: Vintage, 1967), 12.

10 Marable, *Malcolm X: A Life of Reinvention*, 121.

11 Ibid., 7.

12 Ibid., 8.

13 Marika Sherwood, Review of *Malcolm X: A Life of Reinvention*, http://brothermalcolm.net/marable/pdf/sherwood.pdf. See also Marika Sherwood, *Malcolm X: Visiting Abroad April 1964 – February 1965*, Los Angeles, CA: Tsehai Publishers, 2011.

14 Jared Ball, "Who's Malcolm X? Amiri Baraka and Bill Fletcher Debate," *VoxUnion*, posted April 9, 2012, http://www.voxunion.com/whos-malcolm-x-amiri-baraka-and-bill-fletcher-debate.

15 Marable, *Malcolm X: A Life of Reinvention*, 28.

16 Greg Thomas, "Proud Flesh Inter/Views: Sylvia Wynter," 1999, http://www.africaresource.com/proudflesh/issue4/winter.html.

17 Magnus Bassey, *Malcolm X and African American Self-Consciousness: Black Studies*. New York: Edwin Mellen, 2005.

18 Sylvester Stewart, "Stand," San Francisco: Stone Flower Productions, 1969.

19 Carter G. Woodson, *The Mis-education of the Negro* (New York: The Associated Publishers, 1933), 52.

20 Manning Marable, *The Great Wells of Democracy: The Meaning of Race in American Life*, New York: Basic Civitas Books, 2003; Marable, *Race, Reform, and Rebellion: The Second Reconstruction and Beyond in Black America, 1945–2006* (3rd ed.), New York: Palgrave, 2005; Myrlie Evers-Williams and Manning Marable, *The Autobiography of Medgar Evers: A Hero's Life and Legacy Revealed Through His Writings, Letters, and Speeches*, New York: Basic Civitas Books, 2006; Marable, *Beyond Boundaries: The Manning Marable Reader*, New York: Paradigm, 2011.

21 Marable, *Malcolm X: A Life of Reinvention*, 34.

22 Ibid., 43.

23 Elliott Rudwick, "CORE: The Road from Interracialism to Black Power," *Nonprofit and Voluntary Sector Quarterly*, *4* (October 1972), 13.

24 Stokely Carmichael, Amiri Baraka, Sonia Sanchez, Angela Davis, Fundi (a.k.a. Bill Abernathy).

25 Maulana Karenga, *Reinventing Malcolm with Marable: (Part III)*, May 5, 2011, http://www.lasentinel.net/Reinventing-Malcolm-with-Marable-Part-III.html.

26 Malcolm X quoted in Peter Louis Goldman, *The Death and Life of Malcolm X* (Champaign-Urbana: University of Illinois Press, 1979), 16.

27 Paulo Freire and Donaldo Macedo, *Literacy: Reading the Word and the World*, New York: Praeger, 1987.

28 James Baldwin, *Notes of Native Son* (New York: Library of America, 1998), 26.

29 W. E. B. Du Bois, *The Souls of Black Folk* (Avenel, NJ: Gramercy Books; 1994/1903), 7.

30 Manning Marable, *Living Black History: How Reimagining the African Past Can Remake America's Racial Future*. New York: Basic Books, 2006.

31 Ibid., 124.

32 Ossie Davis, Eulogy delivered at the funeral of Malcolm X, Faith Temple Church of God, Harlem, New York City, February 27, 1965, httm://www.malcolmx.com/about/eulogy.html.

33 In 2002, Marable also tried to get C. L. R. James's papers transferred to Columbia University, but the C. L. R. James Cricket Research Centre Library at the Cave Hill Campus of the University of West Indies impeded this effort somewhat.

34 Columbia University Center for Contemporary Black History, Institute for Research in African-American Studies, "The Malcolm X Project at Columbia University," http://www.columbia.edu/cu/ccbh/mxp.

35 Basil Davidson, *The Black Man's Burden: Africa and the Curse of the Nation State*. New York: Three Rivers Press, 1993.

36 Amiri Baraka, "Manning Marable's Malcolm X Book," May 4, 2011, http://theBlacklistpub.ning.com/profiles/blogs/amiri-baraka-reviews-manning.*

37 Ibid.

*This essay also appears in this volume.

CHRISTOPHER M. TINSON

Manning Marable and the Triumph of American Liberalism in *Malcolm X: A Life of Reinvention*

This essay seeks to challenge the late Professor Manning Marable's reading of Malcolm X as "quintessentially American." As several other scholars in this volume have noted, Malcolm X: A Life of Reinvention *downplays the significance of the nationalist tradition out of which Malcolm X emerged. What results is a liberal reading of Malcolm X as, at best, a militant reformer who ultimately believed in the possibility of America to reform itself, not a fierce radical who worked toward revolution. By briefly tracing American liberalism as it unfolded under President Lyndon B. Johnson and revisiting Malcolm's appeal among Black radicals, and through a close reading of the Basic Unity Program of the Organization of Afro-American Unity (OAAU), this essay argues that Marable's recasting of Malcolm X in liberal terms contradicts the dynamic form of radicalism he espoused toward the end of his life.*

Give me my freedom
lest I die
for pride runs through my veins
not blood
and principles
support me so that I
with lifted head see
Liberty . . . not sky!
For I am he who
dares to say
I shall be Free, or dead—
today . . . [1]

A LIE OF REINVENTION

SIXTIES LIBERALISM, CIVIL RIGHTS, AND MALCOLM X

As far as African Americans were concerned, the height of President Johnson's Great Society reforms centered around the granting of civil rights to US racial minorities. According to historian Bruce J. Schulman, "Central to the Great Society, at the core of Johnsonian liberalism rested liberal universalism—belief in the fundamental unity and sameness of all people. For universalists, every person possessed the same intrinsic worth, deserved the same opportunities, shared the same basic aspirations."[2] Though this view was worthy of some applause, Johnson underestimated the intransigence of the southern Democrats and miscalculated the will and endurance of like-minded liberals in bringing his universalist approach into material reality. How these "same basic aspirations" would be pursued hung in the balance. Ultimately, the liberal consensus he envisioned was forced to confront the stark realities of African American life and the racial militancy that ensued.

For African Americans, the success of liberal reform would be measured by the acceleration of African Americans into the civic, political, and economic life of the country. Would they be considered American in the same way and with the same protections as White Americans? To answer this question, mainstream Civil Rights organizations such as the National Association for the Advancement of Colored People (NAACP) pushed for a strategy that emphasized integration.

Integration quickly became the watchword of the Civil Rights movement. In many ways, integration continues to define the entire era. Yet, as a central component of American liberalism in the 1960s, integration and the granting of political rights failed to generate the results it promised. Many understood quite early on that empty calls for integration without material improvement amounted to no change at all. As Steven Steinberg has written, "The demand for 'something more' than legal equality precipitated a crisis among white liberals."[3] The crisis confronting White Americans was increased racial militancy at a time when liberalism suggested that America was moving in the right direction in resolving social inequality.

Journalist Louis Lomax, writing in 1966, stated the problem of White liberalism accordingly:

> . . . white liberals don't know Negroes; they have made an intellectual commitment to be one with a people whom they have been taught to fear and have not yet learned to love. The end result of all this is a kind of awkward, up-side-down white liberal modus operandi which allows the gifted, individual Negro through the chicken wire; he is lionized; the mass Negro, however, is still denied the right to be ordinary—which is what most people, Negro and white, are. But—economic and political power; that is the thing! And white liberals are notoriously stingy with it.[4]

As far as his status as spokesperson for African Americans went, Malcolm spoke on behalf of the "mass Negro." Even in his years with the Nation of Islam (1952–1964), he argued against integration as a signifier of inevitable progress. His disagreement with the widespread usage of the term continued after his departure from the Nation of Islam (NOI). He frequently reminded audiences that integration was not equality and that it certainly was no substitute for liberation. Through his consistent criticism of American civil society's infatuation with integration, Malcolm attracted numerous younger militant activists who also perceived the shortsightedness of the approach. For them, blind appeals toward integration were anathema to the liberated future many of them envisioned.

MALCOLM AND BLACK RADICALISM

Following his departure from the NOI, Malcolm pursued a united front strategy and displayed a willingness to work with Civil Rights activists whom he had vehemently opposed earlier. The NAACP, one of the leading organizations of the Civil Rights establishment, espoused integration as early as the 1930s. Years later, it became the word most used to describe the inclusion of Black people into American civic, social, and economic life; ultimately becoming a "grand synonym" for the movement as a whole.[5] Even as he sought to establish himself among such mainstream organizations and leaders, Malcolm never substituted integration or civil rights for full dignity, respect, and human rights. He called for and imagined much more for Black people than the Civil Rights movement, the passage of legislation inspired by that movement, or American society could offer. He remained in search of true and complete human liberation, and he perceived American society as an impediment toward that end.

The radical critic Harold Cruse is considered one of the earliest theorists to identify the contradictory call for integration. Writing in the pages of *Liberator* magazine, one of the radical publications of the period, Cruse penned a two-part article, entitled "The Roots of Black Nationalism," to demonstrate the development of that belief and strategy. According to Cruse:

> The NAACP was then, as now, the leading integrationist organization among Negroes. But it is noteworthy that the word "integration" was not in vogue at that time as a synonym for "civil rights." Integration as a slogan appears to have gained wide usage during World War II and after because of the urgency of the campaign to "integrate" the armed forces.[6]

Like Cruse, Malcolm realized the limitations of the Civil Rights establishment's faithful adherence to the idea of integration. His fiery characterizations of that realization endeared him to radicals young and old. As younger radicals struggled with ways to implement and expand Malcolm's ideas, older radicals, such as the furiously critical Cruse, pushed him to identify a plan for Black liberation. However, Cruse was not alone in the call for such a plan.

Liberator magazine had tracked Malcolm's rise to national prominence since the police murder of Ronald Stokes in Los Angeles in 1962.[7] One of Malcolm's earlier interviews with the Black radical press following his break with the NOI was a conversation with *Liberator* staff writer and editorial board member Carlos Russell in May 1964.[8] In the subsequent article, Russell pressed Malcolm to provide a clear definition of his program. As his perspective evolved, however, Malcolm strained to give a precise explanation of the direction in which he was headed. Russell seemed eager to get at the core of Malcolm's thinking and probed Malcolm for a blueprint. He raised questions about Malcolm's definition of Black Nationalism, whether or not he had a position on socialism as a possible solution for Black people's needs, and whether or not a coalition with the Civil Rights establishment was worth the effort and how it would materialize. Fresh from his break with the Nation of Islam, Malcolm discussed the necessity for like-minded Black Nationalist leaders to come together and "formulate the best approach towards this end"; that approach, he sagely noted, "will not be unilateral."[9]

Russell expressed his dissatisfaction with Malcolm's answer and later editorialized his criticism, writing: "It became apparent to me that the Minister, like all of the present Negro leaders, is caught in just this trap: the 'how' to achieve their aims. The problem of the Black man in America has become a cliché, but the solution is still forthcoming. This is the real tragedy of the Black struggle—it borders on futility."[10] During the conversation, Russell directly posed the question: "Speaking of socialism . . . how come neither you nor any of the other leaders ever use the term socialism as an alternative?"[11] Malcolm responded by hinting that socialism might in fact be an answer but one that people were not prepared to contemplate, much less organize toward. Russell went on to ask Malcolm why he saw fit to join the Civil Rights struggle and if this move was contradicting his anti-interracialist perspective toward social transformation. Malcolm replied that he intended to demonstrate the ineffectiveness of fighting for civil rights in America. He further claimed that because civil rights were denied to Blacks in America, the United Nations perhaps afforded a better opportunity and a more appropriate stage on which to indict America's practice of procedural discrimination.

Given his internationalist vision, Malcolm concluded that the condition of Black people in the United States was a violation of human rights—that is, the rights belonging to people as human beings—and not merely civil rights or those belonging to a people as citizens of a given nation. This human rights approach was a hallmark of Malcolm's perspective toward the end of his life. His worldview held that Black people were a part of a world community of struggling people of color fighting for an end to their social, political, cultural, and economic subjugation under imperialism, colonialism, and American racism.

At the conclusion of his meeting with Malcolm X, Russell editorialized the following:

> Reflecting on Malcolm's remarks, I felt that there was much truth in what he said; yet, somehow, something was lacking. He gave answers, but they were slogans, ready remarks. He knew the problem, but I felt that he was struggling with the solution. One thing is sure—Malcolm X is indeed a charismatic leader; if he were able to fully integrate all of the loose ends which, at the moment, seem to escape him, in terms of economics and politics, he would indeed become the most formidable leader Black people have ever known. Secondly, he is badly in need of an organization; his mosque will not suffice.[12]

These comments reveal that Russell, though an admirer of Malcolm, perceived certain limitations in Malcolm's approach. Malcolm was evolving, but in Russell's view, he had not formed a clear path toward liberation by that point.

The *Liberator* interview especially reflects the growing expectations and interests in Malcolm among many radicals of his day. Some seemed to disparage his commitment to Islam, perhaps because they viewed that such ties distracted him from a broader, secular fight for Black liberation. Others anticipated sweeping changes from Malcolm, a program that could be quickly implemented or an organization that could carry out the work Malcolm identified as essential. Having just left the maelstrom of the NOI and facing the uncertainty of the future, a request for a precise definition from Malcolm was a remarkably tall order.

Liberator editors and staff writers Dan Watts, Larry Neal, Askia Touré, and Len Holt joined Russell in their increasing attraction to Malcolm. They watched his efforts closely and frequently opened the magazine to analyses of his ideas. As key figures of the Black Arts movement, Neal and Touré explored Malcolm's impact in the cultural as well as the political sphere.[13] In their view, Malcolm came closest to the radical politics the periodical represented. Hardly an issue passed that did not contain at least one article, letter to the editor, or editorial on Malcolm's ideas. *Liberator*'s coverage of Malcolm perhaps is best described as support peppered with criticism, though undoubtedly Malcolm was headed in a direction the publication could easily endorse.

Aside from periodic references to Malcolm and the Nation of Islam sprinkled throughout *Liberator* since the Stokes murder, several significant articles stand out. In the April 1964 issue, for example, Malcolm was pictured on the magazine's cover. Inside, Dan Watts' editorial discussed Malcolm's challenge to African Americans: to either submit to racist violence or organize for self-defense.[14] In July 1964, the periodical published a letter from Malcolm detailing his recent arrival in Ghana and his experience of being among the African American expatriate community.[15] Malcolm once again drew headlines in *Liberator*'s January 1965 issue, followed by an article discussing his significance on the international political scene.[16]

Expectedly, coverage of Malcolm's life and ideas increased after his death. In March 1965, Dan Watts' editorial, "Malcolm X: The Unfulfilled Promise" appeared.[17] In April, Malcolm was again pictured on the magazine cover, followed by an analysis of his murder collectively written by leaders of the Revolutionary Action Movement, who placed Malcolm in a revolutionary nationalist context and argued that Malcolm was killed because he had become a real threat to the American government. In the same issue, *Liberator* staff writer and Malcolm devotee Ossie Sykes penned an article recalling the week that Malcolm X died.[18] In May, staff writer C. E. Wilson's article, "Malcolm: A Tragedy of Leadership" appeared; and in June, the famed cultural critic and poet

A. B. Spellman wrote of "The Legacy of MX."[19] But more than dwelling on the questions surrounding his death, the magazine took the opportunity to call for the advancement of Malcolm's work.

In February 1966, a year following Malcolm's assassination, *Liberator* devoted an entire issue to his honor. Veteran activist and attorney Len Holt's article in that issue warned against the misuse of Malcolm's legacy. Importantly, Holt observed that, since Malcolm's death, even liberals had come around to quoting him. Worse, they were beginning to define Malcolm according to their own political beliefs. He wrote: "Before the assassination, Malcolm was the bogey-man the Civil Rights organizations (with the exception of Snick, the Student Non-Violent Coordinating Committee) castigated as 'racist' and [an] alienator of the Black masses from 'responsible' leadership. . . . Since his death they have made him a budding integrationist en route to their 'truth.'"[20] For his part, Revolutionary Action Movement member Askia Touré (then Rolland Snellings) wrote in that issue that Malcolm was an "international statesman"; but he went further, stating: "To say that he was an international statesman is simply not enough! Malik was Armageddon, the Black Nation, the soul of it, the spirit, voice, and conscience to the Dark Soul of the world."[21] Black Arts critic par excellence, Larry Neal, called Malcolm "the Conscience of Black America."[22]

Neal's article provides perhaps the best description of Malcolm's attraction to a host of younger radicals who had lost faith in the American Dream and had begun to look for alternatives to Civil Rights era liberalism. In his view:

> Malcolm forced us to see—and we were very reluctant to see it—that our "negro leaders" were begging for entry into a system, a way of life which at its root [is] corrupt and spiritually dead. Not only was there no room for us in this integrated dream; we came more and more to understand that integration meant joining with white America in the oppression of the rest of the non-white world. . . . He exposed us to ourselves.[23]

Later in the same issue, *Liberator* book reviewer Roy Johnson reviewed *The Autobiography of Malcolm X as Told to Alex Haley*. "We do not recommend this book," read the review's first line, in bold type. Johnson went on to indicate why the book failed, noting that, for him, there was "not enough emphasis on the latter part of [Malcolm's] life as international statesman and ambassador for Black America to the Bandung World."[24] Collectively, such analyses placed *Liberator* on the cutting edge of Black radical politics in this period. Though solutions to conditions facing Black life were difficult to resolve, many younger Black radicals believed Malcolm came closest to charting the way forward.

In 1968, Harold Cruse provided a genealogy of Black Power that accounted for the shift from Civil Rights liberalism to Black radicalism. Explaining the Student Nonviolent Coordinating Committee's (SNCC) radical turn, he spoke to the lack of sufficient planning in the movement as a whole, writing:

> We have a situation wherein Stokely Carmichael, who has been the most vocal exponent of Black Power within SNCC, is described as a spokesman whose strong points are not structure and plan (i.e., program); his gift is speech. The same was true of Malcolm X, who could inspire but who did not plan, structure, or plot an organized course.[25]

Though the same could be said of nearly all of radical efforts in the 1960s, the lack of a clearly defined plan was not enough to keep militants of various stripes from drawing on Malcolm for inspiration.

Malcolm's attraction amongst radical thinkers and activists was made easier by mainstream Civil Rights leaders' distance from him. For one, he had steadfastly refused nonviolence as a philosophy. While in the NOI, he was forced to hold fast to a nonviolent, or more accurately, a nonretaliatory approach to dealing with White violence toward African Americans. His thinking on this question, however, remained consistent throughout his life. Well up until his death, Malcolm maintained that the Black community had every right to defend itself against racist violence.

Unlike many of the leaders with whom he shared the political spotlight, Malcolm never saw the granting of civil rights as a panacea. It may have been a means to an end, but Malcolm never confused the two; to him, civil rights did not guarantee material improvement in Black peoples' lives. Another liability of Civil Rights liberalism for Black radicals, in Malcolm's view, was that it framed Black peoples' struggle in largely domestic terms. In other words, there was little accountability to international struggle beyond tepid endorsements of universal freedom. Undoubtedly, Civil Rights establishment leaders understood the significance of the Vietnam War and anticolonial struggles throughout Africa, Asia, and Latin America, as well as the effects of the Cold War on their political fortunes. However, it was a nonideological association. On the whole, the Civil Rights establishment extolled American interests abroad, and US-based hostility toward Soviet influence was at a premium.[26]

As the *Liberator* interview reveals, Malcolm was not one to tout socialism explicitly as the quintessential revolutionary course to pursue, although he perceived the possibilities it entailed. As a critic of global capitalism, he realized that Black liberation would include fundamentally rethinking American society and its economic structure because the masses of Black people were, as he put it, "catching hell" in all areas of their lives.[27] Malcolm's indictment of American society as a whole put him on the cutting edge of radical politics. He was far more than the "racial avenger" depicted in *A Life of Reinvention*.[28] As a result, his ideas and analyses—though still in development—formed the centerpiece of radical political perspectives available in the period.

MALCOLM AS LIBERAL: A QUESTION OF POLITICS AND IDENTITY

Marable writes that Malcolm came to look favorably on the possibility of changing the political system from within.[29] Indeed, Malcolm supported political leaders such as Congressman Adam Clayton Powell Jr., as well as local New York City activists like Jesse Gray and

Milton Galamison. This support should not be mistaken for a general belief in the political system, however. More accurately, Malcolm urged grassroots mobilization and local organizing with a critical gaze on government policy. He sought to use whatever means available to grant African Americans more control over their lives. Thus, he represented a militantly defiant engagement with American political culture.

Marable's notion that Malcolm came around to believing in a system of government that undermined Black progress is misleading. It suggests that Malcolm was beginning to back away from his earlier indictments of American society. Worse, it suggests that Malcolm somehow had pegged America wrong, and it could be reformed after all. In coming to this conclusion, Marable ignores Malcolm's frequent analogy of colonialism in describing Black life as it related to the state. Partially a result of his teachings in the NOI and partially the result of his own analysis, Malcolm argued that African Americans were more of an appendage to the state rather than full citizens. He therefore urged all Americans, especially those of African descent, to avoid uncritical, unexamined patriotism in the name of American exceptionalism. He opposed the sense that America was somehow different and unique on the world stage. Malcolm's speech at Corn Hill Methodist Church in Rochester, New York, on February 16, 1965, makes clear his views:

> The spirit of nationalism on the African continent began to collapse the powers, the colonial powers. They couldn't stay there . . . It wasn't that they wanted to go. It wasn't that all of a sudden they had become benevolent. It wasn't that all of a sudden they had ceased wanting to exploit the Black man of his natural resources. But it was the spirit of independence that was burning in the heart and mind of the Black man. . . . The colonial powers didn't leave. But what did they do? Whenever a person is playing basketball, if you watch him, if the players on the opposing team trap him and he doesn't want to get rid of or throw the ball away, he has to pass it to someone who's in the clear, who's on the same team as he. And since Belgium and France and Britain and these other colonial powers were trapped—they were exposed as colonial powers—they had to find someone who was still in the

> clear, and the only one in the clear insofar as the Africans were concerned was the United States. So they passed the ball to the United States. And this administration picked it up and ran like mad ever since.[30]

Malcolm's indictment of the US stretched from the domestic to the international, and it illuminates the major problem with Marable's quest to "read" Malcolm X as quintessentially American: it allows the ideal of American exceptionalism to shroud his contributions, thereby reducing them to a tradition of disgruntled Americanness rather than attribute his impact and ideas to the indigenous Black radical nationalist tradition to which he belongs. Malcolm X was a product of the long tradition of internationally conscious Black Nationalism rooted in eighteenth-century Black resistance to oppression, yet Marable does not attempt to connect him to the different strands of American radicalism, even if a case could be made to that effect. Instead, he opts to situate Malcolm in a liberal context of agitation, racial militancy, and reform.

A Life of Reinvention ultimately suggests a liberal reading of Malcolm's political trajectory. Whether this is done to make Malcolm more palpable to a White liberal audience or whether it is attributable to Marable's own thinking is up for debate, but if Marable does place Malcolm in liberal light, we must ask ourselves why. What is the advantage to be gained from liberalizing Malcolm? Does it amount to a de-radicalizing of Malcolm and what he represented?

According to Marable, Malcolm was beginning to rethink what it meant to be American toward the end of his life. As Marable writes: "Instead of a bloody jihad, a holy Armageddon, perhaps America could experience a nonviolent, bloodless revolution. At some point, Malcolm must have pondered the unthinkable: it was possible to be Black, a Muslim, and an American."[31] To be certain, the identity question lay at the heart of Malcolm's ideas and those of Black radicals he inspired, but nowhere in Marable's questioning of identity is Malcolm's African consciousness. If Malcolm was rethinking his relationship to the United States, he was also embracing a worldview that emphasized the Africanness of African Americans. He ultimately came to see African Americans as a dispersed African people, and he embraced a radical transnational consciousness that expanded the definition of African American to include any African descendant community anywhere in the Americas.[32]

The Basic Unity Program of the OAAU directly addresses the question of identity. In particular, it explains the move away from the term "Negro." In its place, the document states, ". . . we accept the use of Afro-American, African, and Black man in reference to persons of African heritage."[33] Given that Marable's objective was to cloak Malcolm in Americanness and in the ideals of American exceptionalism, he also should have explored the relevance of Malcolm's consciousness as an African descendant. By leaving this point unexplored, however, he reduces Malcolm's self-consciousness to that of a tattered American identity.

Perhaps the most difficult-to-digest example of Marable's liberalism is his questioning of Malcolm's unwillingness to "integrate" the OAAU. "Despite his newfound reluctance at being described as a Black nationalist," Marable writes, "Malcolm still perceived political action in distinctly racial categories, which may further explain why he made no moves to integrate his groups."[34] Here, Marable seems to have ignored the tradition of independent Black institutions. As Ernest Allen has pointed out, the form of integration that might have included the disappearance of historically Black institutions such as the Black church was out of the question even for mainstream advocates of integration.[35]

Marable glosses over the contentious nature of the question of interracial alliance in the Black Power era. The death of liberalism for many Black radicals included the abandonment of a steadfast belief in Black and White political alliances. Malcolm was not alone in his attitude that Whites could do more for Black people's causes by organizing among their own interest and identity groups than they could by joining Black organizations. It was commonly held that Whites did not join organizations but took control of them instead. Writing of this phenomenon during the period, Louis Lomax noted, "Thus it is that white liberal money and bodies have moved in and taken over every national Civil Rights organization with the exception of ACT, CORE, and the Student Nonviolent Coordinating Committee."[36] Rather than provide the context for why a Black organization such as the OAAU would prefer to restrict its membership to African descendants, Marable instead measures Malcolm's organizations by liberal standards of integration as if such a strategy would have brought the struggling new organization the stability it lacked. Such a reading suggests that liberal organizations were somehow more enlightened than Malcolm's efforts to put into practice the concepts of racial unity, autonomy, independent politics, and solidarity with anticolonial movements around the world. In liberal terms, it makes perfect sense that Marable would find fault with a racially exclusive organization; however, it is also a gross misreading of the radicalism that emerged in direct opposition to the liberal politics and ideas of the period.

Though Marable mentions the Left throughout the book, he never seems to take its politics seriously. The Left appears to stand in the way of liberalism, which is defined by gradual, incremental progress. In this regard, Marable posits Black radical perspectives as out of step and irrational. Again, readers of *A Life of Reinvention* would do well to return to the words of Harold Cruse, who ardently sought to explain the emergence of Black Nationalist thought from the perspective of a Black activist theoretician. Cruse's 1962 essay, originally published in the journal, *Studies on the Left*, entitled "Revolutionary Nationalism and the Afro-American," provides a detailed historical explanation for the development of nationalistic thinking among African Americans. In it, he effectively traces the roots of Black Nationalist thought and the emergent organizations that explicitly rejected American liberalism:

> The coming coalition of Negro organizations will contain nationalist elements in roles of conspicuous leadership. It cannot and will not be subordinate to any white groups with which it is allied. There is no longer room for the revolutionary paternalism that has been the hallmark of organizations such as the Communist Party. This is what the New Left must clearly understand in its future relations with Negro movements that are indigenous to the Negro community.[37]

Earlier in his essay, Cruse sought to provide an explanation for the emergence of the Nation of Islam. Though Malcolm outgrew that organization, it does not mean that he eschewed all of the approaches to liberation that group espoused. Indeed, Malcolm maintained the NOI belief that Black people should organize themselves and work toward their own political interests and that they should decide for themselves who their leaders were. He never abandoned racial unity despite his ongoing search for the most accurate descriptor (*nationalist, Black Nationalist, Pan-Africanist, Black internationalist, Black Muslim*, etc.) to describe his personal identity and political program.

MALCOLM AND THE OAAU CRITIQUE OF LIBERALISM

To read Malcolm's trajectory from a liberal gaze is to read him intentionally and egregiously in reverse. Malcolm frequently argued, for example, that both of America's political parties and all its branches of government were accountable for the conditions confronting Black life. He additionally claimed that the failure of the government to protect African Americans from White vigilante and state violence was a core reason many African Americans became disillusioned towards liberalism. Integration meant little to him if it could not guarantee protection of Black life. As I have stated earlier, however, integration was the key tenet of the liberal state in the 1960s as regards Black people. This realization led Malcolm X to realize the need to address the question of integration directly, and he did so in the Basic Unity Program of the OAAU, one of its founding documents. Under the heading "national concerns," in a section that outlined the group's general terminologies, that document identifies the need for Black self-determination and states emphatically that, "the exclusive ethnic quality of our unity is necessary for self-preservation." Central to this discussion, however, is the OAAU's statement on integration, which reads:

> We consider the word "integration" a misleading, false term. It carries with it certain implications to which Afro-Americans cannon subscribe. This terminology has been applied to the current regulation projects which are

> supposedly "acceptable" to some classes of society. This very "acceptable" implies some inherent superiority or inferiority instead of acknowledging the true source of the inequalities involved.
>
> We have observed that the usage of the term "integration" was designed and promoted by those persons who expect to continue a (nicer) type of ethnic discrimination and who intend to maintain social and economic control of all human contacts by means of imagery, classifications, quotas, and manipulations based on color, national origin, or "racial" background and characteristics.[38]

And finally:

> Careful evaluation of recent experiences shows that "integration" actually describes the process by which a white society is (remains) set in a position to use, whenever it chooses to use and however it chooses to use, the best talents of nonwhite people. This power-web continues to build a society wherein the best contributions of Afro-Americans, in fact of all nonwhite people, would continue to be absorbed without note or exploited to benefit a fortunate few while the masses of both white and nonwhite people would remain unequal and unbenefited [sic].[39]

Adding to this straightforward discussion of integration, the OAAU charter makes specific reference to two historic documents: the United States Constitution and the United Nations Charter of Human Rights. Marable mentions that the OAAU founding documents reference the Constitution, but he pays little attention to the emphasis they placed on the UN human rights charter as a document carrying equal weight. As the Basic Unity Program states: "We encourage the Afro-Americans to defend themselves against the wanton attacks of racist aggressors whose sole aim is to deny us the guarantees of the United Nations Charter of Human Rights and of the Constitution of the United States."[40]

The reference to these documents was part of Malcolm's well-known efforts to assert the human rights of African descendants. In his interviews and speeches, he frequently referenced the American Revolution, not in an effort to assert proudly his Americanness but rather to show

African descendants in the United States the politically contentious roots of American society. As an avid reader of history, Malcolm's goal in that regard was to explain the contemporary state of African Americans through a critical examination of America's historical underpinnings.

CONCLUSION

Despite the recent efforts to liberalize Malcolm into an iconic and acceptable American dissident, it should not be forgotten Malcolm X was a product of American repression. He was a son of America's violence and its harsh negation of Black life, not its exceptionalism. His ideas were seen as threatening to American society, and during his lifetime, his thinking was never perceived as an advancement of American ideals.

Looking for a moment at the current political era, it is hard to imagine Malcolm X as an apologist for imperialist wars or the bombing of African nations, especially under a Black presidency. Recall his consistent critique of Black traitors of Black people, most notably Moïse Tshombe in Congo.[41] Malcolm repeatedly directed fierce critique at Tshombe, labeling him a "stooge" of Western imperialism.

Malcolm X was about getting down to the source of a problem, which is the very definition of radicalism. His analyses were tight and unflinching, even as his ideas evolved and his experiences broadened. Not only was he the "Black shining prince" of radicalism,[42] he was "the apostle of defiance."[43]

Malcolm was no American patriot. He was a citizen of the African world.

ENDNOTES

1 Mari Evans, "The Insurgent," in *For Malcolm X: Poems on the Life and The Death of Malcolm X*, edited by Dudley Randall and Margaret G. Burroughs (Detroit: Broadside Press, 1969), 4.

A LIE OF REINVENTION

2 Bruce J. Schulman, *Lyndon B. Johnson and American Liberalism, A Brief Biography with Documents*, 2nd edition (Boston and New York: Bedford/ St. Martin's, 2007), 90.

3 Steven Steinberg, *Turning Back: The Retreat from Racial Justice in American Thought and Policy* (Boston: Beacon Press, 1995), 110.

4 Louis E. Lomax, "The White Liberal" in The Editors of Ebony, *The White Problem in America* (Chicago: Johnson Publishing, 1966), 44–45.

5 Ernest Allen, "Black Power and *Brown v. Board of Education*," unpublished essay, 2004.

6 Harold Cruse, "The Roots of Black Nationalism," *Liberator, 3* (March 1964), 6.

7 Daniel H. Watts and Lowell P. Beveridge Jr., *Liberator, 5* (May 1962), 3. See also, Frederick Knight, "Justifiable Homicide, Police Brutality, or Government Repression? The 1962 Police Shooting of Seven Members of the Nation of Islam," *Journal of Negro History, 2* (Spring 1994), 182–96.

8 Carlos E. Russell, "Exclusive Interview with Malcolm X: What Does Malcolm X Want?," *Liberator, 5* (May 1964), 12–13, 16.

9 Ibid., 13.

10 Ibid.

11 Ibid.

12 Ibid., 16.

13 James Smethurst, "Malcolm X and the Black Arts Movement," in *The Cambridge Companion to Malcolm X*, edited by Robert E. Terrill (Cambridge, MA: Cambridge University Press, 2010), 78–89.

14 Dan Watts, "Malcolm X: Self-Defense vs. Submission," *Liberator, 4* (April 1964), 1.

15 Malcolm X, "We Are All Blood Brothers," *Liberator, 7* (July 1964), 4–6.

16 Pearl Black, "Malcolm X Returns," *Liberator, 1* (January 1965), 5–6.

17 Daniel H. Watts, "Malcolm X: The Unfulfilled Promise," *Liberator, 3* (March 1965), 3.

18 Ossie Sykes, "The Week That Malcolm X Died," *Liberator, 4* (April 1965), 4–7.

19 C. E. Wilson, and Ossie Sykes, "Malcolm: A Tragedy of Leadership," *Liberator, 5* (May 1965), 7–10; A. B. Spellman, "The Legacy of MX," *Liberator, 6* (June 1965), 11–13.

20 Len Holt, "Malcolm X: The Mirror," *Liberator, 2* (February 1966), 4–5.

21 Askia Touré, "Malcolm X as International Statesman," *Liberator, 2* (February 1966), 6–9.

22 Lawrence P. Neal, "Malcolm and the Conscience of Black America," *Liberator, 2* (February 1966), 10–11.

23 Ibid., 10.

24 Roy M. Johnson, "Review of *The Autobiography of Malcolm X*," *Liberator, 2* (February 1966), 23.

25 Harold Cruse, "Behind the Black Power Slogan," in *Rebellion or Revolution?* (New York: Morrow, 1968), 200.

26 Mary Dudziak, *Exporting American Dreams: Thurgood Marshall's African Journey* (Oxford: Oxford University Press, 2008); Dudziak, *Cold War Civil Rights: Race and the Image of American Democracy* (Princeton and Oxford: Princeton University Press, 2000).

27 Malcolm X, "The Ballot or the Bullet," (Speech delivered April 3, 1964), in *Malcolm X Speaks,* Edited by George Breitman (New York: Grove, 1990/1965), 36.

28 Manning Marable, *Malcolm X: A Life of Reinvention* (New York: Viking Press, 2011), 300.

29 Ibid., 302.

30 Malcolm X, "Not Just an American Problem, but a World Problem," in Malcolm X, *February 1965: The Final Speeches* (New York: Pathfinder, 1992), 180–181.

31 Ibid., 285.

32 This perspective can also be found in the thinking of Afro–Puerto Rican bibliophile and archivist Arthur Schomburg at the turn of the twentieth century. See Elinor Des Verney Sinnette, *Arthur Alfonso Schomburg: Black Bibliophile and Collector, a Biography* (Detroit: Wayne State University Press, 1989). See also, Winston James, *Holding Aloft the Banner of*

Ethiopia: Caribbean Radicalism in Early Twentieth-Century America (New York: Verso, 1998), 195–231.

33 OAAU Basic Unity Program, in Malcolm X, *February 1965: The Final Speeches*, 266.

34 Marable, *Malcolm X: A Life of Reinvention*, 407.

35 Allen, *Black Power and Brown v. Board of Education*.

36 Lomax, "The White Liberal," 46.

37 Harold Cruse, "Revolutionary Nationalism and the Afro-American" in Harold Cruse, *Rebellion or Revolution?* (New York: Morrow, 1968), 96.

38 OAAU Basic Unity Program, 264.

39 Ibid., 264–265.

40 Ibid., 263.

41 For more on the Congo crisis, see Ludo De Witte, *The Assassination of Lumumba*, translated by Ann Wright and Renée Fenby (London and New York: Verso, 2001). For African Americans' identification with struggles on the African continent, see James H. Meriwether, *Proudly We Can Be Africans: Black Americans and Africa, 1935–1961* (Chapel Hill: The University of North Carolina Press, 2002).

42 Ossie Davis, Eulogy delivered at the funeral of Malcolm X, Faith Temple Church of God, Harlem, New York City, February 27, 1965, http://www.malcolmx.com/about/eulogy.html.

43 Mburumba Kerina, "Malcolm X: The Apostle of Defiance—An African View" in *Malcolm X: The Man and His Times*, edited by John Henrik Clarke (New York: Collier Books, 1969), 114–119.

TODD STEVEN BURROUGHS

Coda: Objectivity vs. Memory

One day when I was lost, I discovered a Black writer by the name of Manning Marable. I was studying journalism, in a private, predominantly White Catholic university in the midst of the Reagan era, with the clear goal of one day writing for the *New York Times*. I had just turned eighteen, a second-semester freshman working as a freelancer for the New Jersey edition of the *Afro-American* weekly newspaper chain. It was just a newspaper to me. I was a reporter, and we both (the newspaper and I) just happened to be Black.

The New Jersey *Afro* carried the national *Afro*'s opinion page, and I found there a column called "From the Grass Roots" and its weekly entry titled "Challenge to Black Journalists." The author of the piece was Manning Marable. "The white media generally refuses to admit that virtually all journalism is a form of 'propaganda' in the interests of certain political, economic and social class interests—and that Blacks' interests never surface on that agenda,"[1] Marable wrote, directly contradicting the so-called objectivity I had been taught to entrench in my reporting. I read on:

> When we read *Le Monde*, does anyone doubt that we are encountering the interpretations of French journalists, with all the historical, cultural, and political baggage of that tradition? When we read *Pravda* and *Izvestia*, no one doubts that the perspectives of Soviet writers advance a particular view on society and politics. And when one reads the *New York Times*, everything

> from the selection of stories to the orientation of the editorials represents a type of bias towards the white corporate establishment...[2]

Not surprisingly, I had a hard time absorbing Marable's perspective. I did not see how his kind of thinking was going to get me a job in White corporate America. But something kept tugging at me, so I kept reading.

> What is the social responsibility of Black journalism in the period of colorblind racial discrimination? Black writers must see themselves part of a rich historical tradition, as the latest generation in the heritage of free, democratic-oriented journalists....What is a Black journalist? As writers, as part of this tradition of Afro-American critical thought, we have a responsibility to comprehend that racism still exists, and that we should never apologize for taking an uncompromising attitude against racial inequality in our work.
>
> Poverty and hunger still exist, and are becoming worse. Unemployment, educational underdevelopment, and political underrepresentation have not yet been overcome. And our task and challenge, as Black writers, is to raise questions revealing these problems, and to write with a critical vision of social justice and human equality, the basic values which were embodied by the lives of previous generations of Black writers.[3]

I clipped out the column and put it in a notebook. It took me a few years to agree with Marable's positions, but eventually I came to terms with it and him. I even cited his work in my doctoral dissertation fifteen years later. And that is the Manning Marable I will always remember.

But that day, almost thirty years ago, has nothing to do with this day, at least not consciously, but I'm getting a little bit ahead of myself. Let's go back about a year...

So I'm getting out of a cab across the street from the Schomburg Center for Research in Black Culture in Harlem. I had decided to attend the 2011 Harlem Book Fair in general and the panel at the Schomburg on *Malcolm X: A Life of Reinvention* in particular. The panelists were poet Sonia Sanchez, one of the legends of the Black Arts Movement; Zaheer Ali, the Columbia University graduate student who had made the talk-show rounds after Marable's death and the almost-simultaneous release of that book, for which he served as Marable's head researcher; Peniel E. Joseph, the Tufts University history professor whose work chronicles aspects of the Black Power Movement; and Herb Boyd, the venerable journalist, historian, and activist (and a great friend and mentor of mine). The moderator was Yohuru Williams, associate professor of African American history at Fairfield University.

The panelists collectively praised Marable for what he did do in his life and work and were polite, not harsh, in their criticism of what he did not do. It was a scene that we journalists objectively term a "marked contrast" to the torrent of often public, often private criticism that emanated from left-of-center Black scholarly and activist circles after *A Life of Reinvention*'s publication. I looked around in vain for what newspaper reporters would term "the veteran Black activists" to literally get in line to blast *A Life of Reinvention*. When they did not appear, I began to feel a sense of tension that I could only partially identify as nervousness and some dread because I knew what had to come next.

When Williams asked for questions—not comments—from the audience, I got up, knowingly breaking the rules, and started talking about the book (the one you are reading) Jared Ball and I were planning. I was only barely able to mention that the book would be coming out soon and thanking both Black Classic Press and Third World Press for committing to publish their respective essay collections critical of *A Life of Reinvention* before Williams abruptly thanked me for my comments and moved on to the next person. Prior to Williams lowering the boom, however, Sanchez interrupted my flow, exhorting my coeditor and me to include as many women as possible in the volume. (*We tried very hard, Sister Sonia*!)

Strangely, that moment at the Harlem Book Fair felt like incidents I had read about in some of the media theory and criticism books I've read and tried to understand. In those books, left-of-center media scholars write about how "objectivity" limits the intellectual range of information given to the public. They argue that those who own and control the media only want an "acceptable" range of criticism aired and printed, with "acceptable" being defined by the owners and controllers themselves.[4] Were the Harlem Book Fair organizers and these panelists essential "operators" of a pre-determined, live, public, televised presentation of ideas? Were they doing to me, an openly harsh critic of Marable's *Malcolm X*, what African American political and cultural activists claim Whites in power have done historically, and still do, to them? (*And just where, by the way, were the veteran Black scholar-activists who were critical of Marable's Malcolm X biography that day? The ones whose powerful, hard-hitting reviews of the book I had read online? The ones who would have pushed me out of the way both that day as well as twenty years ago to critique an equally controversial biography of Malcolm by Bruce Perry, a White man?*[5]) Or, I wondered, were the organizers of the panel, which was being blasted live around the world on C-SPAN 2 and which would be forever embedded in its online archives, trying to protect a fellow New York City activist/scholar/author, now unable to defend himself?

Frankly, I remember thinking: I'm not even close to being important enough to be "censored," and I couldn't discern my censor's motives or intent for only taking questions, not comments. I could recognize, however, the *results* of this one public session: that no one on the panel represented "the harsh critical wing" of the reviewers of *A Life of Reinvention*. No harsh criticism was allowed of Marable or his controversial book on a public, televised panel at a national book fair held in Harlem, known historically as a place where Black writers, artists, activists and their audiences often speak publicly, harshly, and freely.

It all felt very (intra-racially) "objective" to me. So much for public "dialogue"!

The panel's commentary was nuanced and, admittedly—at least to this rule-breaking, sour-grapes audience member—often penetrating.

For her part, Sanchez asserted that Malcolm did not *reinvent* himself because that would suggest an ulterior motive such as the need to package oneself for a market. Instead, she claimed, Malcolm *re-imagined* himself. She questioned the rationale behind and effectiveness of Marable's oft-cited and so-called "humanization" of Malcolm, as manifested in *A Life of Reinvention* by the often-scandalous information inserted throughout on Malcolm's personal life. She also questioned how that type of insertion benefited either the scholarship on Malcolm or the book's readers, and she chided writers and historians for being too preoccupied with voyeurism. What readers should take away from the book, Sanchez concluded, is that Marable *demystified* Malcolm and showed how Malcolm demystified White America by dissecting its police force, White liberal class, government, and so on. She further noted that Marable's book offers important insights about the language of survival and resistance used by Malcolm and other leaders of his time, language she encouraged those of us in the audience to pass along to our children—and especially to President Barack Obama.

Zaheer Ali's comments confirmed something that I had originally suspected: that Marable's book started out as a political biography. Normally political biographies do not contain the extensive research and interviews of a full biography. Upon reading *A Life of Reinvention*, that point makes sense to me on many levels. It explains, for instance, why Marable only interviewed a handful of people and why he apparently did not seem to worry about why he did not interview more.

As Ali noted, Marable taught that history is "a contestation of interpretations over fact." This is a point with which I can wholeheartedly agree, but only if one actually has *all* the facts and has done *all* the research. History, Ali added, is also corroborative, and Marable (whom Ali admitted was "a little flippant" in some parts of the book) did too little of that. Ali also contended that biographers engage in a "certainty-versus-probability" contest, and again, I agree. However, they are not supposed to sacrifice the consistency of verifiable truth for a good yarn.

Nonetheless, Ali defended his mentor's sourcing and documentation, claiming that Marable took pains to label anything circumstantial—including Malcolm's alleged homosexual relationship with a White man—as just that. (*Huh? That statement made me think of how a great Black biographer, Arnold Rampersad, once wrote about how he got in hot water with the gay community because he found no evidence to confirm that his biographical subject of over a thousand or so pages, Langston Hughes, ever had a homosexual or any other kind of romantic relationship—so he simply concluded that Hughes was probably asexual.*[6]) At the Harlem Book Fair event, however, Ali dismissed those folks who were upset about Marable's book reporting of Malcolm's alleged homosexual relationship as being believers in "a 'one-drop' rule of gayness." He also asserted that every controversial allegation in the book had at least three sources. I don't know if that's true, but he may be correct—that is, if you consider secondhand sources as legitimate ones!

Peniel Joseph, a very talented writer who has described the Black Power movement in "new" and "innovative" ways, was the next panelist to speak. He described Malcolm X as a "local organizer who transformed the Black freedom struggle" and who, along with other Black civil rights activists, kept up a "long-running dialogue" with the idea of America and changed American democracy. (Joseph has been rewarded and praised in elite White circles for his portrayal of the Black Power movement in this fashion, with glowing reviews in mainstream media and interviews on public television.[7]) He repeated the claims I have heard from Zaheer Ali, Michael Eric Dyson, and other friends of Manning Marable since the Malcolm biography's publication: that many critics of *A Life of Reinvention* had only read the parts that address Malcolm's personal life and not those addressing his political one.

Herb Boyd was, as always, his very polite self, willing to take both sides in the debate. (*Those of us who are cursed to be around journalists for any length of time have gotten used to this!*) He agreed with Sanchez about squashing Marable's use of the term *reinvention* to describe Malcolm's development, and stated that he preferred instead the term *political evo-*

lution. He also urged the members of the audience to read the book in its entirety and to come to their own conclusions about it with the words: "You have that responsibility."

Normally, I would have given some of the comments I heard at the Harlem Book Fair panel—even the ones I strongly disagree with—a pass. I would have put on my (still-trying-to-be) objective journalist's hat and said, "Well, that's *their* view. Others will have different opinions, but all will have to read the whole book and make up their own minds." I would have taken my notes, written them up, penned an "objective" article, and moved on. However, since reading Manning Marable's Malcolm X book in its entirety, other perspectives—ones that reveal clearly the numerous problems I personally found with the book as well as many, many others I did not find—have demanded my serious attention.

Those additional views are best captured in the exchange of ideas and perspectives that I imagine might have taken place had several of the current volume's contributors come together to form a critical panel of their own focusing on *A Life of Reinvention*. This "invented" panel would serve as an apt and appropriate counterbalance to the "objectivity" of the Harlem Book Fair discussion. Given the comments excerpted below from their compiled essays, the exchange most likely would have gone as follows:

Mumia Abu-Jamal: Marable seems to go for the sensational rather than for that which he can substantiate.

Kali Akuno: It is the contemporary weaknesses of the Black Liberation Movement as a whole, and of its Black Nationalist wings more specifically—buttressed by imperialism's hegemonic cooptation of Afrocentrism and other liberal variants of multiculturalism into the "postracial" politics of American nationalism that define the so-called "Age of Obama"—that co-enabled the production of this work.

Kamau Franklin: Marable's work is the latest to attempt to remake or reinvent Malcolm X and turn him into a political football for political and moneyed interests....[Making Malcolm X] the embodiment of his own ideological viewpoints amounts to what I call an ivory tower assassination attempt on Malcolm X's meaning as an ideological force for Black self-determination.

William Strickland: The problems...are many and multiple. They range from historical gaffes and endless nonsequitors to key historical omissions. Manning thus becomes his own authority, quoting himself as his evidentiary source!

Raymond Winbush: The arrogance of Marable oozes out in so many places throughout the book....Marable's opinion mattered to him, just as the opinions of broadcast media journalists on Fox News and MSNBC matter to those individuals. Their listeners crave their opinions and speculations concerning contemporary political issues, and these commentators get paid, and paid well, to provide just that. Sadly, in the case of Manning Marable and his last work of speculative nonfiction on one of the great persons in the African world, opinion took precedence over originality and speculation superseded scholarship and a reliance on reliable sources and primary research.

Rosemari Mealy: This omission of women's voices amplifies the concerns of African American womanist scholars that Marable's book widens the gap in the existing literature about Malcolm X written by men because it fails to acknowledge the extraordinary contributions that African American women historically have made to constructing the leadership styles of progressive and revolutionary African American male leaders.

Greg Thomas: The noncritical discourse published *under the name* of Manning Marable amounts to simple PR for Marable's name brand, his specific academic signature, and thus for Viking Books and its parent company, Penguin Group—not to mention his institution of employment, Columbia University. Under these mantles, Malcolm X is absolutely questionable, in *every* way, while the brand of Manning Marable (i.e., his writings, motives, methods, dogmata, etc.) is absolutely unquestionable.

Sundiata Keita Cha-Jua: On analytical grounds, the verdict on *A Life of Reinvention* is mixed. For the most part, its readers learn nothing new of significance; Marable merely provides greater detail of things already known.

Eugene Puryear: Putting aside Marable's claims of having produced a definitive biography, *A Life of Reinvention* has raised more questions than answers. Some of these questions may be irresponsible and some may confuse matters that should be crystal clear, but Marable's biography of Malcolm X has at least shown the need to study and debate Malcolm's legacy and the movements from which he sprang.

Karl Evanzz: *Malcolm X: A Life of Reinvention* is an abomination. It is a cavalcade of innuendo and logical fallacy, and is largely "reinvented" from previous works on the subject.

Amiri Baraka: Some of the characterizations in the book are simply incorrect and suffer from its author only knowing about the movement on paper.

Thus, this fictitious panel might have concurred with Peniel Joseph, who stated at the Schomburg that we (meaning Black folks, I presume) "cannot have sacred cows" and that "Malcolm had no sacred cows"; and with Zaheer Ali, who maintained that "Malcolm was not a sacred cow, and neither was Manning Marable." Might then Joseph and Ali, in turn, also agree with the overriding reason for this volume?

A year later, I have finally, fully identified the source of the tension I felt sitting in the Schomburg auditorium that summer afternoon. Part of it was the realization that, at every bit of age forty-four, I am now partly yet increasingly responsible for the present and future of Black history *and* for the propagation of commonsense and proper propaganda. When Herb Boyd asked the audience of about 150 people at the Harlem Book Fair panel, most of whom looked to be under forty years old, if they had read Marable's book, less than a score of hands went up. Although the strength of this book's contributors tells me that I am far from being ideologically stranded alone on an island somewhere, I recognized then how very different the second decade of the twenty-first century is going to be for many of us who were born in the later decades of the century past.

I keep thinking about how this book might not have been necessary if the media systems I grew up with in the New York tri-state area were still in play. If *A Life of Reinvention* had come out in, say, 1988, a Black news-talk radio station named WLIB-AM, 1190 on the New York City dial, would have featured numerous detailed discussions on the book. Other discussions would have aired on a late-night, national program called "Nighttalk with Bob Law" on WLIB's rival, 1600 WWRL-AM, the flagship station of the National Black Network. Those programs would have been moderated by hosts who knew they would be speaking directly and almost exclusively to Black people, so they would not have bothered with "objectivity."

I can imagine hearing John Henrik Clarke and many other Black scholars providing blistering on-air critiques of Marable's Malcolm X biography, educating young listeners like me. I can also picture myself reading a bombastic Brooklyn weekly newspaper called *The City Sun*, which would have published a special section on this intellectual controversy. Those "unapologetically Black" media venues taught by example. They never had a problem criticizing Black public figures harshly and publicly if they failed Black people.

Back then there were also several local and national television shows in the New York area—*Tony Brown's Journal*, *Like It Is*, *Essence: The Television Program*, *Positively Black*, and *Black News/The McCreary Report*, among others—that probably would have presented other balanced (read: critical) discussions and forums focusing on Manning Marable and his *A Life of Reinvention*, all for large audiences. They surely would have explored and explained the depth of Marable's mistakes. All, however, are gone now, one way or another.[8] (Ironically, that is why I think C-SPAN 2's annual airing of the Harlem Book Fair on its "Book TV" program is so important. Like the fair itself, this broadcast event is one of the few mass forums left where Black perspectives can be heard and seen, live and unedited, by large numbers of people.)

In the 1980s, I would have depended on these forums and the activists who sponsored and participated in them, to do the work we, the editors and contributors to this volume, have done today. I would have remained pretty much silent, letting those elders, Black print journalists, and broadcasters take responsibility for finding and promoting my and our collective voice. I would not have even thought twice about breaking the "rules" much less about doing so in front of a national or international television audience on C-SPAN. But clearly too much time has passed. This century demands more of me. I now bear the responsibility for that collective voice.

The remaining source of my tension also became evident as I meditated about all that has occurred around Marable and *A Life of Reinvention*. Two diametrically opposed quotes, both previously scrolling along in a loop at the bottom of my mind's television screen, began to assume prominence. The first was one stated quite plainly by a Presidential candidate in 2008. The candidate was making a great compromise address about some remarks made by his pastor. During the campaign, it was hailed as "The Race Speech" but now it is known as the "A More Perfect Union" address, presumably because it was crafted to allow the candidate to unify perfectly two audiences—the powerful and the powerless—at once. Here is the first quote:

> The profound mistake of Reverend [Jeremiah] Wright's sermons is not that he spoke about racism in our society. *It's that he spoke as if our society was static; as if no progress has been made* [emphasis mine]; as if this country—a country that has made it possible for one of his own members to run for the highest office in the land and build a coalition of White and Black;

> Latino and Asian, rich and poor, young and old—is still irrevocably bound to a tragic past. But what we know—what we have seen—is that America can change. That is the true genius of this nation. What we have already achieved gives us hope—the audacity to hope—for what we can and must achieve tomorrow.[9]

The second (and much shorter) quote, originating from the collective unconsciousness of struggle, contradicts the first more and more as that former candidate's Presidency continues. It states simply the following: "All change is not progress, as all motion is not forward." Upon reflection on that statement, how sadly appropriate it seems that Manning Marable's creation of a presumably race-neutral Malcolm X shares the same space with the racially/culturally born-neutered, or self-neutered, Barack Obama. There are times in which cultural history and cultural reality trumps objectivity, and this is one such time. Manning Marable's biography of Malcolm X occupies the space between the heralding of a new era of Black "progress" versus the ideas and beliefs of Malcolm's expanding ideas, including those "scary" Black Nationalist-Leftist-Pan-Africanist ones. In the new era, if the latter ideas are brought up today, they must be dismissed as intellectually stunted or as belonging to history itself.

The scholarship on Malcolm X has moved as a result of Marable's book, but in what direction? A new generation of Black writers and scholars is finding new ways to interpret old ideas, some of which expand people and movements into new places. However, the cost of moving into these newly gentrified intellectual neighborhoods, for some, may be too high. There are Blacks who may not know what has been lost by this gentrification, and those who understand all too well what has happened will probably be politely silent and "objective," choosing not to remember, at least not publicly.

The late Gil Scott-Heron—a great writer who lived in Harlem as did his hero, Langston Hughes—passed away about two months before the 2011 Harlem Book Fair, but Scott-Heron was crystal clear forty years ago on this problem's consequence. In the lyrics to his song, "Winter in America," a post-revolution lament that still resonates, he sang about how "ain't nobody fighting/'cause nobody knows what to save." Intellectually and historically, that time may be coming sooner than we think.

In many ways, this work's contributors have chosen to argue about a book because it was a book, *The Autobiography of Malcolm X as Told to Alex Haley*, that intellectually birthed so many of us in the first place.[10] The *Autobiography* was the book that allowed Malcolm to enter our minds, where he witnessed our rebirths. For many of us he is still there, advising ever since, like some sort of Race Man *Sensei*. It's his legacy to us.

Manning Marable's legacy is what it is, for good and ill, like every other human. He does not need *our* tribute; others will take care of that. History is more important than any biographer or biographical subject's legacy, including El-Hajj Malik El-Shabazz (Malcolm X). The issue for us is the need to preserve accurate historical memory, and to do so in concrete words and strong deeds. As contributors to this volume, we agree that Marable made decisions that produced poor history—a history that is being absorbed by an anti-intellectual popular culture via snippets of articles, brief broadcast segments, and trending tweets—about a world-historical figure. Ultimately, the biography that Marable wrote can only be countered by another, more definitive one. For us, preserving memory is more important than preserving some sort of intellectual operational unity in deference to Manning Marable's legacy or trying to figure out a way to use, or salvage, what he did with *A Life of Reinvention* for the larger Black liberation movement. The book you are reading is not that biography. Rather, we humbly offer this volume as a collection of notes for that future biography.

This book is harshly critical of Marable and his posthumously published work. Good! Harsh public criticism is the appropriate response to harsh public actions, harsh public cultural distortions, and harsh public accommodations to the first two. It is also necessary when there are too many voices, for whatever reason, that refuse to separate critique from tribute.

The undercurrent of what has been said, or not said, publicly about Manning Marable since his death and the publication of *A Life of Reinvention* has often times been predicated on the idea of not speaking ill of the dead. Bill Strickland reminds us of this in his essay in this collection, which contends that this idea was "a standard Manning did not adhere to himself." Even if he did, however, that would be irrelevant. Still, and I have no empirical evidence to substantiate this, I believe that if Marable had been White, or if he had not been the esteemed Black pioneering scholar his Black defenders claim him to be, the public reaction of many of those defenders to our collective, harsh, public critique would be, to say the least, muted.

Manning Marable should be remembered—for *all* his contributions—and the quality of those contributions should be, and will continue to be, argued and debated. But it is important to note that many of the public defenders of Marable's bad biography were in some way connected to him—personally, professionally, or both. Thus, it is important to note that the vast majority of the contributors to this volume—"as writers, as part of this tradition of Afro-American critical thought"[11]—we did not go to high school or college with Marable, we were not taught by him, nor did we lecture under him at Columbia. So we do not owe him our silence or knee-jerk defense.

But we do *owe history*. We do *owe Africana Studies*. Our larger commitment to historical memory dwarfs any concerns about offending Manning Marable's admirers, colleagues, friends, and students. History is our prime concern. Therefore, we actively and proudly choose to be intellectual squatters in the new historical neighborhoods, openly breaking the rules and happily accepting any consequences of being labeled trespassers.

ENDNOTES

1 Manning Marable, "From the Grass Roots: Challenge to Black Journalists," *The New Jersey Afro-American*, May 3, 1986, 4. Marable's self-syndicated Black newspaper column was called "From the Grass Roots" from its inception in 1976 to 1983, when he renamed it "Along the Color Line." (Apparently, the *Afro-American*, however, kept the original column name and template it made for several years afterward.) For collections of Marable's newspaper columns and some of his other brief essays for non-academic audiences, see: *From The Grassroots: Essays Toward Afro-American Liberation* (Boston: South End Press, 1980); *The Crisis of Color and Democracy: Essays on Race, Class and Power* (Monroe, ME: Common Courage Press, 1992); *Speaking Truth to Power: Essays on Race, Resistance and Radicalism* (Boulder, CO: Westview Press, 1996); *Black Liberation in Conservative America* (Boston: South End Press, 1997), and *Beyond Boundaries: The Manning Marable Reader* (Boulder, CO: Paradigm Publishing, 2011).

2 Marable, "From the Grass Roots."

3 Ibid.

4 There are at least a score of academic books on this topic published in the last three decades. Two classics by Noam Chomsky, the leftist theorist, are *Manufacturing Consent: The Political Economy of the Mass Media* (New York: Pantheon, 2002), and *Media Control: The Spectacular Achievements of Propaganda* (New York: Seven Stories Press, 2002). A list of books for more general audiences, containing insider's accounts of how mainstream mass media objectivity marginalizes many worldviews, could include Amy Goodman's *The Exception to the Rulers: Exposing Oily Politicians, War Profiteers, and the Media That Love Them* (New York: Hyperion, 2005), and Danny Schechter's *The More You Watch, The Less You Know* (New York: Seven Stories Books, 1997). For a history of this media marginalization from the perspective of race, with an emphasis on the development of media of color in the United States, see Juan Gonzalez and Joe Torres, *News for All the People: The Epic Story of Race and the American Media* (New York: Verso, 2011).

5 Bruce Perry, *Malcolm: The Life of the Man Who Changed Black America*. Barrytown, New York: Station Hill Press, 1992.

6 For Arnold Rampersad's specific discussion on Langston Hughes' sexuality versus what he found and documented as Hughes' biographer,

see the "Afterword" of *The Life of Langston Hughes: Volume II: 1914-1967, I Dream a World* (New York: Oxford University Press, 2002), 426-35. Rampersad's first volume is titled *The Life of Langston Hughes: Volume I: 1902-1941, I, Too, Sing America* (New York: Oxford University Press, 2002).

7 For an example, see *The PBS NewsHour*, "From Dark Days to Bright Nights, Reexamining the Civil Rights era," *The PBS NewsHour*, 7:11, January 18, 2010, http://www.pbs.org/newshour/bb/social_issues/jan-june10/mlk_01-18.html. The weeknight newscast did its "Conservation" segment with Joseph, a one-on-one interview, in observance of Martin Luther King, Jr.'s national holiday.

8 For an educational site on the history of Black public affairs programming from the perspective of public broadcasting, see "Broadcasting While Black," http://www.thirteen.org/broadcastingwhileblack. For some background on the shows and stations listed, see Todd Steven Burroughs, "Drums in the Global Village: Toward an Ideological History of Black Media" (Ph.D. diss., University of Maryland at College Park, 2001). For more history on these types of programs, see Devorah Heitner, "Black Power TV: A Cultural History of a National Movement of Black Public Affairs Television 1968-1980" (Ph.D. diss., Northwestern University, 2007), and Tommy Lee Lott, "Documenting Social Issues: *Black Journal*, 1968-1970," in Phyllis R. Klotman and Janet K. Cutler, eds., *Struggles for Representation: African-American Documentary Film and Video* (Bloomington, Indiana: Indiana University Press, 1999), 71-98. For a history of *The City Sun* newspaper, see Wayne Dawkins, *City Son: Andrew W. Cooper's Impact on Modern-Day Brooklyn* (Jackson: University Press of Mississippi Press, 2012).

9 Barack Obama, "A More Perfect Union," Philadelphia, Pennsylvania, March 18, 2008, https://my.barackobama.com/page/content/hisownwords.

10 Malcolm X, *The Autobiography of Malcolm X as Told to Alex Haley*. New York: Grove Press, 1965.

11 Marable, "From the Grassroots."

ABOUT THE EDITORS

Jared A. Ball is the father of two brilliant and adorable daughters, Maisi and Marley, and the fortunate husband of Nelisbeth Yariani Ball. After that, he is an associate professor of Communication Studies at Morgan State University. Ball's research interests include a focus on the interaction among colonialism, mass media theory, and history as well as on the development of underground journalism and cultural expression as mechanisms of social movements and political organization. Ball is the founder and producer of *FreeMix Radio: The Original Mixtape Radio Show*, an emancipatory, journalistic, political mixtape. He also edits and produces a weekly radio column for BlackAgendaReport.com; and produces and hosts *The Super Funky Soul Power Hour*, which airs on Fridays from 10 a.m. to 11 a.m. (EST) on Washington, DC's WPFW 89.3 FM Pacifica Radio. He is the author of a chapter, "Communicating Liberation in Washington, DC," in *Democratic Destiny and the District of Columbia: Federal Politics and Public Policy*, edited by Ronald Walters and Toni-Michelle Travis (Lexington Books, 2010); and the author of *I MiX What I Like: A MiXtape Manifesto* (AK Press, 2011). He can be found online at www.imixwhatilike.org.

Todd Steven Burroughs is a lecturer in the Department of Communication Studies at Morgan State University and a lifelong student of the history of Black media. He is also a journalist with more than twenty-five years of experience in mass media. He is the co-author, with award-winning journalist and historian Herb Boyd, of *Civil Rights: Yesterday and Today* (West Side, 2010); and a former national correspondent, columnist, and news editor for the National Newspaper Publishers Association (NNPA) News Service. Burroughs has written for national magazines such as *The Source*, *ColorLines*, *Black Issues Book Review*, and *The Crisis*; websites such as *AOLBlackVoices* (now *HuffPostBlackVoices*); newspapers such as *The New York Amsterdam News* and *The* (Newark, NJ) *Star-Ledger*; and wire services such as the NNPA, the Capital News Service (of the University of Maryland's Philip Merrill College of Journalism), and the Knight-Ridder Wire. He is currently writing a journalistic biography of death-row journalist Mumia Abu-Jamal.

ABOUT THE CONTRIBUTORS

Mumia Abu-Jamal—Black Panther, journalist, prolific author, and follower of John Afrika and the MOVE Movement–has been incarcerated as a political prisoner in the United States for more than thirty years. He is the author of several books and other commentaries written during his imprisonment, notably *Live from Death Row* (1995). His commitment to the Black liberation movement has been likened to that of Malcolm X by none other than Assata Shakur, perhaps the single greatest symbol of that movement and of political prisoners alive today. Although Abu-Jamal's death-penalty conviction was rescinded in 2011 and he was transferred out of solitary confinement and into general population in 2012, he remains a prisoner of the Pennsylvania Department of Corrections without possibility of parole.

Kali Akuno (*kaliakuno@gmail.com*) is the national organizer for the Malcolm X Grassroots Movement. He previously served as the acting co-director of the U.S. Human Rights Network and as executive director of the Peoples' Hurricane Relief Fund, based in New Orleans, Louisiana. Akuno is a co-founder of the School of Social Justice and Community Development, a public school serving the academic needs of low-income African American and Latino communities in Oakland, California. His organizational as well as intellectual work makes an important contribution to the legacy of Malcolm X and to this volume.

Margo Arnold, a.k.a. Margo Crawford, is an independent scholar of history whose research focuses on the process of "seasoning"— that brutal ordeal through which newly captured Africans were physically prepared for sale in the West Indies and psychologically conditioned for slavery in the Americas—and its impact on current education structures. She has taught African American history at Northeastern Illinois University, Loyola University, Barat College, and Roosevelt University. She is an independent contractor with the City Colleges of Chicago, the Provident Foundation, and the Chicago Public Schools American History Project. She is the former director of the Sonja Haynes Stone Black Cultural Center at The University of North Carolina at Chapel Hill and the former principal of the DePaul University Alternative High School in the Cabrini Green community of Chicago.

A. Peter Bailey (*apeterb@verizon.net*), a former *Ebony* magazine editor, is an original member of the Organization of Afro-American Unity (OAAU), which was founded in 1964 by Malcolm X. Bailey was also the editor of *Blacklash,* the OAAU news organ, *and* he assisted John Henrik Clarke with the editing of *Malcolm X: The Man and His Times* (1991). He is the co-author, with Malcolm X's nephew, Rodnell P. Collins, of *Seventh Child: A Family Memoir of Malcolm X* (2002).

Amiri Baraka is the author of over forty books of poetry, essays, plays, and music history and criticism. Recognized internationally as a poet icon and revolutionary political activist, Baraka has read his poetry and lectured on cultural and political issues extensively in the United States, the Caribbean, Africa, and Europe. His awards and honors include an Obie, the American Academy of Arts and Letters award; the James Weldon Johnson Medal for contributions to the arts; and Rockefeller Foundation and National Endowment for the Arts grants. He is currently professor emeritus at the State University of New York at Stony Brook and the poet laureate of New Jersey. Baraka lives in Newark, where he directs the word-music ensemble, Blue Ark: The Word Ship.

Sundiata Keita Cha-Jua (*schajua@illinois.edu*) is an associate professor in the Department of History and the Department of African American Studies at the University of Illinois. He previously taught in the history department and directed the Black Studies Program at the University of Missouri at Columbia, and taught history at Pennsylvania State University and Southern Illinois University at Edwardsville. In 1992, Cha-Jua received advanced certificates in Black Studies from Northeastern University and from the National Council for Black Studies' Director's Institute. He is a member of several professional associations, including the Association for the Study of Afro-American Life and History, the National Council for Black Studies (of which he is a member of the National Board), and the Organization of American Historians. His research interests include African American community formation, Black radicalism and nationalism, race and racism, historical materialism, and culturally relevant pedagogy. He is the author of *America's First Black Town: Brooklyn, Illinois, 1830-1915* (2000) and several scholarly articles that have been published in *The Black Scholar*, *The Journal of American History*, *The Journal of Black Studies*, *Nature, Society & Thought*, and *Souls*, among other journals.

Karl Evanzz is the author of five books, including *The Judas Factor: The Plot to Kill Malcolm X*, and *The Messenger: The Rise and Fall of Elijah Muhammad.* He is the coauthor of *Dancing With the Devil* with hip-hop artist Mark Curry.

Kamau K. Franklin (*kamaufranklin.wordpress.com*) worked as a community organizer and attorney for over fifteen years in New York City. He is currently based in the South, where, in addition to his work as an activist attorney, he is a leading member of the Malcolm X Grassroots Movement (MXGM), an organization dedicated to human rights advocacy and building grassroots institutions in Black communities. At MXGM, Franklin has helped develop community cop-watch programs, freedom school programs for youth, and alternatives to incarceration programs. He has written articles for various online publications, including *Black Agenda*, *Left Turn*, and *ThyBlackman.com*, on organizing and activism in the United States, and U.S. foreign policy.

Zak A. Kondo is an associate professor of history at Baltimore City Community College, where he has taught since 2005. His is author of *Conspiracys: Unraveling the Assassination of Malcolm X* (1993) and several other works, including the *Black Student's Guide to Positive Education* (1996) and *For Homeboys Only: Arming and Strengthening Young Brothers for Black Manhood* (1991). He has consulted on several films pertaining to Malcolm X, including *Brother Minister*; *Malcolm X: Make it Plain,* and *Malcolm X*. He has also consulted on films pertaining to the Black Panther Party. He is viewed by many as one of the foremost authorities on the life, death, and legacy of Malcolm X.

Rosemari Mealy is an essayist, poet, human rights activist, and facilitator and trainer in the areas of media analysis, conflict resolution, and youth empowerment. She is a former Claudia Jones Fellow in the African New World Studies Program at Florida International University, where she taught critical race theory analysis. Mealy has lived and worked in Cuba, where she collaborated on several projects in support of U.S. political prisoners with exiled freedom fighter Assata Shakur. She is also the author of *Fidel and Malcolm X: Memories of a Meeting* (1993), *Lift These Shadows From Our Eyes* (1979). Mealy's writings have appeared in numerous publications including *Confirmation: An Anthology of African American Women Writers* (1983), *Black Women in the Diaspora, Vol. I-II* (1995), *University of Massachusetts Black Studies Journal, Black Film Review*, *The Black Scholar*, and *Catalyst*. She is currently working on a book detailing the phenomenological experiences of six African American students expelled between 1960 and 1962 from historically Black colleges and universities for participating in the sit-in movement.

Patricia Reid-Merritt (*Pat.Reid-Merritt@stockton.edu*) is an author, educator, scholar, and performing artist. She is a distinguished professor of social work and Africana Studies at the Richard Stockton College in Galloway Township, New Jersey; and the founder and artistic director of Afro-One Dance, Drama, and Drum Theatre, a community-based cultural and performing arts organization. She is the author of *Righteous Self-Determination: The Black Social Work Movement in America*, published in 2010 by Black Classic Press; *Sister Wisdom: Seven Pathways to a Satisfying Life for Soulful Black Women* (2002); and the national

Blackboard bestseller, *Sister Power: How Phenomenal Black Women Are Rising to the Top* (1996). She currently serves as a senior fellow for the Molefi Kete Asante Institute for Afrocentric Studies.

Eugene Puryear, a recent graduate of Howard University, is a Washington, D.C.-based social-justice activist with nearly a decade of involvement in the anti-imperialism movement. At Howard, he served as a key organizer of demonstrations held in support of the Jena 6 both in and outside of the state of Louisiana. He has also helped to organize some of the largest demonstrations against the Iraq War. In 2008, he was the vice-presidential candidate of the Party for Socialism and Liberation. Puryear serves on the editorial board of *Liberation* newspaper; a collection of his writings can be found at www.Liberationnews.org.

William W. Sales Jr. is an associate professor of Africana Studies at Seton Hall University and has expertise in civil rights and political science. He is the author of *From civil rights to Black Liberation: Malcolm X and the Organization of Afro-American Unity* (South End Press, 1994).

William L. (Bill) Strickland teaches political science in the W. E. B. Du Bois Department of Afro-American Studies at the University of Massachusetts Amherst, where he is also the director of the Du Bois Papers Collection. He is a founding member of the Institute of the Black World, an independent Black think tank headquartered in Atlanta, Georgia. Strickland has served as a consultant to both series of the prize-winning documentary on the civil rights movement, *Eyes on the Prize.* He was also the senior consultant for the PBS documentary, *Malcolm X: Make It Plain*, and wrote the companion book for that documentary. He most recently served as a consultant for Louis Massiah's film on Du Bois, entitled *W. E. B. Du Bois: A Biography in Four Voices.*

Greg Thomas is an associate professor of Black Studies in the English Department at Syracuse University. He is the founding editor of *PROUD FLESH: New Afrikan Journal of Culture, Politics and Consciousness*, an e-journal published by the African Resource Center. He is the author of *The Sexual Demon of Colonial Power: Pan-African Embodiment and Erotic Schemes of Empire* (2007) and *Hip-Hop Revolution in the Flesh: Power, Knowledge, and Pleasure in Lil' Kim's Lyricism* (2009). He is also the co-editor with L. H. Stallings of *Word Hustle: Critical Essays and Reflections on the Works of Donald Goines* (Black Classic Press, 2011). His essays and articles have appeared in critical periodicals such as *African Literature Today, Black Camera, CR: The New Centennial Review, The C. L. R. James Journal, Human Architecture, Journal of Pan-African Studies, Journal of West Indian Literature, Présence Africaine,* and *Words, Beats, Life*. He is currently at work on a book on the political-intellectual writings of George L. Jackson, tentatively titled *The Dragon*.

Christopher Tinson (*cmtHA@hampshire.edu*) is an assistant professor of African American Studies at Hampshire College. His interdisciplinary research and teaching focuses on the intersections between Africana radical traditions, Ethnic Studies, Hip-Hop culture, race and sports, critical media studies, the carceral state, and community-based education. His writings have been published in *The Black Scholar*, the *Journal of African American History, The Nation*, and *Radical Teacher*. He has given lectures and conducted workshops at numerous college campuses, high schools, juvenile detention centers and jails throughout Massachusetts, and since 2006 is co-host of TRGGR Radio, a weekly Hip-Hop-rooted social justice radio program.

Raymond A. Winbush is the director of the Institute for Urban Research at Morgan State University. He has taught at Oakwood University and Alabama A & M, Vanderbilt, and Fisk universities. He is the recipient of numerous grants, including one from the Kellogg Foundation to establish a National Dialogue on Race. He is the author of *The Warrior Method: A Parents' Guide to Rearing Healthy Black Boys* (2002) and *Belinda's Petition: A Concise History of Reparations for the TransAtlantic Slave Trade*. Winbush is also the former treasurer and executive board member of the National Council of Black Studies, and is currently on the editorial board of the *Journal of Black Studies*.

300720-500-22-60W